D0875985

How To Know

THE PROTOZOA

A pictured-key for identifying the more common fresh water, marine, and parasitic Protozoa, with elementary discussions of the importance of each group and of interesting facts concerning them.

by

THEODORE LOUIS JAHN, M.Sc., Ph.D.

Professor of Zoology, University of California at Los Angeles;

and

FRANCES FLOED JAHN, M.Sc.,
formerly
Assistant in Instruction, Department of Hygiene and
Preventive Medicine, College of Medicine,
State University of Iowa.

WM. C. BROWN COMPANY
Publishers
DUBUQUE, IOWA

THE PICTURED-KEY NATURE SERIES

"How to Know the Insects," Jaques, 1947

"Living Things—How to Know Them," Jaques, 1946

"How to Know the Trees," Jaques, 1946

"Plant Families—How to Know Them," Jaques, 1948

"Plants We Eat and Wear," Jaques, 1943

"How to Know the Spring Flowers," Cuthbert, 1943, 1949

"How to Know the Mosses," Conard, 1944

"How to Know the Land Birds," Jaques, 1947

"How to Know the Fall Flowers," Cuthbert, 1948

"How to Know the Immature Insects," Chu, 1949

"How to Know the Protozoa," Jahn, 1949

"How to Know the Mammals," Booth, 1949

"How to Know the Beetles," Jaques, 1951

"How to Know the Spiders," Kaston, 1952

"How to Know the Grasses," Pohl, 1953

"How to Know the Fresh-Water Algae," Prescott, 1954

"How to Know the Western Trees," Baerg, 1955

In Both Spiral and Cloth Binding
Other Subjects in Preparation

Printed in U.S.A.

This book is dedicated

to

Richard P. Hall

Professor of Biology, New York University
who first interested one
of us in a study of
the Protozoa and guided him
through several investigations

and to

Robert L. King

Professor of Zoology, State University of Iowa
with whom, for a number
of years, we have discussed
various phases of protozoology,
always with the assurance
that his comments would be
both stimulating and
informative.

CONTENTS

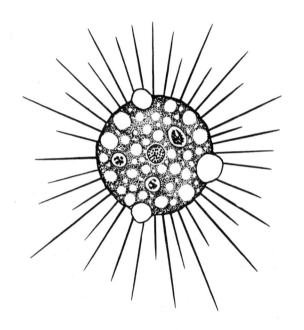

THE PURPOSE AND SCOPE OF THIS BOOK

The study of the Protozoa is one of the most fascinating studies available for people who have microscopes and know how to use them. All too often, the Protozoa are covered in the first week of courses in biology or zoology and quickly dismissed as "simple unicellular animals" long before the students have learned what to look for in studying them. Consequently many students never have an adequate understanding of what the Protozoa are or of the place of the Protozoa in relation to other organisms.

One purpose of the present volume is to present information in what is believed to be an easily assimilable form, so that knowledge of the Protozoa will become more widely distributed. It is the hope of the authors that a better understanding of the Protozoa among beginning students will convince them that no matter how "simple" an animal may look at first glance its morphology and fundamental life processes are just as complex as those of "higher" organisms. The realization of this fact may give a broader outlook on all things biological.

Courses in Protozoology are generally taught only in our larger universities, and the students who take them are usually graduates or advanced undergraduates. Consequently all books devoted to the subject are formal treatises for the use of advanced students or of investigators.

The present book differs from all others in that it is informal and is designed primarily for the less advanced student. However, advanced students who have never made a detailed study of the Protozoa should find it helpful, particularly if it is used in conjunction with an advanced text.

The best advanced text for the purpose is "Protozoology" by R. R. Kudo, published by C. C. Thomas, 1946. There are several other texts which deal primarily with parasitic species, but there is no other recent advanced text which gives a broad introduction to all of the phases of Protozoology and which is also helpful in the identification of both free living and parasitic species. Volume I, "Protozoa through Ctenophora" of "The Invertebrates" by Libbie Hyman, published by McGraw Hill, 1940, contains an excellent discussion of the characteristics of the various groups, but it is not designed especially for identification.

During the course of any prolonged attempt to identify all of the Protozoa that one can find in ponds the student will find many Protozoa that are not listed in the present volume nor in the book by Kudo. After exhausting the usefulness of these aids in the identification of any

1

species the next step is to look in the reference books listed at the end of each chapter in Kudo's book. These articles usually consist of long monographs devoted to a single Class, Order, Family or Genus. Since the present volume is planned chiefly for elementary students such references have been omitted.

In the present book there are a number of sections entitled "What to look for in a flagellate," etc. An attempt has been made to include in these sections the characters which a professional protozoologist would look for in the organism, regardless of whether or not such characters would be placed in a key. In general these directions are similar to the informal questions or instructions that an instructor would give a student who had a specimen under a microscope. In fact, that is how most of them came to the attention of the authors.

The informality of the book is noticeable not only in the text but also in the figures. Since the book is primarily a teaching and learning manual and not a formal treatise, the authors have felt free to make changes in figures copied from other books and published articles. These changes consist of adding or emphasizing taxonomic structures which would be of assistance to the student and of alterations which might facilitate reproduction and enhance the appearance of a third dimension. The figures are not meant to be exact copies of those published elsewhere. However, the name of the original author whose drawing served as a basis for the present drawing is given in parentheses after the size of each organism.

Each species shown in the illustrations was selected for either or both of two reasons: 1) It is common and the student is apt to find it. 2) It is quite different from other species illustrated, and the serious student will be interested in these differences, whether or not he is likely to find it in his own backyard. Fortunately, both reasons apply in the majority of cases.

Most of the work on this book was done at The Iowa Lakeside Laboratory during the summers of 1946 and 1947.
Los Angeles, Calif.
October 1, 1949.

Theo. L. Jahn

Frances Jahn

2

WHAT IS A PROTOZOAN?

The Protozoa comprise that large group of 15,000 to 20,000 species of organisms that are often defined in elementary textbooks as ["simple unicellular animals." This definition is outstanding for the magnitude of the erroneous impression which it gives. No protozoan is simple; some are not unicellular; and some may not, in the strict use of the word, be considered animals.]

The Protozoa can not be considered simple in any sense of the word. Each individual is complete in that it contains, often within a single cell, the facilities for performing all of the body functions for which a vertebrate possesses many organ systems. This concentration of functions into a small bit of protoplasm does not result in simplicity, but only in a reduction of the fundamental problem to a state where the machinery for performing each body function is not so readily visible. The fact that the machinery is not so visible does not imply that it does not exist or that if it does it is simple in nature.

Contraction of the pseudopodium of a shelled ameba, *Arcella*, is not any simpler than the contraction of the muscle of your own arm; the most obvious difference is that in *Arcella* a clear rod of protoplasm, with no structure comparable to that of a complex fiber of striated muscle, is capable of contraction (fig. 1). When a pseudopodium of *Arcella discoides* reaches a certain length it may become attached to the substratum (as shown in the upper sketch) and then contract, thereby dragging the ameba and its shell forward (as shown in the lower sketch). It seems improbable that such a thing as a complex structure could exist permanently in the *Arcella* pseudopodium because just before the pseudopodium contracts it is a flowing liquid. However, the fundamental phenomenon, contraction, is present, and the problem of how contraction occurs is just as complex in *Arcella* as in vertebrate muscle. In one respect it seems more complex because the structure on which we might base an explanation in the case of muscle seems to be entirely missing. The modern explanation of contraction is the same in the two examples. Both the muscle fiber and the pseudopodium have long protein molecules capable of forcibly folding upon themselves and thereby producing a shortening of the structure.

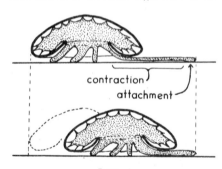

contraction
attachment

Figure 1

3

Similarly the excretion of liquid through the contractile vacuole of Paramecium is not necessarily different from excretion by the mammalian kidney; the complex system of capsules and tubules is absent, but it has been replaced by numerous microscopic and sub-microscopic vacuoles and tubules. The fundamental problem of how the liquid is pumped out of the body fluid by the kidney or by the contractile vacuole is very much the same wherever we find it, and it is just as complex.

If space permitted we could show that in regard to other body functions the Protozoa perform all of the complex body functions per-formed by the Metazoa. The machinery for performing these functions is not simpler in the Protozoa; it merely is not so cumbersome, nor so obvious, especially to the inexperienced investigator.

Are the Protozoa unicellular? First, let us define a cell. Perhaps the simplest and most common definition of a cell is a nucleated bit of living material (protoplasm) which is separated from its environ-ment by a membrane (fig. 2). Ordinarily we consider a cell to con-

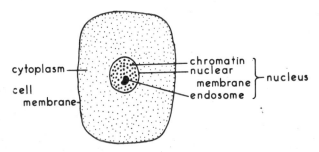

cytoplasm

cell
membrane

chromatin
nuclear
membrane
endosome
nucleus

Figure 2

tain only a single nucleus. Many of the organisms which we call Protozoa contain more than one nucleus: Paramecium has one macro-nucleus and one, two, or several micronuclei (fig. 298). Arcella has two nuclei which are similar in structure (fig. 202), and many of the flagellates found in the intestine of insects as well as ciliates found in the intestine of amphibia have numerous nuclei (fig. 270). The giant free living ameba, Chaos carolinensis has several hundred nuclei (fig. 194). Therefore, we can not define the Protozoa as possessing a single nucleus.

Secondly, let us consider the question of whether the protoplasm of the Protozoa is divided into compartments by cell membranes. Usu-ally it is not. In Chaos carolinensis or in Opalina, a ciliate that lives in the intestine of frogs, there are many nuclei, but the surrounding cytoplasm is not divided into compartments (figs. 194, 270). However, the lack of compartments does not prevent Chaos or Opalina from performing all of their body functions. They differ from Metazoa not in that they are unicellular but in that they are not divided into cells. We may consider them as being non-cellular or acellular.

On the other hand there are many species of colonial Protozoa in which many individuals, each with a limiting membrane and usually with only a single nucleus, live together in a cluster that we refer to as a colony. Why do we not consider a colony to be a single individual and therefore a multicellular organism?

In the case of colonies it is customary to draw an arbitrary line between Protozoa and Metazoa. As long as every cell of a colony is capable of performing every body function, except perhaps reproduction, the cells are considered to be separate individuals and the group is said to be a colony of Protozoa. In such a colony the cells are physiologically independent, i.e., division of labor for most body functions does not occur. If, however, the cells are dependent upon each other for the performance of some body function, such as digestion, excretion, or movement, then we consider the group to be a single individual or a multicellular organism, that is, it belongs either to the Metazoa or Metaphyta. In a protozoan colony division of labor, as we know it in multicellular organisms, exists only for the process of reproduction; every cell is capable of performing all other body functions.

In the formation of the spore of the Cnidosporidia (e.g., *Myxobolus*, fig. 257) there is a true differentiation of cells to form the polar capsules and spore membranes. Nevertheless, the Cnidosporidia are considered to be Protozoa. If one does not wish to call them Protozoa the next question is "What are they?" A person who is confronted with this question may consider various possibilities of where to classify them and will then decide that they certainly do not belong to any of the other phyla. One possibility would be to erect an entirely separate phylum. However, it is simpler and just as good to have them classified among the Protozoa.

Are the Protozoa necessarily animals? Can we draw a reasonable distinction between the Protozoa and the algae? No matter what sort of distinction we try to make, difficulties eventually seem to arise. One arbitrary distinction might be the presence or absence of chlorophyll. However, many of the chlorophyll-bearing flagellates are very closely related — in fact in some cases (e.g., *Cryptomonas* and *Chilomonas*, or *Euglena* and *Khawkinea*) the only difference between two genera is the absence of chlorophyll. If we were to place *Cryptomonas* and *Chilomonas* in different kingdoms we would be separating two very closely related individuals into the two major groups of organisms and would have to call one of them (*Chilomonas*) an animal and the other (*Cryptomonas*) a plant. We would also be forced to do the same thing with *Euglena* and *Khawkinea* and with several other pairs of genera which differ from each other only by the presence or absence of chlorophyll.

Another criterion which has been used for separating plants from animals is the presence or absence of cellulose. On this basis two orders of flagellates included in this book might be considered plants. The Phytomonadida are probably the most plant-like of the flagellates since most of them contain chlorophyll and all of them have cellulose walls. Many of the Dinoflagellida have a cellulose cell wall, but many of them posses no chlorophyll and are also holozoic, that is, they ingest solid food. In the order Dinoflagellida there are closely related organisms, some of which contain chlorophyll and a cellulose wall and others which have no cellulose wall but capture and digest other small animals (e.g., copepods). Must we call some dinoflagellates plants and others animals?

Another criterion which is often used for separating plants from animals is that of locomotion. If it is alive and moves, it is an animal; if it is alive and does not move it is a plant. However, many algae have motile stages; and many Protozoa (e.g., the Suctorea) are attached to rocks or plants and have no means of locomotion in the adult condition. Therefore, this criterion is just as defective as those mentioned above.

That leads us to the next question. Is it necessary to make a clear cut distinction between plants and animals? If a natural distinction were to exist we would like to know what it is. However, it seems as if no such natural distinction exists; all of those found in textbooks are arbitrary rather than natural. We have well recognized criteria by which we can distinguish John Doe from a Petunia, or a cow from the grass she eats, but what right have we to expect that these same criteria should apply to microscopic animals? Are we not trying to apply a highly artificial system of classification to a group of organisms for which it was never designed? Our common definitions of plants and animals lead us into numerous difficulties if we try to apply them to unicellular or acellular organisms, and it therefore seems wise to disregard these distinctions entirely.

Perhaps it would be better to ignore the question of which microscopic organisms are animals and which ones are plants. It seems as if it is far more important to know something about the organisms themselves — how they move, how they obtain their food, how they digest and oxidize their food, how they excrete their liquid wastes, how they eliminate indigestible material, how they reproduce, and how each one is adapted to the conditions under which it lives. The more we know about these subjects the less important seems the question of whether the organism is to be called plant or animal. Among the people who have studied the Protozoa and the algae there is a tendency to smile politely whenever the question is raised, and then (even more politely) to inquire about the details of some of the life processes of the organisms under consideration.

One way out of the dilemma is to create a third classification of organisms which we shall call the Protista to include the Protozoa, fungi, and all unicellular algae which have nuclei. Still another group may be created to include the organisms which do not contain nuclei; this group may be called the Monera. Some authors prefer to create still another group for the Fungi alone. We might also have a separate group for the viruses and bacteriophages. On this basis we may outline the kingdoms of organisms as follows:

1. ARCHETISTA. Submicroscopic organisms, living in animals, plants, or bacteria, in which they cause diseases, e.g., poliomyelitis, mumps, tobacco mosaic disease of tobacco plants, and typhoid bacteriophage.

2. MONERA. Organisms without nuclei, cells solitary or physiologically independent. Includes bacteria, blue-green algae, and spirochetes.

3. PROTISTA. Largely unicellular, with nuclei. Includes Protozoa, green algae, red algae and brown algae.

4. FUNGI. Usually numerous nuclei; contain no chlorophyll; in many species cell walls do not separate the cytoplasm into typical mononucleate cells; usually sessile.

5. METAPHYTA or EMBRYOPHYTA. Organisms with chlorophyll; multicellular; usually sessile.

6. METAZOA. Multicellular; typically holozoic; usually motile.

Such a separation of organisms into six kingdoms has many advantages and seems more reasonable than any of the simpler systems, and is quite superior to the common system which has only two kingdoms — plants and animals. However, we still have some of the same problems in another form. Now we will have trouble drawing a clear separation between the Protista and the Embryophyta because good reasons may be given for placing the colonial Phytomonadida in either group. Also we could place the Sponges and choanoflagellates with either the Protista or the Metazoa because there seems to be a continuous gradation from solitary choanoflagellates to colonial choanoflagellates to true sponges. Furthermore, we could place the Mycetozoida either with the Protista or with the Fungi.

In regard to these questions we may do whatever we please and no serious harm will be done. The classification is primarily a filing system, (cf. p. 40) and one of the most important things about a filing system is to be able to find the items which are filed. Furthermore, very good reasons can be given for considering the six kingdom system superior to the two kingdom system. By far the most important problem for the biologist is to learn about the structure and life of the organism. Which kingdom it belongs to is largely a matter of how we define the kingdoms. Perhaps we should have more than six.

If we had to define the Protozoa in one simple sentence, perhaps we could say that the Protozoa are the organisms described in this book plus their many relatives that had to be omitted to keep the book from being too big. This is obviously a facetious definition which avoids the question.

A more serious definition could be as follows: Protozoa are acellular, complex organisms of the Kingdom Protista. They are usually microscopic and show similarities in most cases to the basic structure of a single cell but also have many collective and individual morphological and physiological characteristics of their own which are not found generally in the cells of Metazoa and Metaphyta. During the course of their ontogenetic development, which may be complex, they do not pass through a two-layered gastrula stage and do not develop tissues specialized for carrying on part of the life processes of the organism.

WHERE TO FIND PROTOZOA

Protozoa live under almost all natural conditions where moisture is found. They have been described from:

1. FRESH WATER PONDS, whether they are clear, cool and spring fed, or stagnant and rich in decaying organic matter. One of the best sources is the shallow semi-permanent ponds often found in farm yards; many Protozoa multiply rapidly in hog wallows. The marshes and sloughs on the margin of lakes are often rich sources, but almost any stream, large or small, or any water hole, large, small, permanent or temporary, is likely to be a valuable source of material.

2. MUD. There are many mud dwelling species, e.g., Euglena is often found as a green scum on mud flats in rivers, especially if a tide is present to keep the mud permanently moist.

3. MOIST SOIL. Many species of Protozoa may be found in moist soil. In general these are not much different from those found in fresh water ponds.

4. MARINE (SALT) WATERS. Two major groups of the Protozoa (Foraminiferida and Radiolarida) are usually found only in marine waters. Foraminiferida are bottom dwelling forms and live at almost any depth up to 2500 fathoms (15,000 feet). Radiolarida are mostly pelagic (floating), but in rough weather they can sink far below the surface. Representatives of all of the major groups of flagellates, ciliates, and amebas, as well as many groups of the Sporozoa can be found in marine waters or in marine Metazoa.

5. BRINE POOLS. A few species are found only in very salty pools or lakes. The Great Salt Lake (Utah) contains several species of flagellates, ciliates, and amebas which have not been described from other places.

6. HOT SPRINGS, such as those found in several of our National Parks.

7. SNOW DRIFTS. *Haematococcus* is often found in snow drifts in our Rocky Mountains and is responsible for some of the green or red scum that is found on the surface of glaciers.

8. PARASITES OF OTHER ORGANISMS. Protozoa are known to parasitize:

a. OTHER PROTOZOA. For example, there is an ameba (*Endamoeba*) which lives in a ciliate (*Opalina*) which in turn lives in frogs. There are also Suctorea which live in the cytoplasm of free-living ciliates, e.g., *Sphaerophrya* which lives in *Paramecium*.

b. OTHER INVERTEBRATES. Common parasites of invertebrates are the gregarines found in insect digestive tracts and in the seminal vesicles of the earthworm. For example, *Monocystis* can be found in great numbers in earthworms, especially in the spring of the year, and *Gregarina* is very common in grasshoppers, especially in late summer and autumn.

c. VERTEBRATES, e.g., man. Some of the most important diseases of man are caused by Protozoa. Well known examples are malaria (almost world wide in distribution), kala-azar (in India and South America), African sleeping sickness, and amebic dysentery (world wide).

The large intestine of frogs is a common laboratory source of *Trichomonas*, *Opalina*, and *Nyctotherus*. Guinea pigs are a good source of *Balantidium*, and rats often have various flagellates in the intestine and *Trypanosoma* in the blood. The coccidia which destroy many thousands of chickens every year are some of the best known parasites of domestic animals.

d. PLANTS. One flagellate genus, *Phytomonas*, causes a serious disease of many plants. An ameba, *Labyrinthula*, and related genera parasitize several genera of aquatic plants. The widespread destruction of such plants may seriously affect the food supply of other organisms such as scallops and ducks (p. 109).

All of the parasites discussed above are found inside of their hosts. However, this is not true of all protozoan parasites. Many are found on the external surface. *Costia* is a flagellate found on the external surface of fishes where it causes a severe skin disease. The *Hydra* which is studied in general biology courses often has either of two species of external parasites, *Kerona* or *Trichodina*.

WHAT EQUIPMENT IS NEEDED FOR STUDYING PROTOZOA?

The most important piece of equipment for the study of the Protozoa is a microscope, preferably the best you can obtain. However, the best one made is by no means necessary. In 1675 Anthony van

Leeuwenhoek discovered the first protozoan known to man (it belonged to the genus *Vorticella*) with a very primitive instrument that gave a magnification of only about fifty diameters. Van Leeuwenhoek made this microscope himself, and it was much more difficult to use than any standard microscope we might meet at the present time. During the succeeding twenty-five years he built many microscopes, one of which had a magnification of 200 diameters. By means of these primitive instruments van Leeuwenhoek saw many of the Protozoa which are described in this book, and many of the drawings he made are easily recognizable as well known species of Protozoa.

If you have a standard microscope with a low power magnification of about 100 times (written 100x) and a high power of 430x you have the most important item of equipment. If you should have an oil immersion lens (which gives twice the magnification of high power and also gives a clearer image) so much the better, especially for small species.

In addition to a microscope the following items are necessary:

1. Slides.
2. Coverslips, preferably no. 1, about ⅞ inch squares or circles.
3. Drawing paper, or 4 x 6 unruled cards.
4. Pencils and erasers.
5. Collecting jars, preferably a dozen or more pint or quart jars with screw tops.

HOW TO COLLECT PROTOZOA

For a beginner the best place to gather Protozoa is in the scum on ponds or among the plants and debris around the edge of shallow ponds and marshes.

The best procedure is to scoop up scum (composed of duckweed, *Spirogyra*, and various other floating or semi-floating plants) by the handsful and push it into quart jars. The lid of the jar may also be used as a scoop for thin layers of scum. Place only a small amount of vegetation in some jars but have others half or two-thirds full. Fill the jars with pond water and replace the lids.

The same procedure is also used for bottom plants and debris (dead plants, leaves). Place the plants in the jars, and fill with pond water, and replace the lids. Even in mid-winter many Protozoa may be found in the debris on the bottom of ponds. If ice is formed it is often a simple matter to chip a hole with an axe and to scoop up debris from the bottom.

When you have brought the loaded jars to the laboratory, remove the lids and place the jars on a well lighted window sill, preferably one that is reached by moderate sunlight. Some Protozoa can be found immediately, but in 24 to 48 hours others that were scattered through the jar will become concentrated at the top where they may be found more easily and in greater numbers. Others may become concentrated near the bottom of the jar or perhaps an inch or so beneath the surface. Intense sunlight may heat the jars too much and kill most of the Protozoa.

The jars should be kept at least several weeks. The species that are most numerous one day may be absent the next day and be replaced by other species. The change in dominance may be slow (over a period of weeks) or rapid (from day to day) depending upon the kind and amount of decaying plant material, the temperature, the amount of sunlight, and the chemical constitution of the water.

The Protozoa which feed mostly on bacteria may be helped by adding a little boiled hay infusion prepared by boiling a small quantity of timothy (or of almost any other kind of hay).

The proportion of hay to water should be enough to produce a color similar to that of strong tea. About twenty-five cubic centimeters of this added to old cultures will usually bring on a revival of protozoan life, especially of *Paramecium*, hypotrichs, and many small ciliates.

Another good way to feed Paramecium is to add malted milk to the culture. Use about one tenth of a standard tablet of malted milk to a quart jar. The tablet should be mashed until it is thoroughly powdered and then sprinkled on the surface. This causes a profuse growth of bacteria. Paramecium and other bacterial feeders eat both the powdered milk and the bacteria.

Many species which are not easily collected may be obtained from commercial biological supply houses. Students who live inland may study the Radiolarida and Foraminiferida by examining prepared slides of the skeletons of these organisms. Then the student should obtain some of the unassorted and unmounted dredgings from the ocean floor. These usually contain skeletons of these Protozoa mixed with the skeletons of other small marine animals. Such dredgings are known as foraminiferan ooze and radiolarian ooze. Selecting protozoan skeletons from the ooze and making slides of them is a pleasant way to spend several laboratory periods. Separating protozoan skeletons and shells from those of molluscs, sponges, bryozoans, and annelids is one way to test your knowledge of the various phyla.

For fresh specimens of parasitic species it is necessary to examine the part of the host ordinarily infected, such as blood, spleen, and intestinal contents. The method used is different for various species and the less obvious details will be discussed later.

Prepared slides of the important protozoan parasites of man and domestic animals are readily available commercially. Permanent slides of the parasites of malaria, amebic dysentery, kala-azar, and African sleeping sickness of man and coccidiosis of rabbits or chickens should be available for all students of Protozoology.

HOW BIG ARE PROTOZOA?

The range of size found among the various species of Protozoa is considerably greater than that found among any phylum of animals. The extent of this range can readily be seen in the following list. The sizes are given in microns (abbreviated by μ). One micron is 1/1000 of a millimeter or 1/25,000 of an inch.

Greatest linear dimension	Organism
1 to 4 μ	*Leishmania donovani*, the cause of kala-azar in man.
3 to 4 μ	*Microsporda*, e.g., *Nosema bombycis*, the cause of pebrine disease in silkworms.
125 to 350 μ	The common species of *Paramecium*, e.g., *P. aurelia*, *P. caudatum*, and *P. multimicronucleatum*.
600 μ or more	*Amoeba proteus (Chaos diffluens)*, when elongated and moving rapidly.
1000 to 3000 μ (1 to 3 mm.)	*Spirostomum ambiguum*, *Stentor coeruleus*, and other large ciliates.
1000 to 5000 μ (1 to 5 mm.)	*Chaos carolinensis*, the giant ameba.
up to 63,000 μ (63 mm. or 2½ inches)	Foraminiferida, e.g., *Cycloclypeus carpenteri*. Fossil species even larger.
up to 70,000 μ (70 mm. or 2¾ inches)	Largest plasmodia of *Myxobolus*.
several feet	Mycetozoida plasmodia, which crawl over rotting logs, and function like supergiant amebas.

A rapid glance over the above table will convince anyone that the size range of the Protozoa is enormous, even if we were to omit the Mycetozoida (because they might also be classed with the Fungi).

If one calculates the difference in volume (rather than the linear dimension as shown above) the size difference is even more striking. For any given shape the volume varies as the cube of the diameter. If, for purposes of comparison, we consider the organism to be spherical we find that the volume of *Leishmania* or *Nosema* is roughly $4/3 \times 3.14 \times 1.5^3$ or 9.4 cubic microns, for a diameter of 3 μ, whereas that of *Myxobolus* is $4/3 \times 3.14 \times 35,000^3$ or 18,000,000,000,000 cubic microns. A *Myxobolus* plasmodium is therefore roughly 2,000,000,000,000 times the volume of *Leishmania*. The size range is about 10^{12}.

The difference in weight would be roughly proportional to the volume, and the weight difference among the Protozoa can be compared with that between one of the smallest known vertebrates, a tropical frog which weighs about 0.1 gram, and one of the largest, the Sulphur-Bottom Whale, which weighs 147 tons or about 135,000,000 grams. The size range of the vertebrates, therefore, is about 10^9, whereas that of the Protozoa is 10^{12}.

HOW TO ESTIMATE THE SIZE OF A PROTOZOAN

One of the first things a beginning student of the Protozoa (or of any other group of microscopic organisms) should learn is how to obtain a fair idea of the size of any object seen through the microscope. The process is much simpler than most people seem to think.

If one knows the diameter of the field then one can judge with a moderate degree of accuracy the size of any object which is less than the diameter of the field provided it is not less than about one-fifth the field diameter. With an ordinary student microscope the low power lens has a magnification of ten times (written 10x) and the ocular has a magnification of 10x, therefore the total magnification is 10 x 10 or 100x. Such a microscope has a field diameter of about 1600 microns (written 1600μ). A micron (μ) is 1/1000 of a millimeter or 1/25,000 of an inch.

If an animal seen in the field is one half as long as the field it is about 800 μ. If it is one fifth the size of the field it is then about 320 μ. (Fig. 3).

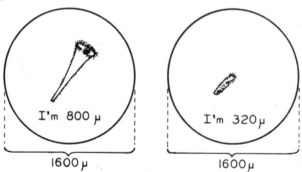

I'm 800 μ

1600 μ

I'm 320μ

1600μ

Figure 3

Under a standard high power objective (43x) and a 10x ocular the size of the field is about 372 μ, and objects one half the diameter of the field will be about 186 μ and those one fifth the size of the field will be about 75 μ.

If you do not know the diameter of your low power field you can estimate it by looking through the microscope at a millimeter celluloid rule or at a piece of millimeter graph paper.

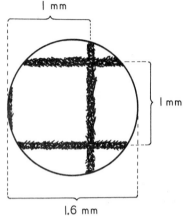

I mm

I mm — If a single square on a piece of millimeter graph paper looks like Fig. 4, then the diameter of the field is about 1600 μ.

1.6 mm

Figure 4

If you use the same ocular for both low power and high power you may obtain an estimate of the diameter of the high power field by dividing the diameter of the low power field (let us say, 1600 μ) by the ratio of the magnification of the high power to the low power objective. You may find these magnifications stamped on the objectives. Usually they are 43x and 10x. If so, then the size of the high power field is

$$1600 \, \mu \div \frac{43}{10} \quad \text{or}$$

$$1600 \, \mu \div 4.3 = 372 \, \mu.$$

If the object to be measured is less than one fifth the diameter of the field one should use an ocular micrometer. This is a calibrated scale which can be placed inside the ocular. The most convenient type is one which divides the field into 100 parts, and the field of a microscope equipped with such a micrometer looks like fig. 5.

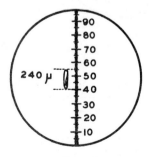

If the diameter of the field is 1600 μ then each small division is 16 μ. If the diameter of the field is 372 μ, then each unit, of course, is 3.72 μ.

Figure 5

14

If the animal to be measured is brought near or under the scale it is a simple matter to determine that it is, let us say, 15 units long. That means it is 15 x 16 μ or 240 μ long if we are using low power or 15 x 3.72 μ or 55.8 μ long if we are using high power. An animal that is 15 units long under low power would, of course, be 64.5 units long under high power.

An accuracy of 10% in measurement is sufficient for the purpose of identifying Protozoa. The reason is that the specimens of any given species are subject to a size variation of at least that much. This is true not only of Protozoa but of all animals, e.g., *Homo sapiens*.

Sometimes students may study a protozoan intently for several hours and not know whether it is approximately 10, 100, or 1000 microns in length. Such ignorance is inexcusable, and is as bad as looking at a horse for an hour and then not being able to say whether it is approximately 1, 10, or 100 feet in length.

HOW TO STAIN A PROTOZOAN

Whenever possible Protozoa should be examined while alive and in their normal aqueous medium. For purposes of identification a fixed and stained preparation is usually a poor substitute for the live and active organism. There are exceptions to this statement, and these exceptions include all of the blood parasites which fortunately can easily be stained by Wright's stain.

However, the beginning student will find several stains useful for special purposes. It will be found that these stains are generally more useful after the organism has been studied alive. The more commonly useful staining methods are listed below:

1. *Intra-vitam staining.*

   a. Food vacuoles. Chinese ink or powdered carmine mixed with the fluid containing the animals is often ingested by ciliates. Acidity or alkalinity of food vacuoles is demonstrated by the use of neutral red which is red in acid and yellow in alkaline solutions. A small drop of stock solution of 1/20% neutral red in absolute alcohol is placed on the slip or cover and allowed to evaporate, then animals are added. Or an aqueous solution of 1/10,000 or weaker may be used and added directly to the material under observation. Neutral red also stains vacuoles other than food vacuoles which are referred to as the "vacuome."

   b. Mitochondria. Use janus green or janus green B in 1/20% alcoholic solution as for neutral red. Aqueous solutions of 1/10,000 or weaker may be added directly to the material under observation.

2. *Temporary killing and staining methods.*

   a. Inks as used for *Paramecium*, p. 188.

   b. Lugol's solution: Potassium iodide 6 grams, iodine 4 grams,

15

distilled water 100 cc. Dilute 1 to 5 or 10 and add to material under observation. Useful for staining Protozoa in feces.

    c. Alcohol: 35% solution to demonstrate pellicle of *Paramecium*, etc.

    d. Acidulated methyl green: ½% methyl green in 1% acetic acid kills and stains the nuclei.

    e. Noland's solution: Phenol, sat. aqueous solution, 80 cc, formalin 20 cc., glycerine 4 cc., gentian violet 20 mgms. Mix a drop of the reagent with a drop of the fluid containing Protozoa. Flagella, cilia, nuclei, etc. are stained.

3. *Permanent mounts.*

    a. Relief stains: 10% nigrosin, china blue or opal blue. Place a drop of material containing the organisms on the middle of a clean slide and near it a drop of stain. Mix thoroughly and spread in a thin layer with a toothpick; dry thoroughly in air. Cover with damar or balsam and cover slip, or use uncovered with an oil immersion objective. Excellent for surface sculpturing of *Paramecium* and for counting flagella.

    b. Histological methods. These are beyond the scope of the present volume, and the student should consult Kudo or any good book on microtechnique.

Figure 6

    c. Wright's stain for blood parasites. A blood film is prepared by dragging a drop of blood across a slide by means of another slide, as shown in fig. 6. The upper slide is touched to the drop of blood and then moved in the direction of the arrow. With a pipette cover the film with a known number of drops of undiluted stain and let stand horizontally 3 to 5 minutes. Then add the same number of drops of neutral distilled water (or a neutral buffer solution supplied with a stain). Rinse in neutral distilled water. Dry. Cover with cedar wood oil and cover slip or use uncovered with an oil immersion objective.

SLOWING DOWN A PROTOZOAN

Many Protozoa move so rapidly that students are continually seeking methods of slowing them down. Whenever a protozoan moves too rapidly for accurate observation one of the greatest assets of the observer is patience. Sooner or later the organisms will usually slow down by themselves. Slowing caused by slight drying of the preparation is often advantageous. However, severe drying causes distortion and should be avoided except for special purposes, e.g., watching the contractile vacuole of *Paramecium*.

One of the best chemicals for slowing Protozoa seems to be methyl cellulose (trade name, Methocel). Methocel solutions have a high viscosity which reduces the rate of locomotion, often with only slight distortion of the animal. Mix 10 grams of Methocel with 45 cc. of boiling water and allow to soak 20 minutes. Add 45 cc. of cold water. Cool to 10°C. until transparent. Place in dropping bottles.

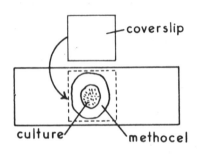

Figure 7

This gives a viscous solution with the approximate consistency of honey.

In using Methocel make a small ring of the Methocel solution on the slide, place a drop of culture in center of ring, and then cover with cover slip (fig. 7). As the organisms swim outward from the center they will move more and more slowly because of the increasing viscosity.

WHY DRAW PICTURES OF THE PROTOZOA?

The drawing equipment is recommended because, as Louis Agassiz once stated, "the best aid to the eye is a sharp pencil." If you make a sketch of an animal you are likely to look for details you would not see otherwise. Many times you are not able to see all of the essential details in a single specimen, but if you draw what can be seen in several specimens and then add these in a composite sketch, the result will be a record recognizable by other protozoologists as well as by yourself.

During the course of your study you will undoubtedly meet many species over and over again. The second time you meet one you can say, "Oh, I saw him yesterday (or last week or last year)." You may then shuffle your drawing cards, find the right one and say, "This is what I thought he looked like then. That's not a bad sketch. He looks pretty much the same now. But here, I didn't sketch (or see) that contractile vacuole quite right. And look at that undulating membrane! He certainly didn't stick it out like that last time!" In such a manner your knowledge of particular species, and thereby of the whole phylum, may increase at a surprisingly rapid rate.

In the study of insects, plants, and of most organisms of moderate size you should keep a collection of the specimens you have identified. With the Protozoa that is not so feasible, mostly because for purposes of identification the organisms should usually be seen in the living state. A stained, permanent slide is quite different from a live, active, swimming or crawling protozoan. For that reason your drawings are much more important as a record of what you have found than they are in entomology or botany.

One relatively painless way to learn classification is to write the name of the subphylum, class, subclass, order, family, genus, and species in the upper left hand corner of your drawing card (fig. 8).

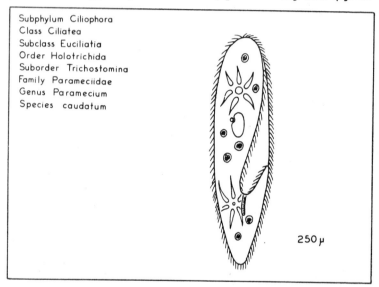

Subphylum Ciliophora
Class Ciliatea
Subclass Euciliatia
Order Holotrichida
Suborder Trichostomina
Family Parameciidae
Genus Paramecium
Species caudatum

250 μ

Figure 8

You may then file the cards by taxonomic groups and you should have little trouble in remembering how to classify any of the animals you find. You can also write the name of the place from which the species was obtained and the date of the observation on the back of the card. The next time you find the same species you may record the new place and date just under that of the previous record. You can also make notes on the back of the card.

Your drawings, together with the notes you take about each organism will become your "collection."

WHAT DO PROTOZOA DO FOR A LIVING?

The many species of Protozoa have various means of making a livelihood. They live under diverse conditions and obtain their food in a variety of ways. The modes of life may be grouped into two major groups: 1) free living, and 2) associative with larger organisms.

By "free living" we mean living in ponds, streams, soil, or similar habitats, and forming no intimate associations with other organisms. Those which are associated with larger organisms may live on the surface or within the other organisms. Those which live on the surface are referred to as *ectozoic* and those which live within another organism as *endozoic*. Both ectozoic and endozoic organisms may be *commensal, parasitic,* or *symbiotic.* These modes of life are outlined below.

1. *Free living.* Free living protozoa may absorb dissolved food materials through the cell membrane (or pellicle) in which case we refer to them as being *saprozoic* or *saprobic.* If they ingest solid food we say they are *holozoic.* Holozoic protozoa may ingest bacteria, algae, other protozoa, or small Metazoa, e.g., copepods. The flagellates which contain chlorophyll are capable of manufacturing the carboyhydrates and proteins from carbon dioxide, water, salts and sunlight. The best term for this plant-like mode of nutrition is *phototrophic.* However, synonyms which are often used are *holophytic* or *photosynthetic.*

2. *Commensal.* We define as a commensal any organism which lives on or in another organism and does not harm or benefit the other organism. Many protozoan commensals obtain food from the larger animal; others use the larger animal merely as a means of transportation and obtain their food from the environment. Commensals may be either saprobic or holozoic, and a few are even phototrophic. *Ectocommensals* live on the outside of larger organisms and *endocommensals* live on the inside.

3. *Parasitic.* A parasite is defined as an organism which lives on or in another organism to the detriment of the latter, i.e., the second organism (the *host*) is definitely harmed by the presence of the parasite. In many instances the harmful effect is very obvious (as in malaria and other protozoan diseases of man). In some instances the harmful effect is very slight. Many times when Protozoa are found living in or on another animal it is not known whether or not a harmful effect is produced. Such organisms are commonly referred to as "parasites" even though they may be quite harmless (i.e., commensals). Parasites may be saprobic or holozoic.

Parasites are called *ectoparasites* if they live on the outside of the body of the host and *endoparasites* if they live inside the host. Endoparasites are often referred to as being *cytozoic, coelozoic* or *histozoic,* depending upon where they live in the host. If they live inside of the cells they are called cytozoic, e.g., *Leishmania* which lives inside of the cells of the human spleen, or *Plasmodium,* the cause of malaria, which lives inside of human blood cells. Common examples of coelozoic parasites are *Gregarina* which lives in the digestive tract of insects or *Trypanosoma* which lives in the blood stream (but not in the blood cells) of man and many other animals. Common *histozoic*

19

parasites are the Myxosporida which parasitize fishes and live in the tissues (muscle, brain, etc.) in between cells where no cavity normally exists.

4. *Symbiotic.* Whenever two organisms live together for mutual benefit we speak of the relationship as *symbiosis* and the organisms involved as *symbionts.* The Protozoa are involved in two main types of symbiotic relationships:

a. Protozoa and chlorophyll-containing organisms. These chlorophyll-containing organisms live in the cytoplasm of the Protozoa, and manufacture carbohydrate which is transmitted to the protozoan. The chlorophyll-bearing organism may be a green alga *(Chlorella,* commonly known as zoochlorella when it is found in an animal), a blue-green alga, or a yellow cryptomonad (known as zooxanthellae when found in an animal). Zoochlorellae are found in *Paramecium bursaria, Stentor polymorphum, Prorodon ovum,* and many other ciliates. They are found in naked amebas, shelled amebas, and heliozoans. Symbiotic blue-green algae are found only in a few flagellates. Zooxanthellae are found in several ectoparasitic ciliates (e.g., *Trichodina),* Foraminiferida, and very commonly in Radiolarida.

b. Protozoa and xylophagous (wood eating) insects. Two groups of xylophagous insects, the termites and certain wood eating cockroaches (the genus *Cryptocercus),* are capable of eating wood but can not digest it without the aid of their intestinal Protozoa. The xylophagous cockroaches live mostly in the woods where they eat dead trees; termites also live in the woods but seem to be especially fond of eating the wooden houses of human beings. Without Protozoa both the termites and the cockroaches would starve to death. The Protozoa are not able to live under natural conditions outside of the bodies of termites and cockroaches. This is a true symbiosis; neither organism can live without the other.

The Protozoa symbiotic in insects belong to three orders of animal-like flagellates, the Protomastigida, Polymastigida, and Hypermastigida. These flagellates are holozoic and ingest the particles of wood which the insect has chewed into small fragments. These particles are digested (i.e., dissolved) by the flagellate; some of the dissolved material is used by the flagellate, and some is used by the insect.

The flagellate, but not the termite, may be killed by any of three methods:

a. Exposure to 100% oxygen for 24 hours or more.

b. Incubation at 36°C. (or 96°F.).

c. Starvation for six to ten days.

Termites treated by any of the above methods will starve to death in spite of the fact they may eat large quantities of wood (or filter paper) The food simply passes through their bodies undigested. However, if they are fed the feces or intestinal contents of untreated termites, they become reinfected with flagellates and are then able to receive cellulose digested by the flagellates, and therefore, do not starve to death.

HOW THE PROTOZOA INCREASE IN NUMBERS

Protozoans are usually very susceptible to chemical and physical changes in the environment. A severe decrease in the food supply, or a change in the acidity or in the oxygen concentration or in the temperature of the medium, or most of all, a drying up of the medium, is apt to cause death of large numbers of the organisms. However, in spite of a very high death rate the average number of Protozoa in the world (but not in any particular habitat) remains more or less constant. Therefore, there must be for each species a mechanism of reproduction that, on the average (but not instantaneously) balances the death rate.

Reproduction of most unicellular organisms is by some form of cell division and is therefore asexual. In many instances division is immediately preceded by the temporary or permanent fusion of two cells or by the permanent fusion of two nuclei. Fusions of cells and/or nuclei are regarded as sexual phenomena and the cell divisions which immediately follow them are often regarded as sexual reproduction. From this viewpoint the term sexual reproduction has quite a different meaning from what it has in higher animals where two cells fuse to give rise to a new individual. This so-called "sexual reproduction" of Protozoa immediately after fusion of two cells is strictly comparable to the early divisions of the fertilized egg and may be considered as asexual. What should be considered true sexual reproduction, however, does occur in the Foraminiferida (p. 128), in the Phytomonadida (p. 75), in the Eugregarinida (p. 151), and perhaps in other groups.

The reproductive and sexual processes of Protozoa may be considered separately. In many species reproduction can not be continued indefinitely unless sexual phenomena occur at more or less definite intervals. In other species sexual phenomena which are known to occur are apparently not necessary for the continued existence of the species, and in still other species no sexual phenomena are known.

A. *Reproduction.*

The exact mechanism of reproduction varies considerably for different groups of the Protozoa but most of the methods of reproduction may be grouped under the following fundamental types:

1) *Binary fission* is division of one organism into two organisms. We often speak of this as the division of a "mother" cell to form two "daughters." Such reproduction, however, is purely asexual and we could just as well say the division of a father cell to form two daughters or sons, or division of a parent to form two offspring or two filial

cells. The usual feminine notation is merely a matter of custom, and the asexual nomenclature, i.e., parent cell and filial cell, seems to be preferable.

In binary fission of flagellates the nucleus divides by mitosis and the cell usually begins to divide at the anterior end, splits longitudin-

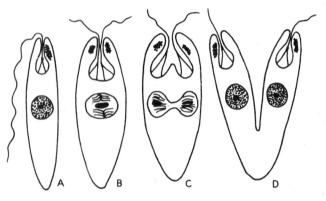

Figure 9

ally and eventually constricts into two. Fig. 9 shows the division of *Euglena*. (After Hall). A. Cell just before division. B. Nucleus dividing by mitosis; each chromosome divides longitudinally. The gullet has already divided and the flagellar apparatus has been duplicated. C. Later stage with nuclear division complete but cytoplasm still continuous. D. Division almost complete. Two complete filial cells will soon be formed. Division of the genus *Trypanosoma* (shown in fig. 135) is similar to that of *Euglena* but looks different because of the location of the flagellum and undulating membrane.

In all ciliates, except the peritrichs, binary fission is transverse.

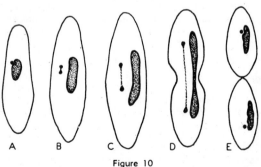

Figure 10

Fig. 10 shows division of *Paramecium caudatum*. A. Animal just before division, with one macronucleus and one micronucleus. B. Micro-

22

nucleus dividing, macronucleus elongated. C. Micronucleus divided, macronucleus more elongate. D. Cytoplasm constricting. E. Division complete. Each young cell now has one macro- and one micronucleus. The micronucleus always divides by mitosis and the macronucleus by amitosis. Since division in all ciliates except the peritrichs is transverse, any free swimming ciliate seen to be constricted across the longitudinal axis may safely be assumed to be dividing. (Cf. conjugation, fig. 15).

Division of *Epistylis*, a stalked peritrich, is shown in fig. 11. A.

Figure 11

An animal just before division. B. Division of the macronucleus and the micronucleus. C. Two animals still attached to the same stalk. D. Each animal has grown a short new section of stalk. By repeated division in this manner, large dichotomously branched colonies of dozens or hundreds of individuals may be formed. In *Vorticella*, which is not colonial, one of the filial cells swims away and grows a new stalk elsewhere (fig. 15).

Paramecium may divide by binary fission once, twice, or even three times a day, depending upon the chemical and physical conditions of the culture. *Glaucoma*, a smaller ciliate, has been observed to undergo as many as eight divisions a day and *Didinium* at least four. *Euglena* also may divide at least four times a day. If such rapid growth rates were unrestricted and were not balanced by equally high death rates a single individual of any of the above species could soon increase to a volume equal to that of the earth. For *Paramecium*, at one division a day, the time required for such unrestricted growth to give rise to a mass of organisms equal to the volume of the earth would be about 113 days. (Calculation by R. L. King).

2) *Multiple fission*. In multiple fission the nucleus divides a number of times and then the cytoplasm divides equally. This type of division occurs in the schizogony of the malarial parasite (fig. 252) in

the schizogony of coccidia (fig. 241), and in the gamogony of gregarines (fig. 246). The process is shown diagrammatically in fig. 12.

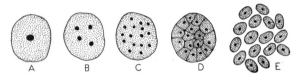

Figure 12

A. A cell just before division. B. Same cell after two nuclear divisions. C. After four nuclear divisions. D. Division of the cytoplasm. E. Numerous small cells each with a single nucleus and known as merozoites, have been produced (see also fig. 252).

3) *External budding.* In some few organisms the cell divides unequally to form numerous small cells and one large one which remains in the adult condition. An example is *Ephelota,* a suctorean. Fig. 13 consists of a series of three diagrams showing multiple external

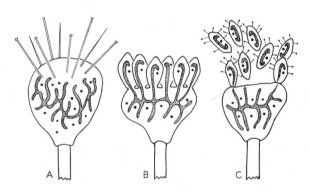

Figure 13

budding of *Ephelota.* A. An animal just before division. There are many micronuclei, but only one macronucleus, and the macronucleus is greatly branched. B. A group of small cells is being formed at the top of the animal. Each cell is receiving one micronucleus and a branch of the macronucleus. C. The small cells have developed tentacles and are becoming detached; the "parent" cell continues its existence as an adult suctorean. Each filial organism may now move to a new place, develop a stalk and grow into an adult.

4) *Internal budding* consists of the formation of a bud or young cell inside of the cytoplasm of the parent cell. The young animal is

then released either by rupture of the parent cell (Myxosporida, fig. 257) or by passing out through a birth pore (Tokophrya, fig. 366).

The most common method of reproduction among the Protozoa is binary fission.

B. *Sexual phenomena.*

1). *Permanent fusion* of cells and nuclei. Among the Sporozoa and in certain flagellates (e.g., *Volvox*) and ciliates (e.g. *Opalina*) and Sarcodina (e.g., *Foraminiferida*) there is a complete fusion of two cells known as *gametes* to form a single cell known as a *zygote*. The zygote usually undergoes repeated division to give rise to a large number of organisms, or, in the case of *Volvox*, to a new colony, or in the Foraminiferida to a new individual many times larger than the gametes. The fusion of two cells with the ensuing fusion of the nucleus is designated as a sexual phenomenon comparable to the union of the egg and sperm of Metazoa and Embryophyta (Metaphyta).

In *Volvox* the comparison is a good one because the gametes are small and the resulting colony is large, and the new colony can truly be regarded as arising from the gametes of the parent colony which may still exist.

What may be considered as true sexual reproduction also occurs in the Foraminiferida (fig. 222). One large individual undergoes rapid division to form many small gametes which fuse, and each zygote grows without cell division into a large individual which is properly considered the next generation—a true sexual reproduction. This large individual may undergo rapid division and produce numerous small cells each of which grows directly into another large individual. This seems to be true asexual reproduction—similar to sexual reproduction but it does not involve fusion of the small cells. The life cycle of the Foraminiferida, therefore, may properly be considered as an alternation of sexual and asexual generations.

In the Coccidia and Schizogregarinida there is a period of repeated multiple fission which constitutes a definite asexual reproductive cycle which is, in turn, followed by fusion of gametes (fig. 240). The zygote divides and the immediate filial cells are regarded as the new generation resulting from fertilization (or sexual reproduction). Therefore, this may be considered as an alternation of asexual with sexual generations. The gametes sometimes differ in size from each other (microgametes and macrogametes) but the average size is not much different from that of the cells of the same species which divide asexually.

In the Eugregarines (e.g., *Gregarina*, fig. 246) the large "adult" divides into thousands of gametes, and these fuse with other gametes produced by another "adult," and there result thousands of zygotes each of which is a new individual which grows into an "adult." This may be considered as a true sexual reproduction; asexual reproduction of the adult does not occur.

2) *Conjugation;* temporary fusion of cells, with nuclear exchange. In all Euciliata and in the Suctorea the fusion of the cells is only temporary, but the fusion of the micronuclei is permanent. This phenomenon is known as *conjugation.* During conjugation two ciliates become attached to each other by their oral surfaces. The micronuclei divide several times in each cell. Then one micronucleus from each cell migrates to the other cell and fuses with a micronucleus of the other cell. The macronuclei of both cells then degenerate (i.e., dissolve in the cytoplasm). In this way one *zygote nucleus* is formed in each cell and all other nuclei degenerate. The cells then separate. The zygote nucleus divides several times and thereby gives rise to new macro- and micronuclei. Then the cytoplasm of each cell divides twice or several times until each filial cell has the number of macro- and micronuclei appropriate for the species (e.g., one of each for *Paramecium caudatum;* one macro- and two micronuclei for *P. aurelia).*

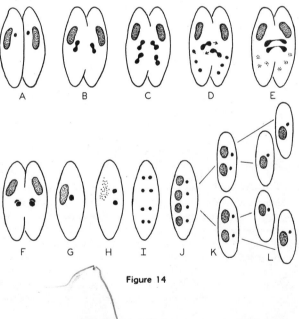

Figure 14

Figure 14. The process of conjugation in *Paramecium caudatum.* A. Two animals attached, each with one micro- and one macronucleus. B. Micronuclei dividing. C. Micronuclei dividing the second time. D. Two micronuclei (one in each cell) dividing the third time; the other three micronuclei in each cell do not divide. E. Migration of one filial nucleus of each cell to the other cell as indicated by arrows in D; the six micronuclei shown in D which did not divide are degenerating (dissolving in cytoplasm). F. Fusion of two micronuclei in each cell; of each pair that is fusing, one member came from the other cell. This completes the process of conjugation; each micronucleus may now be considered as a zygote nucleus, i.e., as a nucleus which has been fertilized by union with the nucleus of another cell. G. An exconjugant which has just been formed by the separation of the pair shown at F and the complete fusion of the two micronuclei in each to form the zygote nucleus. H. Cell with two micronuclei formed by division of zygote nucleus; macronucleus degenerating. I. Cell with eight micronuclei formed by three divisions of zygote nucleus. J. Cell with four macro- and four micronuclei; the macronuclei have developed from four of the micronuclei shown in I. K. Two cells each with two macro- and two micronuclei, formed by cytoplasmic division of J. L. Four cells each with one macro- and one micronucleus. Each of these may divide by fission (fig. 10) many times before the next conjugation.

Conjugation is often considered a method of sexual reproduction. However, this temporary fusion of cells is followed by separation and then by division of the same cells to form filial cells. The new "individuals" comparable to the next generation of multicellular organisms lose their identity and become merely the organisms which are formed by binary fission of the parents which have conjugated. Each of these individuals that arise from the exconjugants has a new nuclear complex which is derived from the zygote nucleus. We may consider conjugation a sexual phenomenon which is immediately followed by repeated asexual reproduction. It certainly is not sexual reproduction in the usual sense of the term, i.e., fusion of cells to form a new individual. It does, however, involve a fusion of nuclei.

It is very easy for students to distinguish conjugating ciliates from dividing ones. In all euciliates except the peritrichs division is transverse and in conjugation the two oral surfaces are apposed. This is shown in Fig. 15. In A, B, C, and D are shown the division of

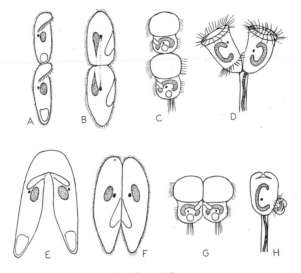

Figure 15

Metopus, Paramecium, Urocentrum, and Vorticella. In the first three species division is obviously transverse. In Vorticella division is in the longitudinal direction of the bell as shown for Epistylis, fig. 11, A-C. However, in Vorticella one of the filial cells develops a ring of basal cilia and swims away rather than remaining attached as in Epistylis. In E, F. G, and H are shown the conjugation stages of Metopus, Para-mecium, Urocentrum, and Vorticella. The first three species are ar- .
ranged side by side with their oral surfaces attached. In Vorticella one conjugant is free swimming and is much smaller than the other and becomes attached to the side of the larger individual. Nuclear processes in all four genera are similar to those shown in fig. 14.

3) Autogamy, endomixis, and cytogamy. There are several other nuclear phenomena in Paramecium which are considered to be sexual in nature. Three of these are autogamy, endomixis, and cytogamy. Autogamy is similar to conjugation except that only one animal is involved. The micronucleus divides several times, and two of these filial nuclei fuse to form a zygote nucleus. All other nuclei degen-erate and the zygote micronucleus divides to form a new macro- and a micronucleus for the individual. Endomixis is similar to auto-gamy except that there is no fusion of micronuclei. Cytogamy is a process similar to conjugation in that two individuals become at-

tached and undergo nuclear changes, but differs from conjugation in that exchange of micronuclei (as shown in fig. 14, D, E) does not occur.

In higher animals we may give clear cut definitions of sex and reproduction, and the vast majority of instances of either may be readily classified. In the so called "simple Protozoa," however, the known facts, as outlined briefly above, do not permit so easy a classification. The sexual phenomena of the Protozoa vary from true sexual reproduction as it occurs in higher organisms to instances where it is not so easy to answer the questions "Is it sex?", "Is it reproduction?", and "Is it both?"

HOW DO PROTOZOA MOVE?

The locomotor organelles of Protozoa are used in separating them into the major taxonomic groups — subphyla and classes. There are three general types of locomotion (fig. 16); by means of

1. Cilia
2. Flagella
3. Protoplasmic flow

Figure 16

LOCOMOTION BY MEANS OF CILIA

Cilia beat with a motion that is not much different from that of a man's arms when he is swimming the breast stroke as shown

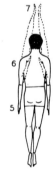

in fig. 17. (Motion of legs is omitted from sketch). When the arms are pulled downward during the power stroke (positions 1-4) the body is pulled forward. During the return stroke (positions 5-7) the body is not being pulled by the arms but is actually being slowed down slightly by the motion of the arms.

power stroke   return stroke

Figure 17

Fig. 18 shows the power and return stroke of a cilium. The cilium is quite rigid during the power stroke and pushes backward, thereby driving the animal forward. On the return stroke it is flexed and does not reach out so far and therefore does not "pull so much water."

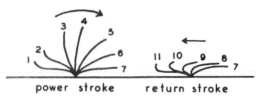

power stroke   return stroke

Figure 18

In most ciliates the cilia are arranged in longitudinal rows, and all the cilia of a row do not beat in phase. If we were to look at such a row from the side the cilia would look something like fig. 19. When some cilia are in the power stroke others are in the return stroke.

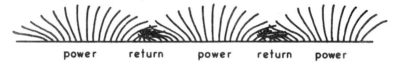

power   return   power   return   power

Figure 19

Fig. 20 shows a comparison of the action of cilia in a large holotrich to the oars of a Roman galley or of a multi-oar racing hull.

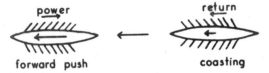

forward push   coasting

ACTION OF OARS IN ROMAN GALLEY

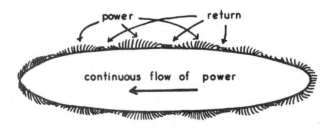

continuous flow of power

ACTION OF CILIA OF LARGE HOLOTRICH

Figure 20

30

During the power stroke the oars or cilia push backward and drive the animal or hull forward. However, in a ciliate the cilia in a longitudinal row do not move in phase as do the oars of a galley. At any one time some cilia of large ciliates, especially of holotrichs, are in the power stroke and others are in the return stroke (fig. 18). This results in a continuous flow of power, and the ciliate moves not by jumps but with a smooth forward movement.

This smooth movement is characteristic of most ciliates, especially Holotrichida, and in many cases may be used to distinguish them from flagellates, most of which move in a more jerky manner. However, there are exceptions on both sides, and to be certain of whether an animal is a flagellate or a ciliate one should really find the structure causing the movement and determine how it beats.

LOCOMOTION BY MEANS OF FLAGELLA

Flagella are usually few in number (except in one order, the Hypermastigida) and move with a whip-like motion which results in their pushing the animal forward either in a straight path or in a spiral .

A flagellum is essentially a whip-like fiber (an axoneme) which is covered by a sheath formed by a projection of the pellicle or outer covering of the flagellate. Fig. 21 shows

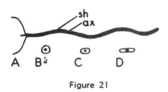

Figure 21

a flagellum in its simplest form. A, longitudinal view; sh, the sheath; ax, the axoneme. B, C, and D are cross sections of the flagellum and show that it may be round, oval, or flat. In many flagellates there are small projections (mastigonemes) which are attached to the flagella, and flagella may be classified on the basis of the arrangement of mastigonemes.

Figure 22. A. Acronematic flagellum with single terminal mastigoneme; found in Phytomonadida and some Zoomastigophorea. B.

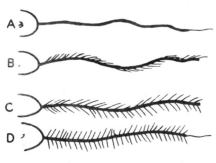

Figure 22

Stichonematic flagellum with single row of mastigonemes; found in Euglenida and transverse flagellum of Dinoflagellida. C. Pantonematic flagellum with at least two and probably several rows; found in Chrysomonadida. D. Pantacronematic, same as pantonematic plus a terminal mastigoneme; found in Choanoflagellidae. Some flagellates (e.g., Trichomonas) have no mastigonemes.

31

Mastigonemes usually can not be seen under an ordinary microscope but may be seen if one uses a dark field microscope, an electron microscope, or nigrosin relief or special mordant staining methods. The function of mastigonemes is at present unknown.

The mechanism by which the flagellum causes movement of the flagellate has been carefully worked out by a number of investigators. However, this is one subject which is very poorly explained in most textbooks.

The simplest type of flagellar movement is shown diagrammatically in fig. 23.

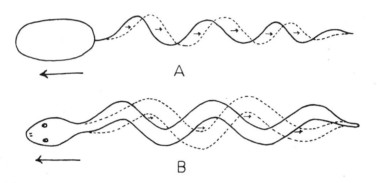

Figure 23

Let us assume that in this diagram the flagellum which is undergoing a wave-like motion is represented as being in the position denoted by the solid line. A wave-like motion passes down the flagellum which moves to the position denoted by the dash line. This wave-like motion is brought about by the active bending and straightening of the flagellum and not by a wiggling motion of the body of the flagellate. In actively bending and straightening in this wave-like manner the flagellum exerts a force on the water as indicated by the small arrows. This force results in an equal and opposite force being exerted on the organism, as indicated by the large arrow. The organism is then driven in the direction of the large arrow as a result of being pushed forward by the flagellum. This type of flagellar movement is found in spermatozoa of some animals and perhaps in some flagellates.

This is the same kind of motion produced by a snake swimming in water or even when moving on land through the grass. Let us suppose that the snake's head is the body of the flagellate and the snake's body is the flagellum. An active wave-like motion of the snake's body resulting from successive contraction and relaxation of the muscles of the vertebral column propels the animal forward. A similar movement is responsible for most of the locomotion of fishes and is particularly noticeable in any long slim fish, especially as seen from above.

The locomotion of most flagellates is much more complex than that shown in fig. 23. The motion of the flagellum is not confined to one plane (as is the body of a swimming snake) but is more in the form

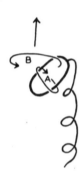

of a spiral, and this spiral movement causes the cell to rotate on its long axis as it is pushed forward, as denoted by curved arrow "A." Furthermore, the body of the flagellate tends to become arranged obliquely to the path of progression as shown in fig. 24. The straight arrow denotes the general direction of movement. The oblique position of the body, together with the rotation, produces a gyration which results in a spiral path as the flagellate moves forward. The small curved arrow (A) denotes the rotation of the body and the larger curved arrow (B) the gyration. As a result of this spiral path the body of the animal acts as an inclined plane and the speed of locomotion is greatly increased.

Figure 24

These complexities are exemplified in the locomotion of *Euglena*. If we watch a specimen of *Euglena* swim freely (so that it does not bump into the slide, coverslip, or other objects in the water) we will note that the path of movement is a spiral and that the flagellum is held at an angle to the body as shown in fig. 25. The organism will move

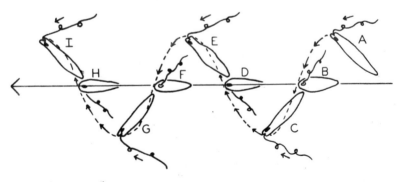

Figure 25

in the general direction of the long arrow, and the posterior end will not deviate much from the path denoted by the straight line. The anterior end, however, will gyrate around this path and will tend to move in a spiral as denoted by the dotted line. At the same time the cell rotates on its long axis because of the action of the flagellum. As seen from the side of the path the flagellum seems to beat backward as shown in the figure. This backward beat of the flagellum tends to push the animal forward as shown by the short arrows. However, the flagellum beats not directly backward but in positions A, C, E, G, and I at an angle of about 45° with the plane of the paper. At positions A, E, and I the flagellum would tend to push the animal through the paper toward the reader and at C and G through the paper away from the reader. This angle of the flagellum results in a gyration of the animal around the general path of locomotion.

We have seen now that the flagellum gives rise to a forward component that pushes the organism forward, that it causes rotation of the cell on its long axis, and most important of all it causes a gyration about the general path of locomotion. This gyration alone is also able to cause the organism to move forward. In fact, in some organisms, such as *Rhabdomonas*, the forward component of the flagellum does not exist, (fig. 42) and gyration alone (or gyration and rotation) is responsible for forward movement.

Gyration causes the whole animal to act as an inclined plane. In fact, it causes the whole animal to act just as the blade of a propeller. The function of the flagellum is merely to cause the gyration, and the gyration causes the forward movement. You can demonstrate this principle very easily if you have a small slow speed motor available. Place a cork on the end of the shaft and on the cork place a piece of wood shaped more or less like *Euglena* (or like a fairly fat cigar). Fig. 26 shows the arrangement.

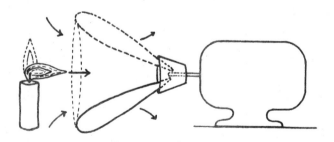

Figure 26

As the piece of wood gyrates air will flow along the path denoted by the arrows. You can test this by bringing a lighted candle near the axis of gyration. The flame will be sucked into the center of gyration. If the imitation *Euglena* were free to move it would be pulled in the direction from which the flame is sucked, i.e., forward. A more complex aquatic model can be constructed in which the imitation animal does move forward and the medium (water instead of air) is pushed backward only slightly.

The next time you go swimming you can demonstrate to yourself how gyration can produce forward movement by performing the

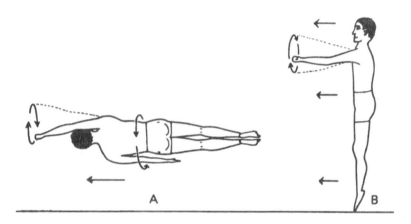

Figure 27

movements shown in fig. 27 with your arm. Not only your arm but your whole body will tend to move in the direction shown by the straight arrows. In position A your body will also tend to rotate. In these experiments your arm is comparable to the body of *Euglena*. The flagellum would merely be the force which causes the *Euglena* to gyrate.

One fundamental difference between flagella and cilia is that in the movement of a flagellum there is no necessity for a return stroke. In the movement of a cilium each complete beat consists of a power stroke and a return stroke. The movement of a flagellum, however, is a continuous undulation. Each bending movement exerts power, and so does bending in the opposite direction. The flow of power is therefore continuous. However, the movement of a flagellate is likely to be jerky for other reasons, namely because of the cell rotation and gyration which are explained above.

LOCOMOTION BY MEANS OF PROTOPLASMIC FLOW

A pseudopodium is an elongate extension of the protoplasm formed by the flowing of protoplasm outward from the main mass of the body. Protoplasmic flows which do not result in elongate extensions are not referred to as pseudopodia. In *Amoeba proteus* the endoplasm flows forward to form the pseudopodium. The pseudopodium is not the cause of the movement but rather the result. The animal really moves merely by flowing, and the protoplasmic flowing may or may not result in the formation of pseudopodia. Movement by flowing is therefore of two types: 1) directed by pseudopodia; 2) not directed by pseudopodia.

1. *Locomotion directed by pseudopodia.* A large ameba such as *Amoeba proteus* is covered by a pellicle. This pellicle is separated from the granular endoplasm by a very thin layer of clear ectoplasm. The endoplasm is granular in appearance, and contains many crystals, a nucleus, usually several food vacuoles, and one contractile vacuole.

The endoplasm is capable of what is known as sol-gel reversibility. This means that it may be in the form of a gel, similar in consistency to that of our common gelatin desserts. It may also occur in the form of a solution, similar in consistency to a warm gelatin dessert that seems to have "melted." The endoplasm is capable of changing rapidly from a gel to a sol state or vice versa, and we refer to it as plasmagel or plasmasol, depending upon whether it is semisolid or liquid.

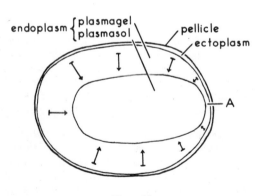

Figure 28

In very diagrammatic form we may represent the structure of an ameba as shown in fig. 28. The square tailed arrows in this figure denote pressure, not movement.

The plasmagel has a tendency to contract so that the plasmasol is under a slight pressure. If this pressure is high enough the plasmasol is likely to flow out of any weak place in the wall of plasmagel, such as the thin region shown at A.

When that happens a pseudopodium may be formed in the weak region, and the ameba moves in that direction. Such a movement is shown in fig. 29.

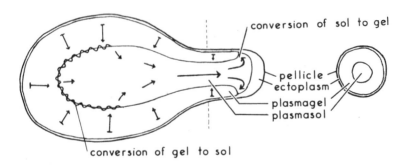

conversion of sol to gel

pellicle
ectoplasm
plasmagel
plasmasol

conversion of gel to sol

Figure 29

In this figure the square tailed arrows denote a pressure but only a slight movement. The tailless arrows denote rapid movement. The small figure on the right is a cross section through the pseudopodium at the level of the dash line. The pseudopodium is a tube of plasmagel through which the plasmasol is forced to flow.

After the plasmasol flows through the center of the pseudopodium it reaches the front end where the arrows are curved. Here it flows around to the front of the tube of plasmagel, and when it reaches this position *it becomes plasmagel.* New plasmasol is formed in the region denoted by the wavy line *by the solution of plasmagel.*

As the ameba flows, plasmagel is converted to plasmasol at the posterior end, this plasmasol flows to the anterior end, and here it again becomes plasmagel. The driving mechanism is the pressure exerted on the plasmasol by the tendency of the plasmagel to contract. This is the basic mechanism of protoplasmic flow as it occurs in amebas. In some species the gel and sol layers are not so easily distinguishable as in *Amoeba proteus,* but the mechanism is very similar.

In some species, for example the shelled ameba *Arcella,* the front end of the pseudopodium may become attached and then it may contract and thereby pull the rest of the animal, including its house if it has one, forward (fig. 1). Such locomotion is different from that described above for *Amoeba proteus* in that the main body is moved by contraction rather than by flowing. Contraction of pseudopodia, however, also occurs in certain naked amebas.

37

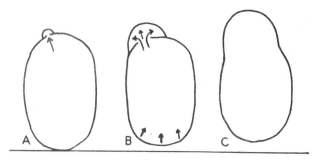

Figure 30

2. *Locomotion not directed by pseudopodia.* Many amebas move by protoplasmic flow without forming pseudopodia. We have defined pseudopodia as elongate extensions of the protoplasm formed by an outward flow from the main protoplasmic mass. Many outward flows are not elongate, and the total projection from the body is not relatively as long as a hemisphere. Fig. 30 shows three stages in the formation of a short blunt extension on an ameba which does not form pseudopodia (elongated extensions). Fig. 31 shows the result of five successive extensions of this type.

Figure 31

Such flows result in movement of the animal because the whole animal may eventually flow through the extension. The basic mechanism is the same as that described above for pseudopodia; the only difference is that the outward flowing propection is broader than it is long.

The two types of locomotor flow, i.e., with and without formation of elongate extensions, ordinarily do not occur in the same species of ameba, and the type of movement is therefore of considerable taxonomic importance.

A few species, however, which normally move by means of several pseudopodia may sometimes move with only one pseudopodium and thereby cause some confusion. For example, *Amoeba proteus* may have one to several pseudopodia and changes readily from one form to another.

HOW TO USE THE KEY

If one has a pictured key to any group of organisms there are two ways in which it might be used in the identification of an unknown: 1) by comparing pictures; 2) by following the key.

The first method involves turning the pages and looking for pictures similar to the organism in question. If the pictures are good and the student knows what taxonomic characters to look for in making the comparison, the method will work in many instances. In fact this method is often used by professionals.

A protozoologist of considerable experience when called upon to identify an organism might say "Oh, that's a little holotrich, probably one of the Hymenostomina." Then he might turn to the part of the key which describes the hymenostomes and after a glance at the pictures of related genera say, "It's probably *Loxocephalus*. No cilia at anterior tip; a long caudal cilium; noticeable transverse row of cilia in anterior quarter of body; mouth very small, hardly noticeable; dark body. That's it."

Proficient use of the first method requires that the student know what to look for in the organism and where to look in the key and that he have a considerable amount of experience in identification. In the example cited above he would have to know that the organism is a ciliate, that it is a holotrich, that it probably has a small mouth with undulating membranes and that in many such small ciliates the mouth is difficult to see, and that the distribution of cilia is one of the taxonomic characters of the group.

In many instances the beginning student will be more certain of his identification if he follows the key. Let us suppose that we did not recognize *Paramecium caudatum* and tried to trace it through the key. How would we go about the job?

The key gives the student usually two choices labelled 1a and 1b, 2a and 2b, etc. In rare instances there are three: e.g., 1a, 1b, and 1c. At the right hand end of each choice there is either a number which refers to the next pair of choices which should be consulted or else there is the name of the group. A description of the group may follow immediately or a page reference pertaining to it may be given.

In the instance of our *Paramecium* we find on p. 169 that the organism fits choice 1a, the Ciliatea, because it has cilia and does not fit choice 1b, the Suctorea, because it does not have tentacles. It might, of course, be a young form of a suctorean; that is unlikely, but we could check the point by looking for pictures of the young forms of the Suctorea. The reference for 1a sends us to 2. There we have choice 2a, the Euciliatia, with two types of nuclei, macro- and micro-nuclei, and choice 2b, the Protociliatia, with nuclei of only one type.

39

We could stain the nuclei in our organism with methyl green and thereby put it in the Euciliatia, or we could rule out the Protociliatia by the fact that all organisms of that group are endozoic.

If we turn to Euciliatia, p. 170 we find a section dealing with the arrangement of ciliary organelles as a basis for further separation and then another section entitled "What to look for in a ciliate." On the basis of the information in those two sections we go to p. 175 and find a key to the orders of Euciliatia. Since there is no adoral zone of cilia on our organism we place it in choice 1a, the Holotrichida, also found on p. 175. Since the organism has a cytostome we take choice 1b and that leads us to 2. Choice 2b leads us to 3. Choice 3b leads us to 4. Choice 4b leads us to 5. Choice 5a leads us to Suborder Trichostomina, p. 186.

We turn to this page and learn that there are 14 families of Trichostomina and that only a few representative genera are included in the present volume. However, by looking over the genera listed and illustrated we determine that our "unknown" belongs to the genus *Paramecium*. From its size, shape, and type of micronucleus we may then identify it as *Paramecium caudatum*.

If we begin our study of the Protozoa by trying to use the key we soon learn to recognize certain groups, and we may then skip the steps leading up to that group. However, it is a good idea to run completely through the key now and then even if we do know the group. Using the preliminary steps in the key will emphasize the characteristics of the group so that they will become more closely fixed in our minds, and it will also serve as a check on our memory when we are inclined to consider an unknown as a member of a group to which it does not belong.

WHAT IS A CLASSIFICATION?

A classification of any group of organisms is simply a filing system, of which one primary purpose is to arrange the available information concerning the various species in such a manner that any of it can be found quickly by a person familiar with the system. For this purpose it is more convenient to file all the material on flagellates under one heading and label it Mastigophora than it is to have this information mixed up with that on ciliates, rhizopods, and sporozoans.

In taxonomy the characters used for separating the various sections of the filing system vary from one group of organisms to another. In general, these characters are chosen on the basis of one or both of the following considerations:

1. Is the character one that can be readily determined by any person familiar with comparable material, i.e., with related species?

A character chosen only on this basis may be designated as an arbitrary character, i.e., it is abitrarily chosen because it is useful. The more easily the characters can be recognized the better, but in many instances the characters chosen are often difficult to determine, simply because there are no easily determinable characters or because the more obvious characters are subject to considerable variation or are known to be of no phylogenetic significance.

2. Is the character of phylogenetic significance? In other words, is the character determined genetically in such a way that various organisms closely related phylogenetically have it and those that are not closely related phylogenetically do not.

If all characters chosen were of phylogenetic significance, and if their order of rank in the taxonomic system were the same as the chronological sequence in which changes in them determined the formation of the various groups of organisms, and if all species which existed in the past were included, then the taxonomic system would be a bird's eye view of the development of the various species concerned. This is often stated as the goal of the taxonomic system. At present, however, for various reasons the goal has been reached only in rather limited groups. The tendency among pioneer taxonomists is to use easily determinable arbitrary characters unless there are known phylogenetic reasons for using others. As more is learned about characters of phylogenetic significance the purely arbitrary characters are discarded, and the taxonomic system is made to conform more nearly to the current ideas concerning phylogeny.

The taxonomic system, therefore, is not static but dynamic. It is continually changing and growing as more facts are accumulated about known organisms, as hitherto undescribed organisms are described and cataloged, and as we change our concepts of the phylogenetic significance of certain characters.

The present key to the Protozoa may be considered simply as a filing system in which the characters have been chosen in accordance with the above principles.

CLASSIFICATION OF THE PROTOZOA; KEY TO THE SUBPHYLA

In the following classification, a uniform series of endings has been adopted. They are as follows: Phylum and Subphylum, —a; Class, —ea; Subclass, —ia; Order, —ida; Suborder, —ina. This system was suggested for all animals by the Zoological Sciences Section (F) of the American Association for the Advancement of Science. The Family names, as in all animals, end in —idae. The groupings used are modified from the report of the Association which was prepared

HOW TO KNOW THE PROTOZOA

by Professor L. E. Noland of the University of Wisconsin after consultation with more than forty protozoologists.

KINGDOM 2 PROTISTA
PHYLUM 1 PROTOZOA

  Subphylum 1 Mastigophora
    Class 1 Phytomastigophorea
      Order 1 Chrysomonadida
      Order 2 Cryptomonadida
      Order 3 Dinoflagellida
      Order 4 Euglenida
      Order 5 Phytomonadida
    Class 2 Zoomastigophorea
      Order 1 Rhizomastigida
      Order 2 Protomastigida
      Order 3 Polymastigida
      Order 4 Hypermastigida

  Subphylum 2 Sarcodina
    Class 1 Actinopodea
      Order 1 Heliozoida
      Order 2 Radiolarida
    Class 2 Rhizopodea
      Order 1 Proteomyxida
      Order 2 Amoebida
      Order 3 Testacida
      Order 4 Foraminiferida
      Order 5 Mycetozodia

  Subphylum 3 Sporozoa
    Class 1 Telosporidea
      Subclass 1 Gregarinidia
        Order 1 Eugregarinida
        Order 2 Schizogregarinida
      Subclass 2 Coccidia
      Subclass 3 Haemosporidia
    Class 2 Cnidosporidea
      Order 1 Myxosporida
      Order.2 Actinomyxida
      Order 3 Microsporida
    Class 3 Acnidosporidea

  Subphylum 4 Ciliophora
    Class 1 Ciliatea
      Subclass 1 Protociliatia
        Order 1 Opalinida

Subclass 2 Euciliatia

Order 1 Holotrichida

Suborder 1 Astomina
Suborder 2 Gymnostomina
Suborder 3 Trichostomina
Suborder 4 Hymenostomina
Suborder 5 Thigmotrichina
Suborder 6 Apostomina

Order 2 Spirotrichida

Suborder 1 Heterotrichina
Suborder 2 Oligotrichina
Suborder 3 Ctenostomina
Suborder 4 Tintinnina
Suborder 5 Entodiniomorphina
Suborder 6 Hypotrichina

Order 3 Chonotrichida

Order 4 Peritrichida

Class 2 Suctorea

KEY TO THE SUBPHYLA

1a With cilia or sucking tentacles.   Subphylum CILIOPHORA, p. 168

1b Without cilia or sucking tentacles............................2

2a (a, b, c) With one or more flagella; with or without pseudopodia.
Subphylum MASTIGOPHORA, p. 50

2b With pseudopodia; without flagella. Subphylum SARCODINA, p. 99

2c Without obvious organelles of locomotion; usually producing spores;
all parasitic.   Subphylum SPOROZOA, p. 142

Many free living Protozoa have numerous fine radiating processes and usually move slowly or not at all. If the radiating processes seem to have knobs on the ends, the organism is a suctorean and the "knobs" are the sucking areas on the ends of the tentacles (fig. 368). If the radiating processes have no knobs they are probably pseudopodia (figs. 160, 166). Some organisms with radiating pseudopodia also have radially arranged spicules of a skeleton, i.e., some Actinopodea. In some ciliates the cilia may cease moving for short periods of time, and the individual cilia may be seen as radiating processes from the body. However, in such cases a few minutes of careful observation will usually be sufficient to detect ciliary movement.

Some Protozoa have both ameboid and flagellated stages in their life history, i.e., the ameba may become a flagellate (with or without pseudopodia) and then this flagellate may lose its flagella and become an ameba. Other species may retain the flagellum permanently and possess pseuodopods during only part of their life history. Such behavior is very confusing to a taxonomist. If the organism does not possess chloroplasts the usual method of classification is on the basis of whether or not the flagella are permanent. Organisms which always have one or more flagella are classed as Mastigophora; those which alternate between flagellate and ameboid stages are classed as Sarcodina. However, if the organism possesses chloroplasts it is considered to belong to the Phytomastigophorea.

Some chloroplast-bearing flagellates have what is known as a *palmella stage*. A palmella consists of many cells without flagella embedded in a gelatinous mass (fig. 71c); sometimes the cells are ameboid. However, they usually have chloroplasts, and the experienced observer can identify them as stages in the life history of a flagellate.

Most free living protozoa have a life cycle which consists of an active or *trophozoite* stage and an inactive stage or *cyst*. In order to form a cyst a protozoan simply becomes rounded and secretes over its surface a more or less impermeable membrane. In the encysted stage the organism may remain alive even though the cysts may be thoroughly dried and blown about by the wind. The principal reason why many species of Protozoa are so widely distributed over the world is that they are carried about in the encysted stage by the wind and on the feet of wading birds.

The Sporozoa are so called because many of them produce spores. A *spore* is a cyst which is formed at a definite point in a complex life cycle. In the Telosporidea spore formation follows fusion of gametes, and in the Cnidosporidea it follows a complex developmental process.

All subphyla contain parasitic species, but the Sporozoa comprise the only subphylum which is completely parasitic.

SUBPHYLUM MASTIGOPHORA

WHAT TO LOOK FOR IN A FLAGELLATE

Does the flagellate have *chloroplasts?* Chloroplasts are bodies in the cytoplasm which contain the bright green material chlorophyll (which is responsible for photosynthesis) and also the yellow pigment, xanthophyll, and one or more reddish pigments known as carotenoids. Chloroplasts may be bright green, yellowish green, or brown, depending upon the proportions of chlorophyll, xanthophyll, and carotenoids present. What color are the chloroplasts?

If chloroplasts are present, do they contain *pyrenoids?* Pyrenoids are centers of carbohydrate synthesis, and in chloroplasts which have them the carbohydrate is formed on the surface of the pyrenoid. Fig. 32 shows a chloroplast of *Euglena* with pyrenoid and with carbohydrate material (paramylum in this instance) attached to the pyrenoid.

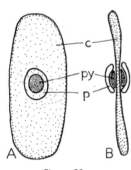

Figure 32

Does the cytoplasm contain highly refractive bodies which have a pale bluish green tinge? These may occur in either chloroplast-bearing or non-chloroplast bearing flagellates. They are carbohydrate food reserves, and are composed of starch or paramylum. Paramylum is very similar in chemical composition to starch, but will not give the blue color reaction as starch does when iodine (Lugol's solution) is added. Chlorophyll is a bright grass green and can always be distinguished easily from carbohydrate reserves after the observer has once seen the two side by side. If the green color is very pale and blue green rather than bright green, you may consider it to be carbohydrate.

If the flagellate has no chloroplasts does it contain food vacuoles, i.e., is it holozoic? Food vacuoles may be almost any color, depending upon what the animal has eaten. Partially digested green algae are yellow to brownish red. Very few flagellates have both chloroplasts and food vacuoles (e.g., some species of Gymnodinium). A few species (e.g., *Noctiluca),* however, are holozoic and also have symbiotic zooxanthellae which live in their cytoplasm.

Size? This may be estimated by any of the methods on pages 13 to 15. In general, Mastigophora are smaller than Ciliophora or Sarcodina.

Shape? Is it short and thick, or long and slim, or intermediate? (Fig. 33).

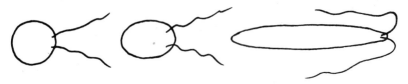

Figure 33

In cross section is it round, flat, triangular, or otherwise?

Fig. 34 shows cross sections of several flagellates. A. *Chlamydo-*

A B C D E

Figure 34

monas, B, *Phacus acuminata*, C, *Euglena trisulcata*, D, *Phacus agilis okobojiensis*, and E, *Phacus trimarginatus*.

Is the body twisted? (Figs. 77, 85).

Figure 35

Does the body change shape? Fig. 35 shows changes in the shape of *Euglena mutabilis* (after Hollande). The pellicle constricts in various ways and squeezes the nucleus and cytoplasm into different shapes.

Does it have a gullet? (Fig. 36). A gullet is an invagination (a pocket-like affair) at the anterior end. It is not necessarily used for

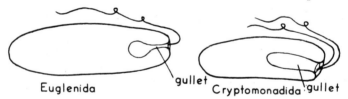

Euglenida gullet Cryptomonadida gullet

Figure 36

ingestion of food. Many flagellates have a gullet but not do ingest solid food. The gullet may be quite inconspicuous. Examine carefully under high power. If gullet is present, Euglenida or Cryptomonadida. In the Euglenida the basal end of the gullet is expanded and appears as a clear vacuole, sometimes called a "reservoir."

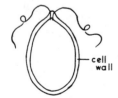

cell wall

Figure 37

Does it have a *cell wall*? (Fig. 37). A cell wall is a lifeless secreted layer that closely covers the cell. It may be composed of cellulose; if so, Phytomonadida.

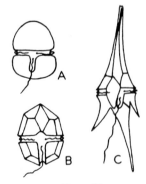

Figure 38

Does the organism have a *transverse groove* around its middle? (Fig. 38). This transverse groove is also called a *girdle, annulus,* or *cingulus.* If so, Dinoflagellida.

If so, is the outer covering thick? If so, is it made of only three pieces (upper, lower, and girdle plates) or are the upper and lower plates subdivided? (Fig. 38 B). If so, are there any horn-like projections? (Fig. 38 C).

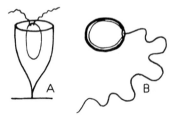

Figure 39

Does it live in a house? If so is the house attached to the substrate (your slide, debris, etc) as in *Stylopyxis,* fig. 39 A, or is the house carried about as in *Trachelomonas,* fig. 39 B? A house is also referred to as a *test,* or *shell,* or as a *lorica.* What color is the test? Brown, yellow, purple? If it is carried about is the test smooth or spiny? If spiny, how big are the spines and how are they arranged? Is there a collar around the opening for the flagellum? What shape is the test? Fig. 40 shows the tests of A, *Trachelomonas raciborskii,* 40μ, and B, *Strombomonas fluviatilis,* $30\,\mu$, which differ in the shape of the test and in the presence of spines.

If you are in doubt about whether a rigid external covering is a test or a cell wall you can smash the animal by pushing the coverslip down on the slide with a pencil or needle. A rigid test will usually break into fragments, and a green flagellate with a red stigma may swim out *(Trachelomonas* or *Strombomonas).*

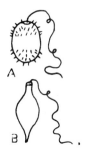

Figure 40

Is the test made of two pieces, i.e., bivalve like a clam shell? If so, *Phacotus.*

Does the organism have a *stigma*? A stigma is a red structure (solid in Phytomonadida, made up of many small granules in Euglenida) at the anterior end (fig. 41, s). It is a part of the mechanism that

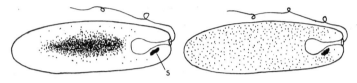

Figure 41

causes certain flagellates (for example, *Euglena*) to migrate toward the light (positive phototropism).

If chloroplasts and a stigma are present, are there other red granules which may be scattered throughout the cytoplasm or massed together in the center of the animal? (Fig. 41). If so, a red species of *Euglena* or perhaps *Haematococcus*.

How many flagella? How many at the anterior end? Posterior end? On the sides? Does one of them lie in the annulus?

What shape is the path of locomotion, and what is the position of the flagellum? Fig. 42 (after Lowndes) shows two positions (A and

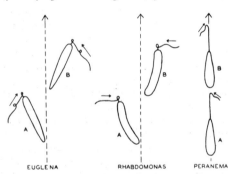

Figure 42

B) in the movement of three common flagellates. The long arrow denotes the general direction of locomotion. *Euglena* and *Rhabdomonas* move in a spiral; *Peranema* does not. Does the unknown flagellate swim in a spiral and does the body rotate as in *Euglena* and *Rhabdomonas*? Or does the body move smoothly forward as does that of *Peranema*? If so, Pera-nemidae. In *Euglena* the flagellum beats backward, and in *Rhabdomonas* the flagellum beats at right angles to the general direction of locomotion. In *Peranema* the flagellum is held directly forward and is bent backward and vibrates only near the tip, and the cell does not rotate.

If Peranemidae, does it have a gullet and a pair of rod-like bodies at the anterior end? If so, *Peranema* or *Heteronema*. If not, *Petalomonas* or related genera.

Does it have one to several blunt pseudopodia as well as a flagellum? If so, *Mastigamoeba*.

Does it have long, thin, non-motile or only slowly motile filamentous projections? These would be axopodia, a special type of pseudopodium used as tactile organelles for gathering food, not used for locomotion.

Does it have a thin, clear, flexible *protoplasmic collar* around the base of the flagellum? (Fig. 129). These are very transparent and usually can be seen only under high power with a careful adjustment of the illumination. If collar is present, a choanoflagellate. With or without a gelatinous test? If test is present, does it have a stalk?

Is it colonial? If so, it may also be bright green. If it is a swimming colony are the cells arranged in the form of a hollow ball, a solid ball, or a flat plate? If so, colonial Phytomonadida. If not green, colonial Protomonadida. Fig. 43 shows two views of a *Gonium* colony.

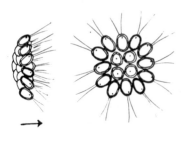

Figure 43

If it is fixed to the slide or to debris (i.e., if it is sessile) what is the shape of the colony? How many cells?

Is it *free living* or endozoic? If parasitic in the blood stream of a vertebrate it may have the flagellum attached throughout most of the length of the body to form an undulating membrane. If so, *Trypanosoma*. If in the intestine and it has an undulating membrane, *Trichomonas*.

If it came from the digestive tract of an insect it may have many flagella. If so, how many nuclei? One (Hypermastigida), two (Dikaryomastigina) or many (Polykaryomastigina)?

If the flagella are numerous, note how they move. This will tell you whether the animal is really a flagellate or a ciliate. If they are relatively stiff and move like oars, then the animal is a ciliate. See fig. 20.

Does it have a rod-like structure, an axostyle, throughout most of its length? And perhaps also an undulating membrane. If so, probably *Trichomonas*.

KEY TO THE ORDERS OF MASTIGOPHORA

The Mastigophora consist of those Protozoa which have one or more flagella. Some Mastigophora also have pseudopodia, but none possess cilia.

The subphylum is usually divided into two classes, partly on the basis of whether or not the cells contain chloroplasts: the Zoomastigophorea, without chloroplasts; and the Phytomastigophorea with or without chloroplasts, those without chloroplasts being similar to the chloroplast-bearing ones in many other ways. This is a confusing system, especially since there are many pairs of species of Phytomastigophorea which differ from each other only in that one has chloroplasts and the other does not. In fact, as far as other characteristics are concerned the Phytomastigophorea may be arranged in two parallel series, one series with and one without chloroplasts. In addition there is a third series, entirely without chloroplasts, which comprise the Zoomastigophorea, and for these organisms there are no similar species which differ from them only in the possession of chloroplasts.

It is known that species may lose chloroplasts during cell division (all of the chloroplasts may go to one of the filial cells) and that once a cell has lost all of its chloroplasts its descendants never regain chloroplasts. Therefore, new non-chloroplast-bearing species are continually arising from chloroplast-bearing ones. For example, let us assume that fig. 44 represents a phyletic tree of the flagellates. The heavy lines denote chloroplast-bearing species and the lighter lines

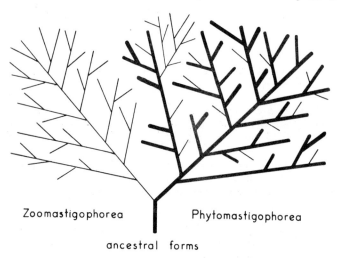

Zoomastigophorea   Phytomastigophorea

ancestral forms

Figure 44

denote non-chloroplast-bearing species. No Zoomastigophorea have chloroplasts; most Phytomastigophorea do have chloroplasts.

During the development of the colorless species of flagellates the loss of chloroplasts has occurred time and time again. Each time the chloroplasts have been lost the loss has been of distinct phylogenetic significance so far as the colorless descendants are concerned. However, since this loss has occurred in so many unrelated or slightly related groups the use of the presence or absence of chloroplasts as a basis for separation of the Classes of the Mastigophora would be in direct contradiction to phylogeny. This is an example of an easily discernible character which has occurred so many times in so many different groups of flagellates that its usefulness as a major taxonomic character has become limited.

In view of the fact that many Phytomastigophorea do not possess chloroplasts the beginning student who finds a flagellate without chloroplasts should try to identify it first in one class, let us say as one of the Zoomastigophorea, and if not successful there to assume that the species is a member of the other class, i.e., of the Phytomastigophorea. In the latter case either the non-chlorophyll-bearing flagellate or another one almost exactly like it except for the presence of chloroplasts will be found among the Phytomastigophorea.

1a With chloroplasts, or a close relative of a chloroplast-bearing flagellate.   Class PHYTOMASTIGOPHOREA, 2

1b Without chloroplasts, and not closely related to chloroplast-bearing flagellates.   Class ZOOMASTIGOPHOREA, p. 82

2a With furrow and transverse flagellum and often with cellulose plates.   Order DINOFLAGELLIDA, p. 58

2b Without furrow and transverse flagellum and plates 3

3a Chloroplasts yellowish to brownish green 4

3b Chloroplasts bright grass green, many species without chloroplasts 5

4a Without gullet; cells not flattened. Order CHRYSOMONADIDA, p. 51

4b With gullet; cells usually flattened. Order CRYPTOMONADIDA, p. 56

5a Without gullet; with cellulose wall; reserve materials starch.   Order PHYTOMONADIDA, p. 75

5b With gullet; without cellulose wall; reserve materials paramylum; many non-chloroplast-bearing species.   Order EUGLENIDA, p. 63

ORDER CHRYSOMONADIDA

Chrysomonads are usually small, i.e., less than 20 μ in length. Chloroplasts are yellowish to brownish green. Some species have ameboid stages. Other species have a test, and some are colonial.

Colonial testate species are often common in water reservoirs. A few species form palmella stages. Nutrition is phototrophic or saprobic. Fresh water and marine.

1a Motile stage dominant; ameboid stage absent or seldom seen.
                              Suborder EUCHRYSOMONADINA....2

1b Ameboid or palmella stage dominant; flagellate stage seldom seen or unknown 6

2a With calcareous or siliceous shell...........................5

2b Without shell or with simple test........................3

3a One flagellum.   **Family CHROMULINIDAE**

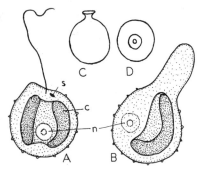

Figure 45

Fig. 45. A. *Chromulina pascheri*, flagellate stage, 15-20 μ (Hofeneeder). Spherical or oval, one flagellum. B. Ameboid stage. C. and D. Cyst stage from side and top.

This is a typical chrysomonad; one or two yellow-brown chromatophores. Some t i m e s present in numbers sufficient to color the water.

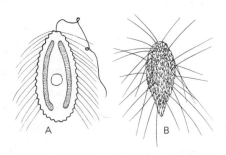

Figure 46

Fig. 46. A. *Mallomonas ploesslii*, 30 μ (Klebs). Body elongate with siliceous scales and spines; many species. B. *M. caudata*, 50 μ (Iwanoff).

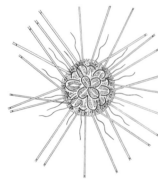

Figure 47

Fig. 47. *Chrysosphaerella longispina,* 250 μ (Lauterborn).

Spherical colony enclosed in gelatinous mass; each cell oval with one flagellum, two chromatophores, and two spines.

3b Two flagella 4
4a Flagella equally long.   Family SYNCRYPTIDAE

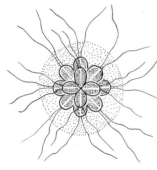

Figure 48

Fig. 48. *Syncrypta volvox,* cells 8-14 μ, colony 20-70 μ (Stein).

Spherical colony, cells embedded in gelatinous mass.

Figure 49

Fig. 49. *Synura uvella,* cells 20-40μ, colony 100-400 μ (Stein).

When present in large numbers in water reservoirs Synura may cause the water to have the odor of ripe cucumbers. Sometimes found in large numbers in winter under the ice on ponds.

4b Flagella unequal in length. **Family OCHROMONADIDAE**

The type genus *Ochromonas* is similar to *Chromulina* except that it has a second and shorter flagellum.

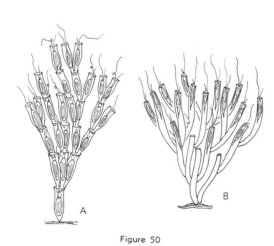

Figure 50

Fig. 50. A. *Dinobryon sertularia,* cells 30-44 μ (Stein).

Solitary or colonial, with hyaline and vase-like test. Each cell has two flagella unequal in length and two yellow-brown chromatophores. When a flagellate di v i d e s one of the filial cells forms a new test on the rim of the test of the parent cell. *Stylopyxis* is similar except that the test has a short stalk and no colonies are formed (fig. 39). B. *Hyalobryon ramosum,* cells up to 30 μ, lorica 50-70 μ (Lauterborn). Similar to *Dinobryon* except for shape of lorica which is tubular instead of vase-like.

5a Bearing calcareous discs or rods; mostly marine. **Family COCCOLITHOPHORIDAE**

Figure 51

Fig. 51. *Coccolithophora wallichi* 20-25 μ (Lohmann).

The surface of the body is covered with secreted calcareous oval discs. Other members of the family have rigid calcareous exoskeletons bearing numerous radially arranged trumpet-shaped tubes. These discs and tubes are picked up by other marine organisms (e.g., Tintinnina, p.215) and used for building arenaceous tests.

5b With siliceous exoskeleton; marine. Family SILICOFLAGELLIDAE

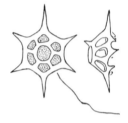

Figure 52

Fig. 52. *Distephanus speculum,* 50 μ (Kuhn).

Six pointed siliceous skeletal framework of unusual shape in which the flagellate lives.

6a Ameboid; each cell usually with chloroplasts; flagellate stage unknown; classed as chrysomonads only because of the chloroplasts.
Suborder RHIZOCHRYSIDINA

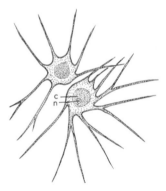

Figure 53

Fig. 53. *Rhizochrysis scherfelli,* 10-14 μ (Scherfell).

Two ameboid individuals with yellowish-brownish green chloroplast and branching pseudopodia. Any group of small amebas each with this color of chloroplast is likely to be this or a related species. Nutrition phototrophic, saprobic, and holozoic.

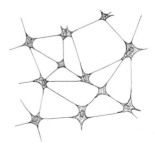

Figure 54

Fig. 54. *Chrysarachnion insidians,* 3-4μ, as many as several hundred to colony (Pascher).

Some individuals have no chloroplast. Individuals much smaller than *Rhizochrysis* and joined to form a network in which small animals are trapped and later digested. Nutrition phototrophic, saprobic, and holozoic.

6b Palmella stage dominant; flagellate stage transient.

Suborder CHRYSOCAPSINA

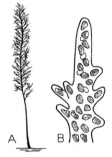

Fig. 55. *Hydrurus foetidus,* 1-30 cm, (Berthold, Klebs).

A. A large olive-green feathery colony. B. The end of one of the branches showing numerous ameboid cells embedded in a gelatinous mass. In running fresh water; sticky to the touch; develops an offensive odor; occasionally encrusted with calcium carbonate.

Figure 55

ORDER CRYPTOMONADIDA

The cryptomonads have one or two yellow-brown chloroplasts; the cells are usually flattened and have one or two flagella and usually a distinct gullet. Some genera do not have chloroplasts. Some genera store starch *(Chilomonas);* others store a slightly different carbohydrate *(Cyathomonas).* Nutrition is phototrophic, saprobic, or holozoic.

1a Truncate anteriorly with distinct gullet.

Family CRYPTOMONADIDAE

Fig. 56. *Cryptomonas ovata,* 20-30μ (Pascher).

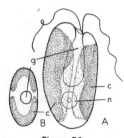

Figure 56

Body flattened, gullet distinct, two flagella, two yellowish to brownish green chromatophores, starch granules. *Chrysidella* is very similar to *Cryptomonas* except that it is less than 10μ long and occurs as a symbiont (zooxanthellae) in Radiolarida and Foraminiferida.

Fig. 57. *Chilomonas paramecium,* 20-40μ.

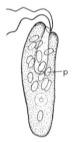

Figure 57

Very similar to *Cryptomonas* except that chloroplasts are absent. Probably the most common flagellate in putrid plant infusions.

Fig. 58. *Cyathomonas truncata,* 15-30μ.

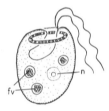

Figure 58

Body somewhat oval; no chloroplasts; gullet very obvious and surrounded by a ring of highly refractile granules. Carbohydrate reserve stains red-violet with iodine. Holozoic, feeding on bacteria.

1b Body kidney-shaped.   **Family NEPHROSELMIDAE**

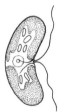

Fig. 59. *Protochrysis phaeophycearum,* 15μ (Pascher).

Figure 59

With a distinct furrow but gullet indistinct or lacking. One or two chloroplasts.

ORDER DINOFLAGELLIDA

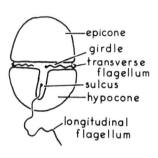

epicone
girdle
transverse
flagellum
sulcus
hypocone

longitudinal
flagellum

Figure 60

The structure of a typical dinoflagellate is shown in fig. 60. The dinoflagellates differ from all other flagellates in possessing a more or less *transverse groove*, also known as a *girdle, cingulus,* or *annulus,* in which there is a flagellum. The groove is usually extended posteriorly in one region to form the *sulcus.* A second flagellum (longitudinal) arises from the sulcus and is directed posteriorly. Nutrition is phototrophic, saprobic, or holozoic. In holozoic species food is ingested in the region of the sulcus. The longitudinal flagellum pushes the animal forward; the transverse flagellum produces rotation and in holozoic species may guide food particles to the sulcus. The part of the cell anterior to the girdle is known as the *epicone* and the part posterior to the girdle as the *hypocone.* The body may be naked, covered with a thin cellulose wall, or with a thick cellulose wall divided into plates. In forms with a cell wall the covering of the epicone and hypocone are designated as the *epitheca* and *hypotheca,* respectively. Some marine species contain two large pink or red vacuoles which are permanently connected by canals to the outside and are called *pusules.* Pusules are probably useful in saprobic nutrition. Many species parasitic in copepods; some on fish. Some species are the cause of "red" or "yellow" water in tropical seas.

Fig. 61. *Gymnodinium aeruginosum,* 35μ.

G. *palustre* is similar, about 45μ. Other species are relatively wider and some are holozoic. Cell without cellulose wall; chromatophores green. Common in fresh water ponds and lakes.

Figure 61

During the "red tide" off the Florida coast in 1947 *Gymnodinium brevis* was present in enormous numbers, as high as 50 million a liter. Enormous numbers of fish died during the "red tide," so many that the coast was littered for miles with tons and tons of stinking carcasses. Death of the fish is caused by a toxin similar to that of *Gonyaulax* (fig. 66).

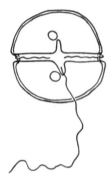

Figure 62

Fig. 62. *Glenodinium monensis,* 25μ (Herdman).

Body covered with distinct cell wall which is not divided into plates. Chloroplasts yellow-green. Sulcus short and extends equally into epicone and hypocone. Two reddish vacuoles (pusules) open into sulcus. Salt or fresh water.

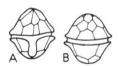

Figure 63

Fig. 63. *Glenodinium cinctum,* 45μ (Eddy).

Similar to *Glenodinium monensis* except for slight difference in shape and the fact that with careful observation the epitheca and hypotheca can be seen to be divided into plates. Common in fresh water. A, B. Viewed from opposite sides of the body.

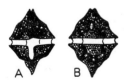

Figure 64

Fig. 64. *Peridinium wisconsiense,* 55-64μ (Eddy).

Peridinium is similar to *Glenodinium* except that the wall is always distinctly divided into plates. Common in fresh water lakes. A, B. Viewed from opposite sides of body.

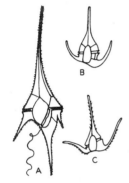

Fig. 65. A. *Ceratium hirundinella*, 95-700μ (Stein).

Body covered with distinct plates; epicone with one long horn-like process and hypocone with 2 or 3. Common in salt water and in fresh water lakes. Numerous varieties. B. *Ceratium tripos*, 225μ (Wailes). Marine.

Figure 65

Fig. 66. *Gonyaulax polyhedra*, 50μ (Kofoid, Lebour).

Similar to *Peridinium* except that the ends of the girdle are not directly apposed but slightly displaced. Ridges along the plate sutures. Surface regularly pitted. Widely distributed. Phosphorescent. One of the chief causes of "red water" in certain areas, e.g., off the California coast. At any one time "red water" may cover an area 60 miles or more in length, and *Gonyaulax* may reach a peak number of six million per liter (Allen).

Figure 66

One species of *Gonyaulax*, *G. catenella*, is known to produce a very toxic alkaloidal material. The amount extracted from 3000 flagellates is about 1 microgram and can kill a mouse; a few milligrams is probably fatal to man. Several epidemics of food poisoning of man have been traced to eating of shellfish (*Mytilus californianus*) which had been feeding on *Gonyaulax*

Figure 67

Fig. 67. *Pouchetia fusus*, 94μ (Schutt).

Sulcus and girdle twisted in a spiral about the body. With a large eyespot or ocellus which consists of a red or black pigment mass and a hyaline refractile body, the two together forming a structure similar to the ocelli of flatworms (*Planaria*, trematodes).

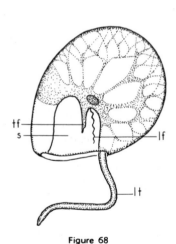

Figure 68

Fig. 68. *Noctiluca scintillans*, 200-2000μ (Kofoid and Swezy).

Body spherical or almost so, without girdle, with deep sulcus, the posterior portion of which is drawn out into a tentacle which pushes food (other Protozoa and small crustacea) into the sulcus. Transverse flagellum attached to pellicle to form a tooth-like process; longitudinal flagellum short and contained in sulcus. Cytoplasm greatly vacuolated with radial strands from a central mass to the periphery.

This species is found in all of the oceans of the world and in some regions is one of the principal causes of phosphorescence. Many phosphorescent granules in the cytoplasmic strands. s, sulcus; lf, longitudinal flagellum; tf, transverse flagellum; lt, tentacle.

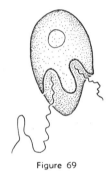

Fig. 69. *Oxyrrhis marina*, 20-33μ (Hall).

Girdle incomplete on side opposite sulcus; posterior margin of girdle absent. Tentacular lobe projects posteriorly between bases of flagella. Colorless. Holozoic, feeding on algae. Movement jerky and rolling. Marine, and in salt lakes. Cosmopolitan; common in laboratory cultures.

Figure 69

Fig. 70. *Oodinium ocellatum*, a dinoflagellate parasitic on marine fish (Nigrelli).

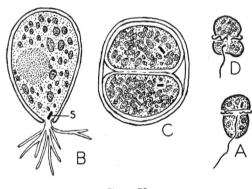

Figure 70

A. A small young dinoflagellate similar in shape to *Gymnodinium*, with stigma (s). This organism becomes attached to fish and then loses its flagella and develops root-like processes which enter the body of the fish and extract nourishment. B. Young attached stage, 12μ. The attached stage increases in size up to 100μ. It then becomes detached and divides by repeated binary fission to form as many as 256 small gymnodinia, as in A. C. Two cell stage of division of recently detached form. D. *Oodinium limneticum*, young gymnodinium stage. Life history similar to that of O. *ocellatum* but with chloroplasts and without stigma; on small fresh water fishes (*Betta, Colisa, Trichogaster, Lebistes, Xipophorus, Platypoecilus, Mollinesia*) for which it is often fatal (Jacobs). This is a good example of a phototrophic organism which is also a serious parasite. During the parasitic stage it is saprozoic. Other species occur on annelids, tunicates, and other aquatic invertebrates.

ORDER EUGLENIDA

The euglenoids consist of both green and colorless flagellates, usually with one or two flagella which arise from an invaginated anterior portion of the cell known as the gullet. Chloroplasts, when present, are almost pure green. Cells usually contain discoid or oval carbohydrate bodies which do not stain with iodine; this carbohydrate is known as paramylum. Nutrition is phototrophic or saprobic in Euglenidae, saprobic or holozoic in Peranemidae, and usually saprobic in Astasiidae. Some genera have a test or lorica; most genera are naked. Some genera are plastic; others rigid.

Although superficially heterogeneous the euglenoids have several important characters in common. For instance, paramylum does not occur in other orders. The nucleus of euglenoids is also quite characteristic and uniform throughout the group. It consists of one or more central bodies and of numerous chromatin granules uniformly distributed between these central bodies and the nuclear membrane.

1a Cells with chloroplasts and stigma.........................2

1b Cells without chloroplasts and stigma....................9, p. 70

2a Cells usually attached to substratum by stalk; palmella stage common; flagellated stage transient.   Family COLACIIDAE

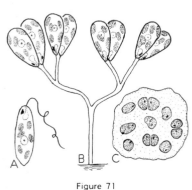

Figure 71

Fig. 71. *Colacium vesiculatum*, 20-30μ (Johnson, Stein).

A. Flagellated stage which is very similar in appearance to Euglena. B. Stalked organisms which are formed when the anterior end of a flagellate becomes attached to the substrate (Cf. *Euglena cyclopicola*, fig. 78) and then secretes an additional stalk on the end of the old stalk, thereby making the extra stalk dichotomously branched. C. Palmella stage consisting of non-flagellated cells embedded in a gelatinous mass. These cells may divide and eventually become flagellated.

2b Cells usually free swimming; without stalk; flagellum also bifurcated at base which is in gullet and visible only in stained specimens. 3
        Family EUGLENIDAE

Genus EUGLENA

The characters used in separating species are: size, shape, and degree of plasticity of body; size, shape, number and arrangement of chloroplasts; number and shape of paramylum bodies; striations or ornamentations on the pellicle; and length of flagellum. Many species. Very common, especially in small barnyard ponds. The genus *Khawkinea* is identical in almost every respect (even to the stigma and flagellum bifurcation) but has no chloroplasts.

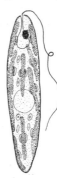

Figure 72

Fig. 72. *Euglena gracilis,* 35-55μ (Johnson).

Body cylindrical, rounded at ends, plastic; nucleus central; flagellum body length; less than 20 chloroplasts; one paramylum body attached to each side of each chloroplast (as in fig. 33). One of the most common species, widely distributed.

One reason for the very wide distribution of *E. gracilis* is its great ability to live in both highly acid and highly alkaline as well as neutral media. The organism grows well between pH 3.5 (quite acid) and pH 9.9. (very alkaline). Other species of *Euglena* are more restricted in their growth by high or low pH values.

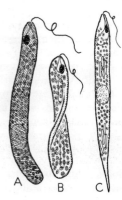

Figure 73

Fig. 73. A, B. *Euglena ehrenbergii,* 190-400μ (Johnson).

One of the largest species. Body cylindrical or flattened, with rounded ends, plastic; pellicle spirally striated; chloroplasts small, discoid, and numerous; paramylum in form of one or two elongate rods, 30-110μ in length. Widely distributed. C. *Euglena acus,* 50-175μ (Johnson). Body elongate spindle form, especially pointed at posterior end, only slightly plastic; chloroplasts numerous and discoid; paramylum bodies numerous and rod shaped; flagellum ¼ body length. Common. E. acutissima is similar but with a more sharply pointed posterior, 120-350μ.

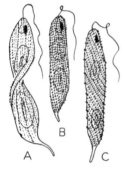

Figure·74

Fig. 74. *Euglena spirogyra*, 80-180μ (Johnson).

Several varieties. Body cylindrical or flattened, clear spike-like posterior; two oval ring shaped paramylum bodies. The distinguishing feature of the species is the rows of conical or pyramidal processes arranged spirally on the pellicle; these are quite refractile and easily detected. Widely distributed but seldom in large numbers. Several varieties. A. *E. s.* var. *suprema*, 140-180μ. B. *E. s. marchica* 85-165μ. C. *E. s. abrupta-acuminata*, 130-145μ.

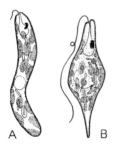

Figure 75

Fig. 75. A. *Euglena deses*, 86-170μ (Johnson).

Body cylindrical with rounded ends, and plastic; chloroplasts numerous; flagellum less than ¼ body length. This species can be distinguished by its worm-like crawling movements; it seldom swims. B. *Euglena rostrifera*, 90-140μ (Johnson) Body usually bulged in middle, tapered anteriorily and posteriorily; chloroplasts numerous with paramylum bodies attached; flagellum body length.

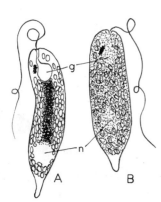

Figure 76

Fig. 76. *Euglena rubra*, 76-168μ (Johnson).

This is the most common of several "red" euglenas. It is very common in the midwestern United States in middle and late summer where it often forms a bright red scum on barnyard ponds, especially in very hot weather. The cytoplasm contains thousands of bright red granules which may be accumulated at the center of the body as in A or may be distributed throughout the cytoplasm or peripherally as in B. When the red granules are concentrated in the center of the cell the green chloroplasts are on the outside and the organism appears green, and the scum it forms is green. When the granules are distributed they cover the chloroplasts, and the organism and the scum it forms appear red. The scum is usually red in bright sunlight, becomes green soon after sundown, and then again becomes red at sunrise. Other organisms also form a red scum, but this is one of the most common causes in fresh water. g. gullet; n. nucleus.

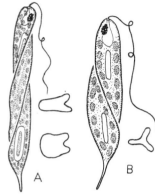

Figure 77

Fig. 77. A. *Euglena oxyuris*, 140-150μ. (Johnson).

Cross sections to right. Body flattened, with longitudinal groove, clear posterior spike-like projection. Two oval ring-shaped paramylum bodies. Widely distributed. B. *Euglena tripteris*, 90-120μ (Johnson). Body with three longitudinal ridges, as shown in cross section to right, and a thin pointed posterior projection; only slightly plastic. Two rod-shaped paramylum bodies. Widely distributed.

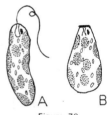

Figure 78

Fig. 78. *Euglena cyclopicola*, 16-32μ (Johnson).

Body cylindrical with rounded ends; plastic. Free swimming or attached by its anterior end to various microcrustacea, e.g., *Daphnia*, *Cyclops*, and *Cypris*. Common.

5a Cell round in cross section and without ridges; two large ring-shaped paramylum bodies.　　　　　　**Genus LEPOCINCLIS**

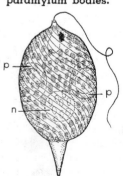

Figure 79

Fig. 79. *Lepocinclis ovum*, 20-40μ.

Body ovoid with short anterior and longer posterior projections; round in cross section. Two ring-shaped paramylum bodies. n. nucleus; p, paramylum.

This genus is readily distinguished from *Euglena* by its rigid body. It is also easily distinguished from *Phacus* by the fact that the body is round in cross section and that it always possesses two laterally placed paramylum bodies.

5b Cell usually flattened; often ridged and twisted; paramylum bodies discoid or ring shaped. **Genus PHACUS**

Phacus differs from *Euglena* in that the body is rigid and in that the chloroplasts are numerous, small, and discoid in all species. The chloroplasts have been omitted from most of the drawings below. The body is usually flattened, but may also be ridged and/or twisted. Very common; many species.

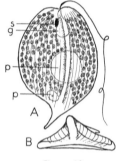

Fig. 80. *Phacus pleuronectes,* side (A) and anterior (B) views, 40-100μ (Allegre and Jahn).

Body flat with one small longitudinal ridge and an oblique posterior projection. Chromatophores small as in all species of the genus. Very common. g, gullet; p, paramylum; s, stigma.

Figure 80

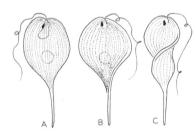

Fig. 81. A. *Phacus longicauda,* 120-170μ (Allegre and Jahn).

Body flattened but not twisted; no ridges; posterior process long. B. and C. *Phacus torta,* 80-100μ (Allegre and Jahn). Similar to *P. longicauda* except that body is twisted 45-60°. *P. t.* var. *tortuosa* is twisted much more.

Figure 81

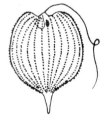

Fig. 82. *Phacus monilata,* 43-54μ (Allegre and Jahn).

Body flattened, pointed posteriorly, incurved anteriorly with small projection; pellicle with about twelve rows of small knobs.

Figure 82

Figure 83

Fig. 83. *Phacus warszewiczii*, 55-72μ (Allegre and Jahn).

A. Side view. B. Anterior view. Body with three wide longitudinal flanges, slightly twisted.

The flanges, or keels, are very noticeable and readily serve to distinguish this from other species of *Phacus*. However, the species is somewhat similar to the three-flanged species of *Euglena* (e.g., *E. tripteris*) which have a slightly plastic and relatively much longer body than the rigid *P. warszewiczii*.

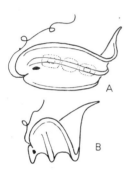

Figure 84

Fig. 84. *Phacus trimarginatus*, 48-60μ (Allegre and Jahn).

A. Side view. B. Anterior view. Body flattened, twisted so that anterior-posterior line does not pass through much of the body. Body smooth on inside of spiral; with three longitudinal ridges on the outside.

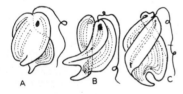

Figure 85

Fig. 85. *Phacus quinquemarginatus* 35-52μ (Shawhan and Jahn).

Three views of the same organism from different sides. Body with five longitudinal ridges, twisted more than 90°.

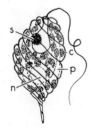

Figure 86

Fig. 86. *Phacus pyrum*, 30-50μ.

Cell pear-shaped, with sharp posterior process; circular in end view, with numerous spiral ridges. c, chloroplast; n, nucleus; p, paramylum; s. stigma.

6a Cell only partially enclosed in lorica which is open at the anterior end; free swimming.   Genus KLEBSIELLA

Fig. 87. *Klebsiella alligata*, 35μ (Pascher).

Yellow to brown test with large opening at anterior end. Free swimming; a good example of the absence of streamlining. Marine. Similar to genera below except for large opening to test.

Figure 87

6b Cell completely or almost completely enclosed in lorica 7

7a Lorica flexible and attached to substratum.

Genus ASCOGLENA

Fig. 88. *Ascoglena vaginicola*, lorica 43μ (Stein).

Lorica flexible, colorless to brown, attached to substratum; solitary; without stalk.

In certain respects (in that it is solitary, sessile, and has a test) *Ascoglena* is reminiscent of certain Chrysomonadida. However, it may easily be distinguished from chrysomonads by the bright grass green color of the chloroplasts which are quite different from the yellow brown ones of the Chrysomonadida.

Figure 88

7b Lorica rigid; free swimming 8

8a Lorica with neck which is continuous with that which covers the body; posterior end usually pointed; no spines on lorica.

Genus STROMBOMONAS

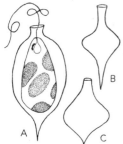

Fig. 89. A. *Strombomonas urceolata*, 45μ (Playfair). B. *Strombomonas gibberosa* var. *longicollis*. C. Lorica of *S. g.* var. *tumida* (Playfair).

The members of this genus are sometimes included in the genus *Trachelomonas*, but because of the large number of species in the genus *Trachelomonas* it seems preferable to split the genus and to place those species in which the neck is continuous with the body in a separate genus.

Figure 89

8b Lorica with or without neck; neck if present is not continuous with body but is more like a standing collar.

Genus **TRACHELOMONAS**

Trachelomonas and *Strombomonas* are very common and differ from *Euglena* only in the possession of a lorica which is usually yellow to dark brown. Often found in numbers sufficient to color the water brown. The lorica of *Trachelomonas* may be smooth or decorated with spines, with or without a collar. If the lorica is crushed by pushing on the coverslip with a pencil the flagellate may swim away. It will be indistinguishable from *Euglena*.

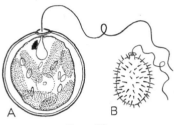

Figure 90

Fig. 90. A. *Trachelmonas volvocina*, 10-20μ (Wilson). B. *Trachelomonas horrida*, 40μ (Palmer).

These are two of the most common species of *Trachelomonas*. *T. volvocina* is very common in the spring and summer, especially in small farm yard ponds in midsummer.

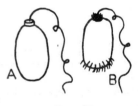

Figure 91

Fig. 91. A. *Trachelomonas teres*, 35μ (Maskell). Ovoid with definite collar. *T. abrupta*, 20μ, is very similar in shape except that the collar is entirely lacking. B. *Trachelomonas armata*, 30-60μ (Lemmermann).

Spines around the opening and over the posterior fourth of the lorica. (See also fig. 40).

9a Only one flagellum and this one is not held almost rigid and directly forward for half or more of its length; locomotion with cell rotation; saprobic only. Family **ASTASIIDAE**

Fig. 92. *Astasia dangeardi,* 50-60μ.

Body plastic; many paramylum bodies; one flagellum; swims with spiral motion as does *Euglena.*

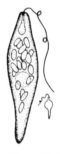

This organism is very representative of the family Astasiidae. One of the interesting things about this family and the following family (Peranemidae) is that all of the species are able to form paramylum, a pale bluish-green carbohydrate very similar to starch, in the absence of chlorophyll. This is, of course, comparable to the synthesis of glycogen, another form of carbohydrate, by other Protozoa and by Metazoa. As demonstrated by Schoenborn, at least one species of *Astasia* is able to live in a medium

Figure 92

containing only inorganic salts, a mixture which is too simple for the growth of *Euglena.* Therefore, *Astasia,* in spite of its lack of chlorophyll, is not so restricted by its environment as some of the chlorophyll-bearing species. In fact, under certain conditions *Astasia* is as independent of organic food as the chemosynthetic bacteria.

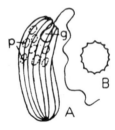

Fig. 93. A. *Rhabdomonas incurva,* 15-25μ (Hall). B. Cross section.

Body rigid, usually clear with longitudinal ridges. Many paramylum bodies. Swims with flagellum at right angles to direction of locomotion (fig. 42). Common. g. gullet; p, paramylum.

Figure 93

Fig. 94. A. *Menoidium cultellus,* 40-55μ (Pringsheim). B. Cross section.

Body flattened; many rod-shaped paramylum bodies. This genus differs from *Rhabdomonas* only in that the body is flattened instead of being circular in cross section.

There are numerous species which differ from each other in size, in body shape as viewed from the side, and in the shape of the paramylum bodies.

Figure 94

9b One or two flagella, one of which is often held more or less rigid, directly anteriorly for part of its length and beats only near the tip. Locomotion usually without cell rotation; saprobic or holozoic.   Family **PERANEMIDAE**

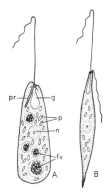

Figure 95

Fig. 95. A. *Peranema trichophorum*, 20-70μ.

Body plastic, cylindrical, sometimes with posterior end truncate; tapered anteriorly. Ordinarily does not rotate as it swims. Two pharyngeal rods on side of gullet. These rods are used for supporting the lip of the gullet during ingestion of food. Feeds on algae and other Protozoa. Paramylum bodies small, numerous. fv. food vacuole; g, gullet; n, nucleus; p. paramylum. There is a second flagellum which is attached to the pellicle for the length of the body and is usually visible only in well stained specimens. B. *Heteronema acus*, 45-50μ (Stein). Similar to *Peranema* except that the second flagellum is free, half as long as the body, and trails during locomotion. Body slightly plastic. *Heteronema mutabile* is highly plastic and may reach a length of 250μ. *Anisonema* is similar except that the trailing flagellum is much longer than the body.

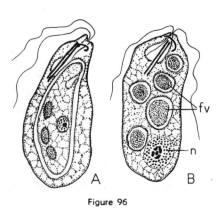

Figure 96

Fig. 96. *Heteronema acus*, showing pharyngeal rods and food vacuoles (Loefer).

Optical sections d r a w n from stained animals. A. shows one with a food vacuole which contains a *Euglena*. B. shows one with several food vacuoles (fv) containing other material and the nucleus (n) which has a structure typical of all euglenoids. Food is taken in through the gullet as in *Peranema*.

72

Figure 97

Fig. 97. *Heteronema spirale*, 24-30μ (Lemmermann).

All of the characteristics of the genus and in addition the body is shaped as shown with several spiral ridges and grooves.

This is a very unusually shaped organism which is sometimes found in rather putrid ponds or plant infusions.

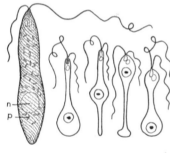

Figure 98

n —
p —

Fig. 98. *Distigma proteus*, 80μ (Lackey).

Similar to *Heteronema* but body is very highly plastic as shown in the series of diagrams; change of shape is rapid and very common. Can swim with flagellum straight in front or by means of cell rotation. n, nucleus; p. pharyngeal rod.

Figure 99

Fig. 99. *Entosiphon sulcatum*, 20μ (Hollande).

Body ridged longitudinally. The characteristic of the genus is that the pharyngeal rods (three) are almost as long as the body and are fused to form a tube, hence the name.

The function of this tube is unknown. It was formerly believed that it was useful in ingesting food. However, the organism is now thought to be saprobic rather than holozoic.

Fig. 100. A. *Petalomonas mediocanellata*, 21-26μ (Shawhan and Jahn).

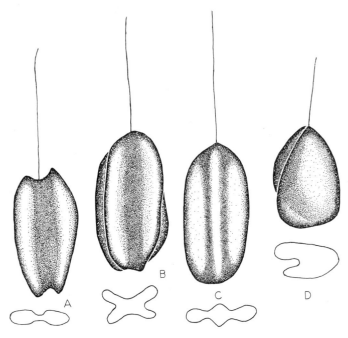

Figure 100

One flagellum held directly anterior. Body flattened, very clear, with median longitudinal grooves, one each on dorsal and ventral sides. B. *P. alata*, 23-25μ (Shawhan and Jahn). With four longitudinal grooves, one dorsal, one ventral, and two lateral. C. *P. bicarinata*, 30-35μ (Shawhan and Jahn). Two keels, one dorsal and one ventral, body thickened toward lateral edges. D. *P. asymmetrica*, 18-25μ (Shawhan and Jahn). Body pyriform with deep groove on one lateral edge. Lower sketches show cross sections for the four species.

Fig. 101. *Notosolenus sinuatus*, 22μ (Stokes).

Similar to Petalomonas except for presence of short trailing flagellum which usually lies in a wide groove.

As seen in cultures it is very difficult to observe the short flagellum unless the organism is viewed with an oil immersion objective.

Figure 101

74

ORDER PHYTOMONADIDA

The phytomonads are small. The cells are usually less than 25μ, and they may be solitary or colonial. Each cell is covered by a cellulose cell wall through which the flagella protrude. Nutrition is phototrophic or saprobic. Stigma present. Colonies are flat or spherical and may be 500 or more microns in diameter. Very common in fresh water ponds, often causing the water to appear green.

1a Solitary; not colonial.....................................2, p. 79

1b Colonial, with 4 or more individuals fastened together; colony discoid or spherical; 1, 2, or 4 flagella per cell. Each cell has the fundamental structure shown for *Chlamydomonas* (fig. 116), i.e., it has one nucleus, usually one green chloroplast, a red stigma, usually two flagella, and a cellulose cell wall. Reproduction by repeated division of each cell to form a colony (fig. 108) except in *Pleodorina* and *Volvox*. **Family VOLVOCIDAE**

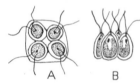

Figure 102

Fig. 102. *Gonium sociale*, cells 10-22μ (Chlordat).

Four cells, each similar to *Chlamydomonas*, arranged in one plane with all anterior ends pointed in the same direction. A. Anterior view. B. Side view. Fresh water.

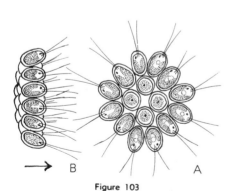

Figure 103

Fig. 103. *Gonium pectorale*, cells 5-14μ, colony up to 90μ (Stein).

Usually 16 cells (rarely 8) arranged in a flat disc with 4 cells central, and 12 peripheral. Common in ponds in spring and summer. Arrow denotes usual direction of movement, but the colonies also often tumble or somersault as they swim. They do not swim edgewise so as to take advantage of the lower water resistance, apparently unaware of the advantages of streamlining in locomotion.

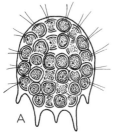

Fig. 104. *Platydorina caudata,* cells 10-13μ, colony up to 165μ (Oltmanns).

Biflagellate; the flagella of the central cells are on alternate sides of the colony which is slightly twisted with several posterior projections.

Figure 104

Figure 105

Fig. 105. *Chlamydobotrys stellata,* cells 15μ, colony 30-40μ (Korschikoff).

Colony of 8 biflagellate cells, arranged in two rings, usually with the tapered posterior ends pointed obliquely outward, hence the specific name. Common in fresh water.

Figure 106

Fig. 106. *Spondylomorum quaternarium,* cells 12-36μ, colony up to 60μ (Stein).

Somewhat similar in appearance to *Chlamydobotrys* except that colony consists of 16 cells and that each cell has 4 flagella. Fresh water.

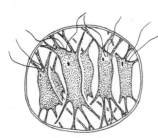

Figure 107

Fig. 107. *Stephanosphaera pluvialis,* cells 7-13μ, colony 30-60μ (Hieronymus).

Colony spherical or almost so; 8 biflagellate cells arranged in ring, not completely filling the colony, but sending protoplasmic processes to the periphery. Fresh water.

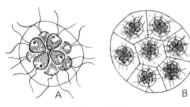

Figure 108

Fig. 108. *Pandorina morum,*
cells 8-17μ, colony 20-50μ, and
occasionally to 250μ (Smith).

A. Trophic colony of 16 cells
arranged in a closely packed
sphere; clear material on outside of cells. B. Reproduction,
in which each cell divides four
times to form a small colony of
16 cells. The membrane of the
parent colony breaks up, and
the 16 small filial colonies are
released.

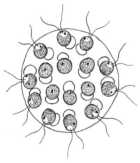

Figure 109

Fig. 109. *Eudorina elegans,* cells 10-24μ,
colony 40-150μ (Goebel).

Colony of 32 cells, equal in size, arranged
in a loosely packed sphere with considerable clear material between the cells.
Common in fresh water. In reproduction
each cell divides to form a filial colony
as in *Pandorina* (fig. 108, B).

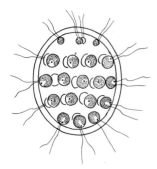

Figure 110

Fig. 110. *Pleodorina illinoisensis* (Kofoid).

Very similar in size and appearance
to *Eudorina* except that 4 cells are smaller than the other 28. These 4 cells are
incapable of reproduction; the other 28
may form new colonies as in *Pandorina*
(fig. 108 B) and *Eudorina.* In *P. californicus* the cells and colony are larger;
cells to 27μ, colony to 450μ.

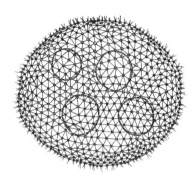

Figure 111

Fig. 111. *Volvox aureus,* colony 350-500μ (Smith).

1000 to 3000 cells arranged as a hollow ball. Reproduction may be either asexual or sexual. In asexual reproduction a few certain cells in a colony become very large and divide to form filial colonies within the space of the parent colony. In this figure four filial colonies are present. These will later be released through an opening in the wall of the parent colony. In sexual reproduction two cells of unequal size (macrogamete and microgamete) fuse to form one cell, a zygote, and then this cell develops into a colony. The larger of these two cells (the macrogamete) is similar to the asexual cells which develop into filial colonies except that it does not develop until after fertilization (union with the microgamete). The microgametes are formed by repeated division of a few certain cells of the colony.

Other species of *Volvox* have from 128 to 10,000 cells in a colony and are 100 to 600μ in diameter. Common in ponds.

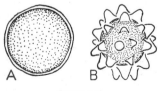

Figure 112

Fig. 112. Zygotes of *Volvox.* A. Zygote of *V. aureus,* 40-60μ, with smooth covering.

Often found attached to the wall of a colony. B. Zygote of *V. globator,* 35-45μ, with a covering of blunt spines (Smith). *Volvox* usually spends the winter in this stage, and in the spring each zygote develops into a colony.

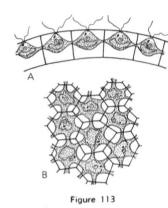

Figure 113

Fig. 113. Diagram of the arrangement of cells in *Volvox globator* (after Janet).

A. Part of the wall of the colony as seen in section. The upper side (with flagella) is external, the lower side faces the interior. Note that the cells are connected to each other by cytoplasmic strands, and that each cell possesses a nucleus, a chloroplast, a stigma, and 2 flagella. B. Same, from surface view, showing how each cell is connected to all of its neighbors.

2a Cell wall a single piece, usually distinct 3

2b Cell wall bivalve, i.e., composed of two parts.
Family PHACOTIDAE

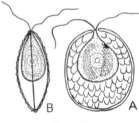

Figure 114

Fig. 114. *Phacotus lenticularis*, 13-20μ (Oltmanns).

Cell wall gray in color and composed of two parts which fit together like the halves of a clam shell. Protoplasm does not fill cell wall. Outer surface of wall is covered with small curved ridges which may give a scaly appearance. Two flagella; stagnant water.

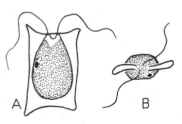

Figure 115

Fig. 115. *Pteromonas aculeata*, 25μ (Smith).

Cell wall winged in plane of suture of the two valves. Two flagella; fresh water.

This organism together with *Phacotus* (fig. 114) comprise the two outstanding exceptions among the phytomonads to the simplicity of the cell wall. A third example is *Dysmorphococcus*, similar to *Phacotus*, but circular in anterior view rather than flattened.

79

3a Two flagella.

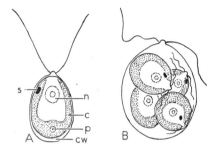

Figure 116

Family CHLAMYDOMONADIDAE

Fig. 116. A. *Chlamydomonas angulosa*, 20μ (Dill). B. Same, dividing.

During division the cell wall increases in size, and the cell divides several times. Eventually the old cell wall splits and the young flagellates emerge. c. *chloroplast;* cw, cell wall; n, nucleus; p. pyrenoid; s, stigma.

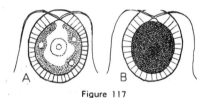

Figure 117

Fig. 117. *Haematococcus pluvialis,* 8-50μ (Reichenow).

Very similar to *Chlamydomonas.* A. Cell showing chloroplast. B. Cell completely filled with red granules. These red granules give the organism a bright red appearance, hence the generic name. Occurs in ponds in temperate climates and also in snow drifts in the Alps and in the Rocky Mountains where it imparts a bright red color to the snow.

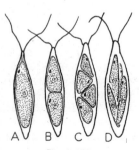

Figure 118

Fig. 118. A. *Chlorogonium euchlorum*, 25-70μ (Dangeard).

One of the larger phytomonad cells. Similar in structure to *Chlamydomonas* but elongate. Very common in pond water. B-D. Stages in reproduction which is similar to that of *Chlamydomonas.* Fresh water.

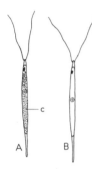

Figure 119

Fig. 119. Comparison of *Chlorogonium* and *Hyalogonium*.

These two species are identical except that *Hyalogonium* has no chloroplasts. c, chloroplast.

The genus *Hyalogonium* is a good example of one of the small colorless branches on the major green stem in the hypothetical phyletic tree in fig. 44.

3b Four flagella.

Figure 120

Family CARTERIIDAE

Fig. 120. *Carteria cordiformis*, 18-23µ (Dill).

Ovoid with slight invagination at anterior end. Similar to *Chlamydomonas* except for the four flagella. Fresh water.

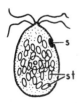

Figure 121

Fig. 121. *Polytomella agilis*, 8-18µ (Doflein).

No chloroplasts. Similar to *Carteria* except for shape and absence of chloroplasts. Fresh water. s, stigma; st, starch.

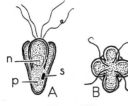

Figure 122

Fig. 122. *Pyramimonas tetrarhynchus*, 20-28µ (Dill).

Similar to *Carteria* except for shape. Four longitudinal ridges in anterior region, elongate posteriorly. n, nucleus; p. pyrenoid; s. stigma.

81

CLASS ZOOMASTIGOPHOREA

This group consists of non-chloroplast bearing flagellates which are not closely related to the chloroplast-bearing. members of the Phytomastigophorea. They may be distinguished from the Astasiidae and Peranemidae by the absence of paramylum and by the structure of the nucleus and from the Peranemidae by the fact that the flagellum does not project directly anteriorly. Pharyngeal rods are absent. Some genera have pseudopodia as well as flagella and others have a brief ameboid stage. Many are important parasites of man and of domestic and wild animals; others are symbiotic in termites and xylophagous cockroaches (p. 19 and 20).

KEY TO THE ORDERS OF ZOOMASTIGOPHOREA

1a With pseudopodia and flagella.

Order RHIZOMASTIGIDA, p. 82

1b With flagella only; no pseudopodia.........................2

2a One or two flagella. Order PROTOMASTIGIDA, p. 84

2b More than two flagella..3

3a Mononucleate; many more than eight flagella.

Order HYPERMASTIGIDA, p. 98

3b Mononucleate, dinucleate, or multinucleate; 3-8 flagella per nucleus. Order POLYMASTIGIDA, p. 94

ORDER RHIZOMASTIGIDA

Members of this order have both pseudopodia and one or more flagella. Pseudopodia are axopodia or lobopodia. Some species (e.g., *Mastigamoeba hylae*) do not develop true pseudopodia but move by protoplasmic flow (p. 36).

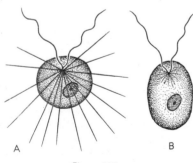

A   B

Figure 123

Fig. 123. *Dimorpha mutans*, 15-20μ (Blochmann).

Axopodia and two flagella. When not moving it appears to be a small heliozoan (p. 101). The observer who first gets this impression is usually greatly astonished to see the organism pull in its axopodia and rapidly swim away. Fresh water. A. Non-swimming form. B. Swimming form.

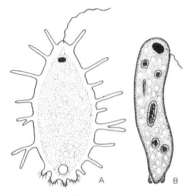

Figure 124

Fig. 124. A. *Mastigamoeba aspera*, 150-200µ (Schulze).

A large flagellated ameba with one anterior flagellum, many small blunt pseudopodia, and a uroid (p. 111). Fresh water. B. *Mastigamoeba hylae*, 80-100µ (Becker). Elongate body, movement by protoplasmic flow; short anterior flagellum. Parasitic in gut of frogs and tadpoles.

This is the largest species of the Rhizomastigida and is highly representative of the order.

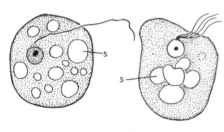

Figure 125

Fig. 125. *Histomonas meleagris*, 8-21µ (Bishop, Wenrich).

Ameboid with one to four flagella. T h e cause of "blackhead," a serious infection of young turkeys, chickens, grouse, pheasants and quail; often fatal. The organism is found as a flagellate in the lumen of the intestine and as an ameba without a flagellum in the liver and the intestinal wall. The comb of the fowl turns black, hence the name. s, starch granules.

The trophozoite is voided in the feces and may contaminate food or drinking water and thereby produce an infection in other birds. The organism can also be transmitted from one bird to another in the eggs of a parasitic nematode, *Heterakis gallinae*.

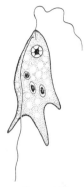

Fig. 126. *Cercomonas crassicauda,* 10-16μ.

With trailing flagellum at least partly attached to body; posterior end actively ameboid, so much so that sometimes the animal seems to be "walking" with the pseudopodia. *Cercobodo* is similar but with trailing flagellum free from body. Both genera are often classed with the Bodonidae, (p. 94).

These genera are common in soil cultures and sometimes in putrid infusions.

Figure 126

ORDER PROTOMASTIGIDA

This is a rather heterogeneous group of colorless flagellates which possess 1 or 2 flagella. Some are important parasites (e.g., Trypanosomidae).

3a Collar enclosed in jelly.   Family PHALANSTERIIDAE

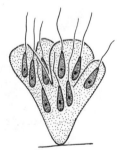

Fig. 127. *Phalansterium digitatum,* cells 17μ (Stein). Cells ovoid, one flagellum; numerous individuals embedded in gelatinous mass, sometimes branching. Fresh water.

Figure 127

4a Without lorica.   Family **CODOSIGIDAE**

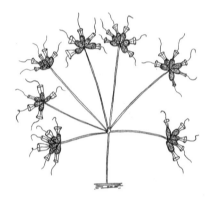

Figure 128

Fig. 128. *Codosiga botrytis*, cells 10-22µ.

One to several cells at end of long clear stalk, simple or branched. Very transparent. Fresh water. *Monosiga* is similar but always solitary.

The structure of these organisms is representative of that of all choanoflagellates. The collar is a thin retractile extension of the protoplasm and is not found elsewhere in the Protista.

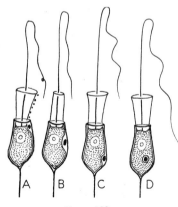

Figure 129

Fig. 129. *Codosiga botrytis*. Method of food ingestion (Lapage).

A. shows food particles being beaten by flagellum into pocket formed between cell and envelope. B. and C. Later stages. Following stage C the body undergoes violent contractions and expansions, and with almost explosive violence the food mass is pushed into the cytoplasm where it is surrounded by a vacuole.

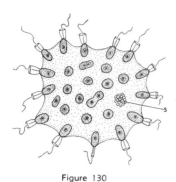

Figure 130

Fig. 130. *Protospongia haeckeli*, cells 8μ, 6 to 60 cells in colony (Kent).

Cells embedded irregularly in gelatinous mass. Collars free. The cells on the outside of the colony are collared; those inside usually possess no collars. In sponges the cells lining the gastro-vascular cavity possess collars. Collared cells are not found in any other group of organisms. Therefore, since they occur only in the choanoflagellates a n d t h e sponges it is assumed that these two groups are closely related. s, mass of spores formed by repeated division of one cell; each spore may start a new colony.

4b With lorica.

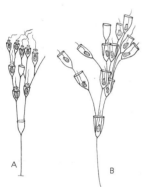

Figure 131

Family BICOSOECIDAE

Fig. 131. A. *Polyoeca dichotoma* (Lang).

Similar to *Monosiga* and *Codosiga* except for vase-like lorica with long stalk. B. *Poteriodendron petiolatum*, cells 21-35μ (Stein). Similar to *Polyoeca* but collars are rudimentary. *Bicosoeca* is similar but without stalk.

In *Poteriodendron* and *Bicosoeca* the collar is not so well developed as in the Codosigidae or in *Polyoeca* and therefore *Poteriodendron* and *Bicosoeca* are probably more closely related to each other than to the other choanoflagellates.

5a Free living.

Family OIKOMONADIDAE

Figure 132

Fig. 132. *Oikomonas termo*, 5-20μ.

Anterior end lip-like. Common in salt and stagnant water.

5b Parasitic.   Family **TRYPANOSOMIDAE**

Members of this family are polymorphic, that is, during their life cycle the body changes in structure. There are several body forms which are designated as *leishmanial, leptomonad, crithidial, herpetomonad,* and *trypanosome.* These are shown diagramatically in fig. 133. The genera are defined as organisms which possess certain body forms but no others, and occur in invertebrates only, or invertebrates and vertebrate hosts, or in invertebrate and plant hosts. The limitations of the genera are also shown in fig. 133.

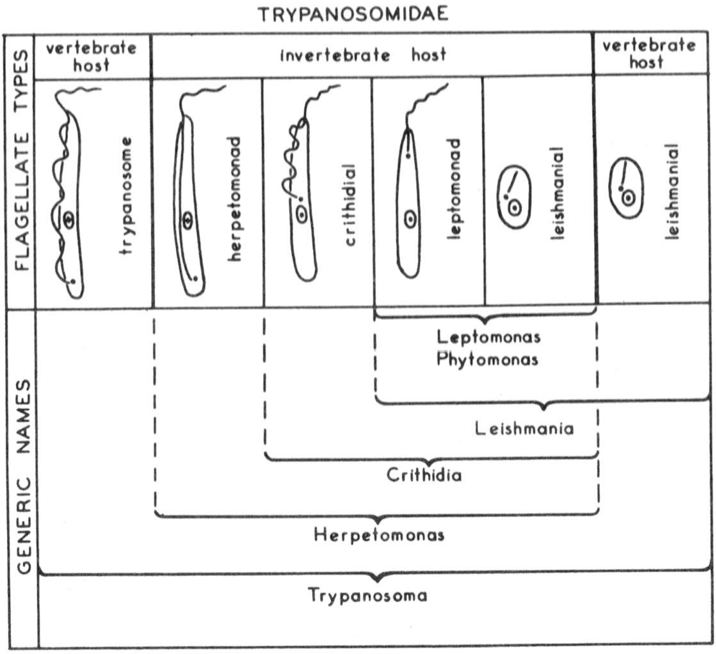

Figure 133

GENUS TRYPANOSOMA

The outstanding morphological characteristic of *Trypanosoma* is that the flagellum is attached throughout the length of the body by a thin double layer of pellicle. This layer of pellicle forms an *undulating membrane* which undulates when a wave-like motion passes down the flagellum. Hundreds of species; in the blood of all classes of vertebrates; many species are highly pathogenic.

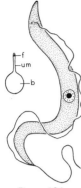

Figure 134

Fig. 134. *Trypanosoma diemectyli,* 46-65μ (Nigrelli).

A common and typical member of the genus, found in the spotted newt, *Triturus viridescens.* Nucleus central. Flagellum arises from a mastigosome (kinetoplast) at one end of the animal, is attached to the pellicle the entire length of the body to form an undulating membrane, and continues posteriorly as a free flagellum. Insert is a cross section showing relation of flagellum to undulating membrane and to body.

Fig. 135. Life history of *Trypanosoma lewisi,* 25μ, found in the blood of rats and in the gut of fleas.

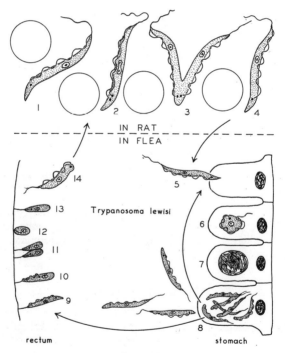

Figure 135

1, 4, normal trypanosomes in blood of rat, scattered among the red blood cells; 2, 3, stages in division which occurs in blood stream. When a flea sucks blood some of the trypanosomes enter the flea's stomach where they enter the epithelial cells (5), round up (6), divide rapidly (6, 7), and then may either repeat the division cycle or pass into the rectum. In the rectum they become attached by the flagellum (9), pass through crithidial (10), leptomonad (11) and leishmanial stages. Division may occur in the leptomonad stage (11). Then the leishmanial forms become leptomonads (13) and finally short stumpy trypanosomes (14) which are called *metacyclic* because they have passed through a cycle of development which involved several body types. The metacyclic trypanosomes pass out in the feces of the flea. Since a flea often defecates immediately after feeding on rat blood the feces are often deposited near the wound made by the mouthparts of the flea when it bites another rat. The new rat may scratch the feces and metacyclic trypanosomes into the wound, thereby becoming infected. Of all of the stages that occur in the flea only the metacyclic trypanosome is capable of starting a new infection in a rat. Development in the flea requires about six days. Fairly common in rats, sometimes becoming very numerous in the blood stream. Infection in the rat persists for several weeks, after which time the parasites decrease rapidly in numbers.

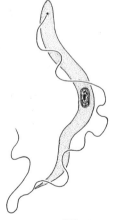

Figure 136

Fig. 136. *Trypanosoma gambiense*, 22μ (Wenyon).

Found in human blood; the cause of Gambian Sleeping Sickness in man, common in West Africa. A similar organism, *T. rhodesiense* causes Rhodesian Sleeping Sickness, present in eastern Africa. Both diseases are transmitted by the bite of the tsetse fly in which the organisms undergo a cyclical development first in the gut and later in the salivary glands. In man the parasites live in the blood stream and the lymph glands (which swell considerably, especially those of

Figure 137

the neck, fig. 137) and eventually get into the cerebrospinal fluid. Then the patient becomes very sleepy and may go to sleep at almost any time. For example, he may take a mouthful of food and go to sleep before swallowing it. This disease was known to the slave traders of the past century who refused to buy African natives with swollen lymph glands. The mortality is very high and death occurs in six months to a year. In the Boruma Islands the population was reduced from 56,000 to 13,000 and in part of Uganda from 300,000 to 100,000 in a seven year epidemic. Treatment by the use of various arsenicals and antimony compounds and by use of Naphuride (Bayer 205) is usually successful in early stages of disease. Prevention involves the elimination of the tsetse fly, usually by destruction of the underbrush in which it breeds close to streams.

Trypanosoma cruzi, the cause of Chagas' disease in South and Central America, is transmitted by several biting bugs, especially *Triatoma* (one of the "kissing bugs"). Cyclical development occurs in the intestine of the bug, and the infective forms pass out in the feces from which they pass into skin abrasions or the wound made by the bite. Usually a serious disease only in children. The parasite is found in wood rats in this country.

Figure 138

Fig. 138. *Trypanosoma rotatorium*, 30μ (Noller).

Found in the blood of frogs, transmitted from one frog to another by the bite of the leech. Cyclical development occurs in the leech gut. Common in frogs, but seldom in large numbers.

This organism is distinctive because of its broad body, its prominent undulating membrane, and its large size. The free portion of the flagellum is as long as 35μ in some specimens and entirely lacking in others. The undulating membrane, however, is always present. The blood of the internal organs (e.g., kidney) of the frog contains more trypanosomes than the peripheral blood. The kinetoplast is small, and the nucleus usually does not stain deeply.

GENUS HERPETOMONAS

This genus does not occur in vertebrates but only in the gut of invertebrates. The herpetomonad body form has a flagellum which runs the length of the body, but the undulating membrane is usually very narrow or lacking. In some instances where the membrane is well developed the form is identical with that of *Trypanosoma*.

Fig. 139. *Herpetomonas lepticoridis,* 9-65μ (Kay).

In gut of the box elder bug, *Leptocoris.* Herpeto-monad, crithidial, leptomonad, and leishmanial forms are found. Cysts containing leishmanial forms pass out in the feces and are ingested by other box elder bugs. *Herpetomonas muscarum,* found in a number of common species of flies, has a similar life history.

Figure 139

GENUS CRITHIDIA

Found in the gut of insects, e.g., *Crithidia gerridis* in water bugs of the genus *Gerris.* Pass through crithidial, leptomonad, and leishmanial stages. Morphology and life history similar to *Herpetomonas,* except for absence of herpetomonad form.

GENUS LEPTOMONAS

Found in gut of insects, e.g., *Leptomonas ctenocephalis,* in gut of flea. Life history includes only leishmanial and leptomonad forms.

GENUS PHYTOMONAS

Similar to *Leptomonas* except that it is found in the sap of plants of the genus *Euphorbia* and of related genera where it causes wilting. Transmitted from one plant to another by sap sucking bug, *Stenocephalus.*

GENUS LEISHMANIA

Organisms which have a leishmanial stage in a vertebrate and leishmanial and leptomonad stages in an insect vector. There are three species which cause diseases of man:

Leishmania donovani, cause of kala azar, a disease common in India, China, and parts of Africa and South America, transmitted by

Figure 140

sandflies. The parasite is a flagellate in the sandfly but is non-flagellated in man. The symptoms consist of irregular fever, greatly swollen spleen and general lassitude. Fig. 140 shows an Indian child with spleen enlargement caused by *Leishmania*. The mortality is 80 to 95 per cent. In parts of Assam this disease was responsible for a 25 per cent decrease in population between 1890 and 1900.

Leishmania tropica, cause of oriental sore, a benign leishmaniasis in which one skin lesion confers an immunity; common along the Mediterranean and Red Seas and eastward to Indo-China.

Leishmania braziliense, cause of espundia or Brazilian leishmaniasis, in northern South America and in Central America. This is a malignant form of cutaneous leishmaniasis which may later attack the mucous membranes of the nose, thereby producing great disfigurement and eventual death.

Treatment of leishmanian infections with several antimony compounds is usually effective.

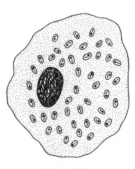

Figure 141

Fig. 141. *Leishmania donovani*, 2-4μ.

A large endothelial cell (from lining of blood capillaries) found in the blood of man. This cell contains dozens of leishmanial bodies.

6a With undulating membrane.

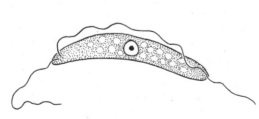

Figure 142

Family CRYPTOBIIDAE

Fig. 142. *Cryptobia helicis*, 6-20μ (Belar).

Parasitic in reproductive organs of snails of the genus Helix. Other species occur in other invertebrates and in the blood and gut of fish.

6b Without undulating membrane 7

7a Flagella equally long.   **Family AMPHIMONADIDAE**

Fig. 143. *Amphimonas globosa*, 13μ (Kent).

Cell spherical, long delicate stalk. Fresh water.

Figure 143

7b Flagella unequal in length 8

8a Without trailing flagellum.   **Family MONADIDAE**

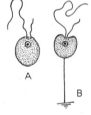

Fig. 144. A. *Monas guttula*, 14-16μ (Fisch). B. *Monas socialis*, 5-10μ (Kent).

Body plastic; actively motile. Both species common among decaying vegetation.

Figure 144

Fig. 145. *Cephalothamnium cyclopum*, cells 5-10μ (Stein).

Colonial with short stalk; attached to body of *Cyclops* and among plankton.

Figure 145

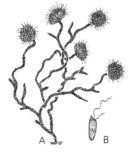

Figure 146

Fig. 146. *Anthophysis vegetans*, cells 5-6μ (Stein).

Stalk rough, branched, and yellow brown in appearance. Very common in stagnant water and plant infusions. A. Branched colony. B. Separate cell. The cells often leave the colony when placed under a coverslip.

8b With trailing flagellum.

Figure 147

Family BODONIDAE

Fig. 147. *Bodo edax*, 11-15μ (Kuhn).

Common in stagnant water and plant infusions.

ORDER POLYMASTIGIDA

The polymastigote flagellates possess 3 to 8 flagella per nucleus and may be mono-, di-, or mutinucleate. In many species there is a rod-like structure approximately as long as the body attached to the nucleus and known as the *axostyle*. Each nucleus with its associated flagella and axostyle (if present) is known as a *karyomastigont*. The order is divided into three suborders on the basis of the number of nuclei or of karyomastigonts.

1a (a, b, c) With 1 nucleus. Suborder MONOKARYOMASTIGINA, p. 94
1b With 2 nuclei.   Suborder DIKARYOMASTIGINA, p. 96
1c With more than 2 nuclei. Suborder POLYKARYOMASTIGINA, p. 97

SUBORDER MONOKARYOMASTIGINA

One nucleus; 3-8 flagella; with or without axostyle.

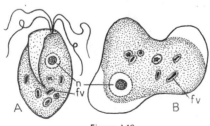

Figure 148

Fig. 148. *Tetramitus rostratus*, 18-30μ (Hollande). A. Flagellated form. B. Ameboid form.

The life cycle consists of an alternation of ameboid and flagellated forms; binary fission occurs in both. Stagnant water; also from cecum of rat.

Figure 149

Fig. 149. *Tetramitus salinus*, 15-30μ (Kirby).

Two flagella anteriorly; two trailing. In California brine pool.

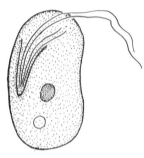

Figure. 150

Fig. 150. *Costia necatrix*, 10-20μ (Moroff).

Body ovoid in surface view, flattened in edge view. Four flagella, 2 short and 2 long, which arise from funnel-like depression. Ectoparasitic on various fresh water fishes; when numerous the parasite forms a whitish coat over the skin of the fish. High fatality for young trout, especially in fish hatcheries where it is one of the worst enemies of young trout.

Figure 151

Fig. 151. *Streblomastix strix*, 15-52μ (Kofoid and Swezy).

Small cup-like sucking disc at anterior end; 4 flagella; very elongate nucleus; 4-8 spiral ridges. In gut of termite.

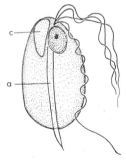

Figure 152

Fig. 152. *Trichomonas augusta*, 18-22μ.

Body ovoid to spindle form; 4 anterior flagella; undulating membrane length of body with continuing free flagellum; axostyle (a). Holozoic; ingestion through anterior cytostomal region (c). This species and the very similar *Trichomonas batrachorum* are extremely common in the large intestine of frogs; they also have been found in liver cysts. These flagellates are easily distinguished from other genera present by the undulating membrane which is very active and by the presence of the axostyle.

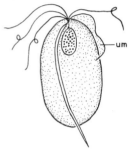

Figure 153

Fig. 153. *Trichomonas vaginalis*, 10-15μ (Kupferberg).

Similar to *T. augusta* except for short undulating membrane and absence of trailing flagellum. In the vagina of women (20% or more of all examined) where it sometimes causes a severe irritation with considerable discomfort; also in the male urinary tract. Treatment with weak acetic acid solutions is usually but not always effective.

In addition to the above there are almost 100 species of Trichomonas found in over 200 species of hosts which include insects, annelids, molluscs, and all classes of vertebrates. Some are symbionts in termites; one (*T. foetus*) causes abortion in cattle; another (*T. columbae*) causes liver degeneration in pigeons. Besides *T. vaginalis*, four other species are found in man; one in the mouth and three in the intestine.

SUBORDER DIKARYOMASTIGINA

Two nuclei; 6-16 flagella; with or without axostyle.

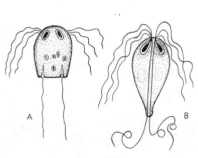

Figure 154

Fig. 154. A. *Hexamita inflata*, 13-25μ (Klebs). Six anterior flagella, three attached to each nucleus, and two trailing, one on each side. Common in stagnant water and plant infusions. B. *Hexamita salmonis*, 10-12μ (Davis).

In intestine of trout and salmon where they divide in the epithelium of the intestine and pyloric caeca; highly pathogenic, often fatal, a serious pest in trout hatcheries. *H. intestinalis*, 10-16μ, very similar to above, is very common in the large intestine of frogs.

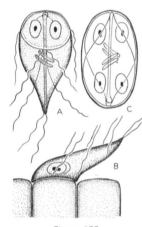

Figure 155

Fig. 155. A. *Giardia intestinalis*, 9-20μ, sometimes called *G. lamblia*.

Eight flagella; axostyle, and two smaller obliquely placed rods, known as *parabasal bodies*. Found in the intestine of man; often the cause of a severe diarrhea which may be cured by atabrine, a drug which is also used for malaria. B. Flagellate attached to epithelial cell. C. Cyst containing two individuals as often seen in feces. During diarrhea the free swimming flagellated forms are found in the feces. However, when the feces are not liquid the flagellated forms occur only in the small intestine, and only the cysts can be found in the feces.   Attachment of the flagellates to the intestinal lining apparently causes considerable irritation and a general digestive disturbance. There are many species of Giardia, and the specific differences are principally in size and shape, some being short and thick, others very long and slim. Found in all classes of vertebrates.

SUBORDER POLYKARYOMASTIGINA
Many nuclei; 3-8 flagella per nucleus.

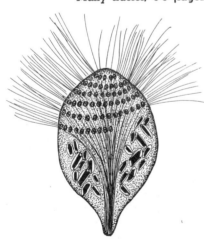

Figure 156

Fig. 156. *Stephanonympha nelumbium*, 45μ (Kirby).

Oval; numerous n u c l e i spirally arranged around anterior end; axostyles form a bundle which projects to the posterior end.   In termite gut; symbiotic.

This genus is representative of a suborder consisting of five genera, all found in termites.   In some genera there are certain groups of flagella which are not connected with a nucleus. Such flagella are connected only to an axostyle, and the complex is called an *akaryomastigont*, in contrast to the typical *karyomastigonts* which are found in the same and in other genera.

ORDER HYPERMASTIGIDA

One nucleus; many flagella arranged in tufts or uniformly distributed. Found only in the gut of termites, cockroaches, and woodroaches; many species are symbiotic (p. 20).

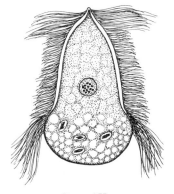

Fig. 157. *Trichonympha campanula*, 144-313μ (Kofoid and Swezy).

In termite gut. Anterior portion consists of nipple and bell, both of which are composed of two layers; nucleus central. Posterior portion ameboid; ingests wood fragments, digests them, and makes digestion products available to the termite. Sexual phenomena at time the termite molts.

Figure 157

Fig. 158. *Trichonympha agilis*, 55-115μ (Kirby).
Similar to *T. campanula* except for shape and size. In termite gut.

Figure 158

Fig. 159. *Holomastigotes elongatum*, up to 70μ (Koidzumi).
Spindle-shaped; few spiral rows of flagella; nucleus anterior; no food vacuoles; saprobic. In termite gut.

Figure 159

SUBPHYLUM SARCODINA

The distinguishing characteristic of the Sarcodina is that they move by protoplasmic flow, and the members of the subphylum are generally recognized either by the flowing of protoplasm or by the presence of pseudopodia. Pseudopodia are temporary elongate extensions of the cytoplasm, and they may or may not be part of the locomotor mechanism. There are five types of protoplasmic extentions, and the type of extension is used in classifying the Sarcodina. The types are:

1. *Axopodia* are long, thin, unbranched projections of the cytoplasm and contain an axial filament which can be seen with an oil lens in stained preparations and sometimes in the living organism (e.g., *Actinosphaerium*, fig. 160 and 161). Axopodia are not locomotor in function.

2. *Rhizopodia* are long, thin, and branched, and the branches tend to anastomose (to fuse with each other) to form a network. They are locomotor in function, and they also serve for food gathering and digestion. Food vacuoles are formed in the network and the products of digestion later pass into the main body of the animal (e.g., *Elphidium*, fig. 222, or *Mycetozoida*, fig. 226).

3. *Filopodia* are long, thin, clear, sometimes branched and pointed extensions of the ectoplasm, but they do not fuse to form a network (e.g., *Euglypha*, fig. 208).

4. *Lobopodia* are relatively large elongate finger-like, blunt ended extensions of the body, and contain both ectoplasm and endoplasm. They may be branched but the branches do not anastomose. Locomotion may occur through the pseudopodium (see p. 36), or the lobopodium may not function in locomotion.

5. *Protoplasmic waves* are wave like extensions of the protoplasm, which result in locomotion without the formation of the elongate process which we call a pseudopodium (see p. 38.)

All of these types are not always as distinct as they may appear in the above outline. For example, the pseudopodia of *Arcella* are large and blunt as are the lobopodia but usually contain only clear ectoplasm as do filopodia, and the radiating pseudopodia of *Astramoeba radiosa* bear a close resemblance to filopodia.

Types 1 to 4 are collectively known as pseudopodia, and a pseupodium is defined as an elongate extension of the cytoplasm.

WHAT TO LOOK FOR IN THE SARCODINA

What type of pseudopodia? Are they long, thin, numerous, radially arranged, and unbranched? If so, axopodia, and the specimen belongs to the Actinopodea.

If the radial processes have knobs on their distal ends, the organism does not belong to the Sarcodina but to the Suctorea (p. 222), unless it happens to be orange in color (Vampyrella, fig. 173).

Are the pseudopodia long, thin and branched? Do the branches tend to anastomose (i.e., fuse with each other) to form a network? If so, rhizopodia, and the organism does not belong to the Amoebida but may belong to any of the other orders (figs. 209 and 222 show typical rhizopodia).

Are the pseudopodia elongate with a blunt end as in Amoeba proteus? If so, lobopodia, and the organism belongs to the Amoebida.

Does the ameba move by means of flowing projections of protoplasm which are blunt but which are not as long as they are wide? If so, they are not properly called pseudopodia but are referred to as "protoplasmic waves" or "eruptive waves." If so, Amoebida.

Does the ameba have a test (ie., a shell or house)? If so, one usually sees the shell first and then looks inside for the ameba. If so, Foraminiferida (marine) or Testacida (fresh water). Is the shell composed of one chamber or many? Testacida are always single chambered; Foraminiferida single or multiple.

Is the ameba very large (up to several inches or more) and is it crawling on decaying wood? If so, Mycetozoida.

If the organism has axopodia, does it have a membrane which separates the cytoplasm into inner and outer layers? If so, it is probably marine and belongs to the Radiolarida. If not, it is probably in fresh water and belongs to the Heliozoida.

KEY TO THE ORDERS OF THE SARCODINA

1a With numerous radiating axopodia; some species, however, have filopodia.   Class ACTINOPODEA, 2

1b Without axopodia, with filopodia, rhizopodia, lobopodia or protoplasmic waves.   Class RHIZOPODEA, 3

2a Without a central capsule; usually fresh water.   Order HELIOZOIDA, p. 101

2b With a central capsule; marine.   Order RADIOLARIDA, p. 104

3a With test or shell..4

3b Without test or shell....................................5

4a Test single chambered; not composed of silicon or of calcium carbonate; usually fresh water.   Order TESTACIDA, p. 124

4b Test single or multichambered, calcareous, siliceous, or arenaceous; usually marine. Order FORAMINIFERIDA, p. 128

5a (a, b, c) With radiating pseudopodia (rhizopodia or filopodia). Order PROTEOMYXIDA, p. 108

5b With rhizopodia; forming plasmodia; usually on decaying wood. Order MYCETOZOIDA, p. 136

5c With lobopodia, without rhizopodia. Order AMOEBIDA, p. 110

CLASS ACTINOPODEA

It is customary for taxonomists to define the Actinopodea as Sarcodina with axopodia, and then when discussing both the Heliozoida and the Radiolarida to include in these orders a number of species which have filopodia but no axopodia, thereby ignoring certain principles of logic and pinning the unwary student on both horns of a dilemma at the same time. Some of these species, moreover, resemble Heliozoa and Radiolarida much more closely than they resemble any other group; the only difference being the type of pseudopodia. Furthermore, some organisms (e.g., *Clathrulina*) have filopodia in the young growth stages and axopodia later.

One way out of this difficulty would be to define the Actinopodea as organisms with radiating filopodia or axopodia, thereby placing most of the Proteomyxida in the Actinopodea. At best, the Proteomyxida comprise a miscellaneous group and some of them may be considered as related to both the Actinopodea and the Rhizopodea. However, in the present treatment the student is left with at least part of this dilemma.

Some day the filing system which we call our "classification" should be revised so that the process of filing (or classifying) will be more logical. The principal difficulty with making such a revision is that the revised system is apt to be as complicated as the sum total of the entire group of organisms and much more difficult to use than the present system which includes a convenient "miscellaneous" group. Similar statements could be made about some of the other taxonomic groups of the Protozoa (e.g., Mastigophora), and of most of the other phyla.

ORDER HELIOZOIDA

The heliozoans are typically spherical fresh water Sarcodina which have numerous radiating axopodia. Axopodia are thin, clear, non-branching pseudopods with an axial filament. There are several genera of organisms which have very thin clear branching pseudopods (filopodia) and these "pseudo heliozoa" (e.g., *Vampyrella*, *Nuclearia*) are sometimes included in this order; in the present key, however, they are placed in the Proteomyxida. Also there are some flagellated genera with axopodia (e.g., *Dimorpha*); these are placed in the Rhizomastigida. Certain organisms have both filopodia and axopodia, either at the same time or at different stages of growth; these (e.g., *Clathrulina*) are included in the Heliozoida.

Heliozoida are holozoic and ingest food, usually algae, by means of lobopodia which flow around the victim, as in most amebas.

WHAT TO LOOK FOR IN A HELIOZOAN

Is the ectoplasm highly vacuolated and distinct from the endoplasm? If so, perhaps *Actinosphaerium*. If not, perhaps *Actinophrys*.

Is the outer margin of the body covered with transparent siliceous plates embedded in a gelatinous envelope? With radiating siliceous spines? Or with a rigid siliceous test? Or is it naked?

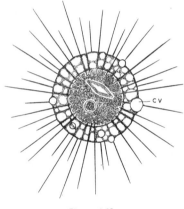

Figure 160

Fig. 160. *Actinosph a e r i u m eichhorni*, body usually 200-300μ, sometimes to 1 mm.

Ectoplasm highly vacuolated, quite distinct from granular endoplasm, but not separated by a membrane as in Radiolarida. Numreous nuclei and food vacuoles usually containing algae or small crustacea in endoplasm; two or more contractile vacuoles. Fresh water, among vegetation and algae. *A. arachnoideum* has both axopodia and rhizopodia.

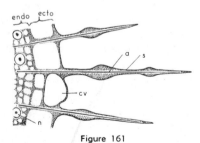

Figure 161

Fig. 161. Small section of *Actinosphaerium eich h o r n i* showing ectoplasm with contractible vacuole (cv), endoplasm with nuclei (n), axopodia with axoneme or axial filament, and cytoplasmic sheath (s).

With a high power lens the axonemes can sometimes be seen in living axopodia, but they usually can not be traced into the body of the cell except in well stained preparations. In *Actinosphaerium* each axoneme ends blindly in the endoplasm. In other genera the arrange-

102

ment is somewhat different. In *Acanthocystis* there is only one nucleus, and it is eccentric; all of the axonemes end in a single central granule. In *Actinophrys* the nucleus is central and each axoneme arises from a different granule near the nucleus. In *Camptonema* each axial filament arises from a separate nucleus.

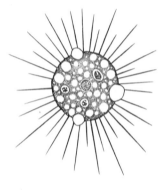

Fig. 162. *Actinophrys sol*, body 40-50μ, commonly called the "sun animalcule."

Central nucleus; several contractile vacuoles; ectoplasmic layer not distinct as in *Actinosphaerium*. Very common among vegetation.

Figure 162

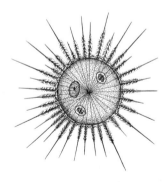

Fig. 163. *Raphidiophrys pallida*, body 50-60μ (Cash).

Outer gelatinous envelope in which are embedded siliceous spicules, especially around the base of the axopodia. Single nucleus. Fresh water; among vegetation.

Figure 163

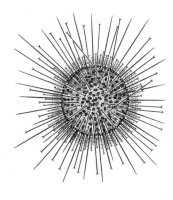

Figure 164

Fig. 164. *Acanthocystis turfacea,* body 48-100μ (Leidy).

Superficially resembles Actinophrys; but body usually contains zoochlorellae and hence the common name "green sun animalcule." Close examination, however, reveals three types of radiating structures: 1) axopodia, 2) long siliceous spicules, 3) short siliceous spicules. With a high power lens (preferably oil immersion) it is possible to see that the spicules have basal plates and are forked at the outer ends. Body with gelatinous covering.

Figure 165

Fig. 165. *Clathrulina elegans,* 60-90μ (Leidy).

Envelope a rigid siliceous basket - like structure, with regular openings and siliceous stalk. Filopodia during growth stages; mostly axopodia after the skeleton is well formed. Fresh water, among vegetation.

ORDER RADIOLARIDA

Radiolarians are pelagic marine organisms, usually with axopodia and a skeleton of silicon or of strontium sulfate. These skeletons eventually sink to the ocean floor where they often form thick layers of mud known as "radiolarian ooze." This ooze may become sedimentary rock and may be buried under other types of rock or perhaps may become the surface of dry land. The Radiolarida, like the Foraminiferida, are therefore of considerable importance to geologists (p. 129).

The Radiolarida are distinguished from the Heliozoida morphologically by the presence of a *central capsule,* a membrane which separates the ectoplasm from the endoplasm. There are four sub-orders (with several synonyms) which are distinguished from each other mostly on the basis of the number of openings in the central capsule.

The ectoplasm is highly vacuolated, and the vacuoles contain a solution with a low specific gravity. This permits the organisms to float in spite of the heavy skeleton. Under the influence of rough weather these vacuoles may collapse and the animal then sinks, to rise again in calmer weather.

The inland student probably will not have living radiolarians available. However, the skeletons, obtained by soaking radiolarian ooze in acid, are very beautiful and well worth seeing. There is a vast array of forms with radiating spines and latticed spheres, some concentric, with hooks, thorns, and various other shapes of protruberances which make the skeletons among the most beautifully intricate objects in nature. One undeveloped possibility would be to use them as models for Christmas tree ornaments; they would put the usual ornaments to shame by comparison.

There are 35 families of which only a few are represented below.

1a Skeleton composed of radial strontium sulfate spines; central capsule very thin with no openings except for rays of skeleton which originate at center of animal.

Suborder ACTIPYLINA or ACANTHARINA

The name Actipylina means "ray gates"; Acantharina emphasizes the "spiny" appearance.

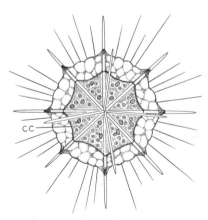

Fig. 166. *Acanthometron elasticum*, skeleton 500μ or more (Hertwig).

The skeleton originates at the center of the body and consists of 20 rays in a regular arrangement. Central capsule (cc) thin. Zooxanthellae in endoplasm.

Figure 166

1b Skeleton of silicon, does not originate in center of body......2

2a Central capsule thick with numerous pores uniformly distributed; very highly vacuolated ectoplasm; skeleton lacking or composed of spicules only in some species; well developed in others.
                    Suborder PERIPYLINA or SPUMELLINA

The name Peripylina emphasizes the openings in the central capsule; the name Spumellina emphasizes the foam-like appearance of the ectoplasm.

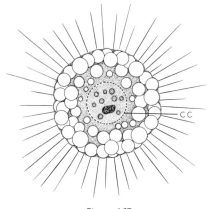

Figure 167

Fig. 167. *Thalassicola nucleata*, 5mm (Huth).

These giant cells contain only a single nucleus, which together with numerous oil droplets are contained within the central capsule (cc). Vacuoles very highly developed, giving the animal the appearance of a large mass of foam, hence one name of the suborder. Related colonial forms may be 4-6 cm in length.

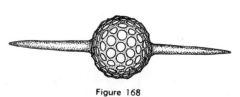

Figure 168

Fig. 168. *Sphaerostylus ostracion*, sphere 175μ.

Spherical with two long spines; another sphere within the one shown. Recent; tropical Atlantic. *Echinomma* has more openings and a dozen spines; *Haliomma* has more openings but no spines.

2b Central capsule with only three tubular openings or with one group of many openings on one side.....................3

3a Central capsule with three tubular openings; one on one side (an astropyle) and two more or less opposite (the parapyles); with brownish gray pigment.
            Suborder TRIPYLINA, PHAEODINA, or CANNOPYLINA

The name Tripylina emphasizes the number of openings to the capsule; Cannopylina their tubular shape; and Phaeodina, the color of the pigment.

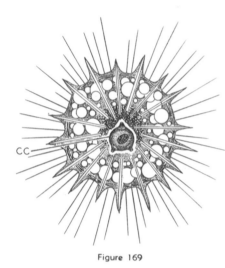

Fig. 169. *Aulacantha scalymantha*, 1400μ (Kuhn).

Skeleton of numerous radial rods and of many small tangential needles. Central capsule with three tubular openings, brownish gray pigment near the astropyle. Recent.

Figure 169

3b Central capsule with only one opening; skeleton of silicon, of various shapes.   Suborder MONOPYLINA or NASSELLINA
The name Nasselina comes from "nass" meaning "fish basket."

Fig. 170. *Lithocircus* (after Haeckel).

Skeleton merely a sagittal ring. Central capsule, with a group of openings at one end, contains nucleus. Cytoplasm fills skeletal ring and pseudopodia extend beyond. Pseudopodia branch and anastomose freely.

Acanthodesima is similar, but skeleton is composed of two such rings.

Figure 170

Fig. 171. *Thysocyrtis rhizodon,* 350μ.

Skeleton is increased in size by addition of new chambers.

Figure 171

CLASS RHIZOPODEA

ORDER PROTEOMYXIDA

Organisms with radiating filopodia or rhizopodia; they may easily be distinguished from the Heliozoida by the fact that the pseudopodia of the Proteomyxida are branched. Some (e.g., *Labyrinthula*) feed on algae by penetrating the cell wall and are therefore considered related to the fungi.

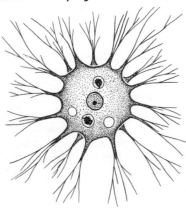

Fig. 172. *Actinocoma ramosa,* 14-26μ (Penard).

Spherical; n u c l e u s with heavy membrane; filopodia, simple or in groups; fresh water. *Nuclearia,* 40-60μ, is similar but multinucleate and sometimes with gelatinous envelope.

Figure 172

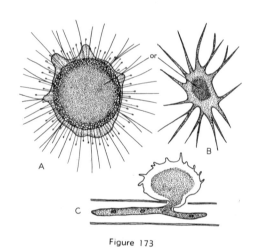

Figure 173

Fig. 173. A. *Vampyrella lateritia,* 30-40μ (Leidy).

Body spherical; usually bright orange in color because of carotenoid granules (or) which have been obtained from algae. Three types of protoplasmic processes: 1) lobopodia or protoplasmic waves for locomotion, 2) filopodia, 3) shorter unbranched processes of unknown function which have knobs on the ends and remind the observer of Suctorea (p. 222). These may be quickly withdrawn or protruded. B. Younger individual without knobbed processes. C. *Vampyrella* entering an algal cell (*Maugeotia*). The rhizopod can produce an opening in the cellulose wall of an algal filament. Then the pseudopodia enter and digest the cell; the organism then moves on to the next cell. In this way *Vampyrella* may cause considerable destruction to filamentous algae.

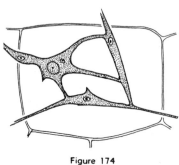

Figure 174

Fig. 174. *Labyrinthomyxa sauvageaui,* 7-11μ (Duboscq) in the alga *Laminaria.*

Body of cell fusiform; ameboid; cell entirely inside of plant; joined to each other by radiating pseudopodia. The genus Labyrinthula is very similar. In 1931 and 1932 *Labyrinthula* attacked the eel grass (*Zostera marina*) along the Atlantic coast. It almost completed eliminated the eel grass and caused the death of most of the scallops and of many ducks (p. 9). In 1947 the eel grass was just getting back to normal and the ducks and scallops could again obtain one of their most important foods.

109

ORDER AMOEBIDA

The Amoebida are naked rhizopods which move by means of lobopodia or protoplasmic waves and do not possess axopodia, rhizopodia, or filopodia. A naked ameba which has rhizopodia is probably a young myxameba or plasmodium of the Mycetozoida. Very small free living amebas with lobopodia or with protoplasmic waves may be the ameboid stage of a flagellate (e.g., *Tetramitus*, fig. 148) or a myxameba (fig. 226).

WHAT TO LOOK FOR IN AN AMEBA

Is the organism free living or parasitic? If parasitic, Endamoebidae.

Is the ameba moving? If it does not move for several minutes it probably is not normal. A few species move very slowly, but for most free living species the method of locomotion is the best if not the only means of identification. If an ameba moves very slowly it may be in bad health for lack of water; add more pond water to the slide and see if the ameba increases its speed.

Is the pellicle relatively inelastic so that as the ameba changes shape the pellicle becomes wrinkled? And does it form longitudinal folds when the ameba is moving? If so, *Thecamoeba*.

Does the ameba have pseudopodia? If so, does it move by means of pseudopodia or by means of protoplasmic waves? (See p. 36). This is a very important character.

In the amebas which move by means of pseudopodia (e.g., *Amoeba proteus*) the entire body eventually flows into the region which was once a pseudopodium (fig. 29). Such a pseudopodium is referred to as "indeterminate" because there is no definite limit to its size; it may continue to push out in one direction and the ameba moves forward through the pseudopodium.

In the amebas which move by means of protoplasmic waves, pseudopodia may or may not be present. (Present in *Mayorella*, absent in *Valkamphia*). If pseudopodia are present they are usually conical in shape, and of a size which is more or less definite for the species. Such pseudopodia are referred to as "determinate" because they reach a definite size and are then withdrawn. No normal ameba under typical conditions has both determinate and indeterminate pseudopodia.

Therefore, if pseudopodia are present find out whether they are "determinate" or "indeterminate." Remember that indeterminate pseudodopodia direct locomotion of the ameba, whereas determinate pseudopodia do not direct locomotion. Amebas with determinate pseudopodia move by means of eruptive waves, and the pseudopodia serve other functions.

Does the ameba possess a uroid? A uroid is a posterior proto-plasmic mass which is often slightly separated from the body by a constriction (figs. 189, 198, 200). Is the uroid covered with many very long thin protoplasmic projections? Or is its surface composed of small hemispherical projections? Uroids sometimes are filled with old food vacuoles which contain the indigestible residue of the food. In such cases all or part of the uroid may become completely con-stricted from the body, and the ameba may move away, thereby leaving its feces enclosed in a small quantity of proto-plasm.

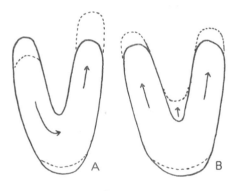

Figure 175

If two indeterminate pseudopodia are formed at the same time and are at a slight angle to each other does one of them eventually reverse and flow into the base of the other? If so (fig. 175, A), Amoeba, Chaos or Meta-chaos. Or does a web form between them? If so (fig. 175, B) Polychaos.

Are the indeterminate pseudopodia round in cross section or do they possess longitudinal ridges (e.g., Amoeba proteus)?

Determinate pseudopodia may be completely withdrawn, or as the ameba moves forward (by flowing) the pseudopodia may be only par-tially withdrawn and the pseudopodial remnants may accumulate at the posterior end to form a uroid (e.g., Mayorella vespertilio).

What kind of nucleus is present? Is it spherical with a compact mass in the center (e.g., Mayorella) or is it shaped like a thick biscuit with refractile granules just under the crust (e.g., Amoeba proteus)? If no nucleus can be found by careful observation the ameba may have very small nuclei (Chaos or Pelomyxa).

Does the cytoplasm contain crystals? If so, what shape are they? (Figs. 193, 196, 197).

Size? Different species of the Amoebida vary from a few microns to several millimeters in length.

Color? Some Amoebida are colorless, some are yellow, others are green with zoochlorella, and still others are dark gray or black with symbiotic bacteria (Pelomyxa).

When disturbed (e.g., by bumping the coverslip with a pencil) does the ameba become rounded? Or does it become rayed so that it resembles Astramoeba radiosa (fig. 190).

111

KEY TO THE AMOEBIDA

1a Free living...2, p. 116

1b Parasitic.   Family **ENDAMOEBIDAE**

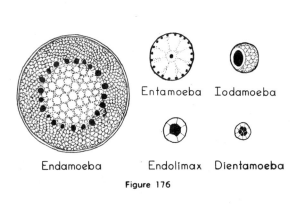

Entamoeba   Iodamoeba

Endamoeba   Endolimax   Dientamoeba

Figure 176

The endamoebas are ordinarily divided into five genera on the basis of the structure of the nucleus. This usually c a n b e seen only in well stained s p e c i - mens. Fig. 176 shows the five nuclear t y p e s and the generic names. Most intestinal species have cysts which pass out with the feces; new hosts become infected by fecal contamination of food or drinking water.

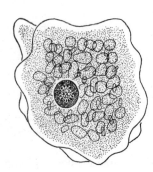

Figure 177

Fig. 177. *Endamoeba blattae*, 10-150μ (Kudo).

In colon of cockroaches; ingest starch grains, which often fill the cytoplasm, and also yeast and bacteria. Cysts often contain as many as 60 nuclei. Very common. Many other species in termites.

The nucleus of members of the genus *Endamoeba* differs from that of the genus *Entamoeba* in that there is no central karyosome and no peripheral chromatin. However, the two genera are often erroneously referred to collectively as *Endamoeba*.

112

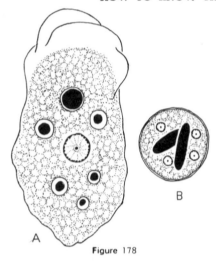

Figure 178

Fig. 178 A. *Entamoeba his-tolytica*, 15-35μ (Kudo).

In human large intestine, cause of amebic dysentery. Very active, with clear ectoplasm at anterior end; movement by eruptive waves; with central karyosome and peripheral chromatin; food vacuoles contain red blood cells shown in various stages of digestion. B. Cyst, containing 4 nuclei and one or more deeply staining chromatoid bodies with rounded ends (Kudo).

This ameba secretes a material which dissolves the intestinal lining and permits the ameba to enter the connective tissue and muscular layers. The lesions are usually flask-shaped, i.e., larger within the wall than on the inner surface. Two or more of these lesions may merge inside the wall and thereby make a hole in the epithelium several inches in diameter. As much as 50 per cent of the intestinal epithelium may be dissolved. Dissolution of the mucosa of the large intestine results in diarrhea (liquid feces) and dysentery (bloody feces). Then the ameba may enter the liver through the portal vein and give rise to large cysts of histolyzed tissue and hemolyzed blood which are sometimes six inches or more in diameter. These cysts contain many amebas and may or may not contain bacteria. They often rupture through the surface of the liver to adjacent organs or into the coelom. Death usually occurs from peritonitis caused by perforation of intestinal wall or from rupture of a liver cyst.

Amebiasis of man is a cosmopolitan disease and is spread by fecal contamination of food or drinking water, either directly, by food handlers, or by flies. Many people have a partial immunity which allows them to act as "carriers." The encysted stage of the ameba can live for weeks in sewage and can withstand ordinary chlorination of drinking water.

Modern methods of treatment, which include the use of emetine, of various organic iodine compounds (diodoquin, anayodin, vioform), and of carbarsone, are very effective.

E. invadens, found in various turtles and snakes, produces lesions in the intestine and liver similar to those of *E. histolytica* in man. It is easily grown in culture, available commercially, looks very much like *E. histolytica*, and can be used as classroom material for the detailed study of a pathogenic ameba. *E. histolytica* is active only at or near body temperature, but *E. invadens* is also active at room temperature.

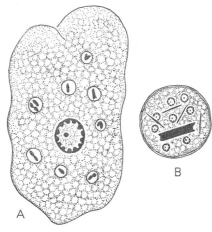

Figure 179

Fig. 179. *Entamoeba coli*, 20-35μ (Kudo).
In human intestine, nonpathogenic, often confused with E. histolytica. Slow moving; food vacuoles contain bacteria, no red blood cells; nucleus large, karyosome eccentric, chromatin very prominent. Cyst with e i g h t nuclei; chromatoid body with jagged ends. Common.

In the trophozoite stage this ameba can be distinguished from *E. histolytica* by the absence of hyaline ectoplasm at the anterior end, by its slow rate of locomotion, and by its relatively large nucleus. The difference in rate of locomotion of the two species is quite pronounced at 37°C. but is decreased by lower temperatures

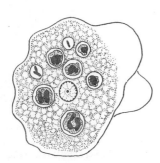

Figure 180

Fig. 180. *Entamoeba gingivalis*, 10-30μ.
In human mouth especially around the base of pyorrheic teeth; probably a contributing cause of pyorrhea. In pyorrhea a dark hard material (tartar) is secreted between the tooth and the gum by filamentous bacteria. The amebas live at the lower edge of this tartar, ingest leucocytes, and probably help dissolve the peridental cement (cartilage) which holds the tooth to the bone. More and more tartar is formed down the side of the tooth, and the bacteria and amebas move closer to the root. When most of the cement is dissolved the tooth loosens and eventually comes out. Pyorrhea is the cause of the loss of about 50 per cent of the teeth lost by adults.

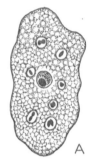

Figure 181

A   B

Fig. 181. A. *Iodamoeba butschlii*, 6-25μ (Kudo).

Common in human intestine; non - pathogenic. Nucleus with large eccentric karyosome and numerous faintly staining bodies. B. Cyst. The cysts contain a large vacuole filled with glycogen which stains brown with iodine. The cysts were found in feces and known as I-cysts before they were known to be the cysts of the ameba; hence the name Iodamoeba.

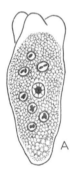

B

A

Figure 182

Fig. 182. A. *Endolimax nana*, 6-15μ (Kudo).

In human intestine; non-pathogenic; nucleus with large irregular karyosome. B. Cyst, usually oval, with 4 nuclei.

The trophozoite is fairly active and movement is somewhat similar to that of *Entamoeba histolytica*. However, it is ordinarily only half the size of *Entamoeba*, and the nucleus is so small (1.5 to 3.0μ) that it is rarely seen in living specimens.

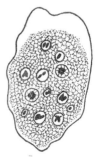

Figure 183

Fig. 183. *Dientamoeba fragilis*, 4-18μ (Kudo). In human intestine; non-pathogenic; nucleus with 4-8 central karyosomes; mono- or dinucleate.

This is the only intestinal ameba of man with two nuclei. However, the number of nuclei is variable, with only 40 to 80 percent of the specimens binucleate. The binucleate condition is apparently an arrested telophase of division; the binucleate cell divides into two mononucleate cells and then the nucleus of each divides prior to the next cytoplasmic division. It has also been suggested that *Dientamoeba* may have a flagellate stage in its life history.

115

2a Small forms, usually less than 20μ, with both ameboid and flagellated stages. Family **DIMASTIGAMOEBIDAE**

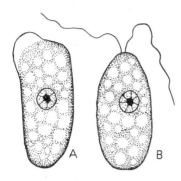

Figure 184

Fig. 184. *Dimastigamoeba gruberi,* ameba, 10-50μ; flagellate, 10-30μ. Ameboid stage resembles *Valkampfia.* Stagnant water or coprozoic.

The genus is also called *Naegleria.* A related genus, *Trimastigamoeba,* has three flagella. These genera are truly intermediate between flagellates and amebas and are arbitrarily classed as amebas only because the flagellum is not permanent. See p. 44.

2b Larger than 20μ; no flagellate stage known 3

3a With unified streaming of granular endoplasm 4

3b Without unified streaming of granular endoplasm; disc-shaped, thick in middle which contains endoplasm; thin clear outer region drags granular endoplasm along. Family **HYALODISCIDAE**

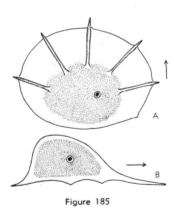

Figure 185

Fig. 185. *Hyalodiscus rubicundus,* 40-60μ (Penard).

A. Top view. B. Side view. Endoplasm thick and granular, orange in color; ectoplasm thin and clear. Endoplasm central or somewhat posterior and does not flow in a unified manner. The ectoplasm flows forward, and the endoplasm is apparently dragged along rapidly without visible streaming of the granules. Sometimes there are several ridges of the pellicle which project from the endoplasm out to and slightly beyond the edge of the ectoplasm, forming short thin spine-like pseudopodia. When suspended in water (i.e., not touching any solid object) it has a rayed stage similar to *Astramoeba.*

4a No prominent longitudinal ridges in pellicle; with pseudopodia or protoplasmic waves 5

4b Pellicle wrinkled and relatively inelastic, with longitudinal ridges when moving; oval to circular in locomotion; wave-like expansions; no pseudopodia. Family THECAMOEBIDAE

Fig. 186. *Thecamoeba verrucosa*, up to 200μ, the "ameba with a skin."

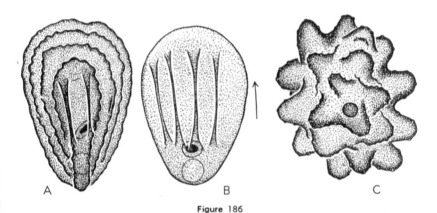

Figure 186

The characteristic of this genus is the distinct pellicle, a tough outer layer which may be thrown into folds, ridges, and wrinkles. Movement is by means of protoplasmic flow without pseudopodia. A. Moving very slowly. B. More rapid movement. C. At rest, with pellicle wrinkled over lumps on the surface. *T. striata* is similar, but smaller (25-45μ), very clear and glassy in appearance, and quite flattened, with three longitudinal ridges. Fresh water.

5a Pseudopodia indeterminate or absent.
Family AMOEBIDAE or CHAIDAE......6, p. 120

5b Pseudopodia determinate, conical or tapering, do not direct locomotion, granular material only near base, are withdrawn after reaching a given size or may form part of uroid; locomotion by protoplasmic flow. Family MAYORELLIDAE

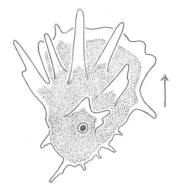

Figure 187

Fig. 187. *Mayorella bigemma*, 100-300μ, usually 125μ (Schaeffer).

Numerous c o n i c a l determinate pseudopodia; locomotion by protoplasmic flow; pseudopodia which are formed toward anterior end become more or less posterior as the protoplasm flows ahead and are then withdrawn. Fresh water.

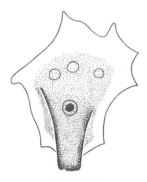

Figure 188

Fig. 188. *Mayorella vespertilio*, 70μ (Penard).

Very similar to *B. bigemma* but smaller. The figure shows an animal moving very rapidly with few pseudopodia; protoplasmic wave very obvious. When moving more slowly the general appearance is that of the figure of *M. bigemma*. Fresh water.

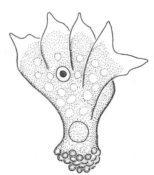

Figure 189

Fig. 189. *Mayorella spumosa*, 50-125μ (Penard).

Somewhat fan - shaped; conical determinate pseudopodia; uroid composed of numerous small bumps; endoplasm always vacuolated with some vacuoles as large as 30μ in diameter. Fresh water.

118

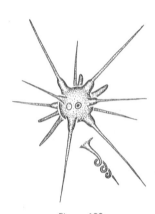

Figure 190

Fig. 190. *Astramoeba radiosa*, body 14-30μ, including pseudopodia up to 135μ.

Very transparent. Locomotion slow and irregular, uncertain; club - shaped or ovoid when moving, sometimes with short pseudopods. Characteristically with numerous long thin pseudopods when suspended in water; may remain in this form for long periods of time. Pseudopodia sometimes thicker at base as shown; may become helical when retracted, as shown in insert. Other genera (e.g., *Flabellula*, *Metachaos*, *Mayorella*) may assume a rayed stage when disturbed, but they usually change to a different form within a few minutes.

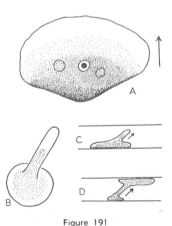

Figure 191

Fig. 191. A. *Flabellula velata*, 60μ, a small ameba, broader than long in locomotion, with a characteristically broad clear layer of ectoplasm across the entire anterior end.

Movement by protoplasmic waves; sometimes a few short conical pseudopodia. Rayed when disturbed. When quiescent it may send out a long blunt exploratory pseudopodium (as in B). If this pseudopodium makes contact with another object it may function as an indeterminate pseudopodium, i.e., the animal may flow through the pseudopodium to reach the other object. In C and D, the horizontal lines represent the slide and coverslip, side view. In C the ameba is putting out a pseudopodium toward the coverslip. In D it has almost completed attachment to the coverslip.

119

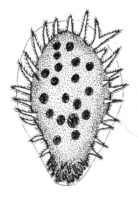

Figure 192

Fig. 192. *Dinamoeba miriabilis*, 150-340μ (Leidy).

With numerous small conical determinate pseudopodia, sometimes branched, which are very rapidly put out and rapidly retracted, with minute processes as shown. Movement is slow and uncertain but by protoplasmic waves. Animal often surrounded by gelatinous layer. A voracious feeder, ingesting long filaments of algae and numerous non-filamentous forms. Uroid sometimes present.

6a Pseudopodia rarely formed; locomotion by wave-like expansions
....7, p. 123

6b Pseudopodia usually present, indeterminate, with granular protoplasm except at advancing tip; pseudopodia direct locomotion, i.e., the animal flows through its pseudopodia.

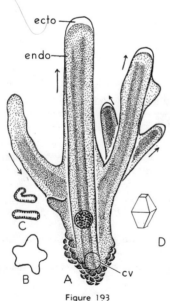

ecto

endo

C

B   A   cv

D

Figure 193

Fig. 193. A. *Amoeba proteus*, also known as *Chaos diffluens*, up to 600μ or more when elongated (Leidy).

One to several indeterminate pseudopodia which contain endoplasm except at advancing tip. Pseudopodia longitudinally ridged. Uninucleate with disc-shaped nucleus sometimes folded (flat view in fig. A, edge view in C) with refractible chromatin granules toward periphery. No web formed between pseudopodia; eventually all of the protoplasm flows through only one pseudopodium as the animal moves forward. Numerous crystals in cytoplasm. B. Cross section of pseudopodium. D. Crystal, 4.5μ.

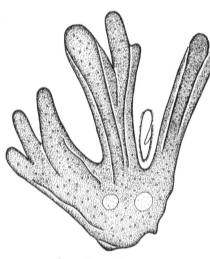

Figure 194

Fig. 194. *Chaos carolinensis,* also called *Amoeba carolinensis,* *Pelomyxa carolinensis,* and *Chaos chaos,* 1 to 5 mm.

The so called "giant ameba," much larger than *Amoeba proteus.* Locomotion by means of ridged indeterminate pseudopodia as in *A. proteus,* but nuclei very small (20μ) and very numerous (several hundred). Rarely found in nature; available commercially; an excellent species for study, especially because of its huge size. The amebas are easily seen with the unaided eye and can be picked out of a culture with an ordinary pipette and placed singly on slides. If paramecia are added to the slide the ameba may ingest them in large numbers, one immediately after another, or as many as twenty in one food vacuole, all ingested at the same time. The figure shows a *Paramecium* which may soon be engulfed by this huge ameba.

This ameba and *Amoeba proteus* both have ridged indeterminate pseudopodia. If this is considered an adequate generic character, then the two species may be placed in the same genus which can be called either *Amoeba* or *Chaos,* depending upon which interpretation one wishes to put on certain historical events. If the differences in size of body and size and number of nuclei are considered important enough to distinguish separate genera then one can use the names *Amoeba proteus* and *Chaos carolinensis.*

Fig. 195 shows the locomotion of *Chaos carolinensis* as seen from the side (Wilber).

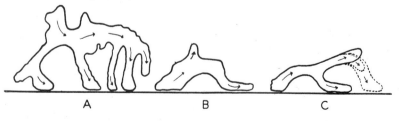

A   B   C

Figure 195

121

A shows how several pseudopodia make contact with the sub-stratum. Arrows indicate flow of protoplasm. B. and C are another animal; in B an upper pseudopod is just forming; in C this pseudopod has passed forward and is shown in three stages of progression. The animal in B and C later "walked" like that shown in A. The loco-motion of Amoeba proteus seen from the side is very similar.

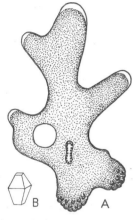

Fig. 196. A. *Metachaos discoides*, up to 450μ (Schaeffer).

Similar to *Amoeba proteus*, but the pseu-dopodia are not ridged and are round or oval in cross section. The whole ameba eventually flows through one main pseu-dopod, as in *A. proteus*. B. Crystal from cytoplasm.

Figure 196

This species is the one most commonly confused with *Amoeba proteus*. The distinguishing feature is the presence of ridges on the pseudopodia of *A. proteus*. These are often not easily seen unless one focusses carefully with a high power objective on an actively advanc-ing pseudopod. Under these conditions, however, the ridges appear as longitudinal folds in the pellicle of *A. proteus* but not in that of *Meta-chaos discoides*.

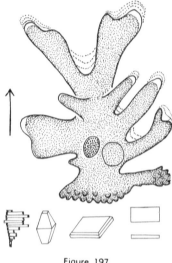

Figure 197

Fig. 197. *Polychaos dubia*, 400μ (Schaeffer).

An average of 12 pseudopodia, not ridged, but oval or round in cross section. The animal moves forward by flowing not only through one pseudopodium as in *Amoeba* and *Metachaos* but through several at the same time; an advancing web is formed between the pseudopodia (as shown by dash lines in the figure) at the same time that the ends of the pseudopodia move forward. The animal, therefore, may move forward and also retain its shape; this gives the appearance of gliding forward without forming new pseudopodia. Actually, however, the protoplasm is streaming within the pseudopodia. The cytoplasmic crystals are of several kinds, as shown at the bottom of the figure.

7a Large (over 100μ) dark in color, usually many food vacuoles.

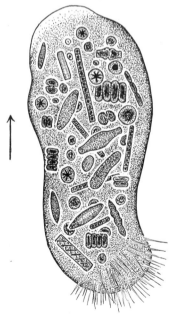

Figure 198

Fig. 198. *Pelomyxa palustris*, 100μ to 3mm, usually above 500μ (Leidy).

This very large ameba moves entirely by protoplasmic waves with little change in shape; seldom forms pseudopodia. Uroid with many fine projections sometimes present. Clear ectoplasm only at advancing front of the protoplasmic wave. A voracious feeder; body may contain a hundred or more food vacuoles. Many small nuclei, usually visible only in stained preparations. Animal often appears gray to black because of bacteria (*Cladothrix*, symbiotic? commensal?) in the cytoplasm.

Whenever this ameba and *Chaos carolinensis* are placed in the same genus it is assumed that the difference in the type of movement, i.e., protoplasmic waves vs. pseudopodia, is not sufficient to warrant a separate genus. The two principal characters which these amebas have in common are the large size of the animal and a large number of small nuclei. However, the type of movement is usually considered of prime importance in the taxonomy of the amebas, and this difference seems adequate to warrant a separate genus.

7b Under 100μ, usually clear or vacuolated with only a moderate number of food vacuoles.

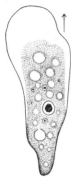

Fig. 199. *Valkampfia limax,* 30-40μ (Kudo).
Small clear ameba; moves rapidly entirely by eruptive waves; no pseudopodia; no uroid. Common. Fresh water. Somewhat similar to *Flabellula* except that it is always longer than broad. Very similar to ameboid phase of *Dimastigamoeba* (fig. 184).

Figure 199

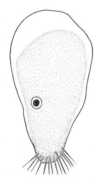

Fig. 200. *Trichamoeba limax,* up to 100μ; other species down to 20μ.
The distinguishing generic character is the uroid with many hair-like projections; otherwise similar to *Valkampfia.*

Figure 200

ORDER TESTACIDA

The Testacida are shelled rhizopoda with only a single chambered test. The test may be chitinoid, arenaceous, or made of plates. Pseudopodia may be rhizopodia, filopodia, or lobopodia. Mostly fresh water, among vegetation.

WHAT TO LOOK FOR IN THE TESTACIDA

What is the color and the general appearance of the test? If it is a uniform brown and its appearance reminds you of the material of an insect exoskeleton, it probably is what is commonly described as "chitinoid." However, this does not mean that it is composed of chitin. It is some other organic compound secreted by the ameba. If so, probably *Arcella*.

Is the test composed of many tiny sand grains or other solid material stuck together by an almost invisible "glue"? If so, the test is arenaceous, i.e., composed of foreign material. If so, perhaps *Difflugia*.

Is the test composed of many tiny plates neatly arranged over the surface of the ameba? If so, perhaps *Euglypha*. These plates are not foreign bodies but are secreted inside of the ameba and then moved to the surface and glued in position.

What is the shape of the test? Is it a flat disc? A thick disc? A hemisphere? Pear-shaped? Does it have spines?

Where is the opening? Is it centrally located or is it to one side?

What type of pseudopodia?

1a **Shell simple and membranous or chitinoid** 2

1b **Shell arenaceous or made up of platelets** 3

2a **Filopodia, or rhizopodia, anastomoses.**

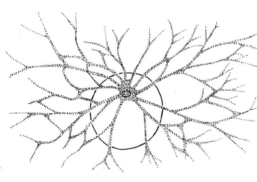

Figure 201

Family GROMIIDAE

Fig. 201. *Gromia fluvialis,* 9 0 - 2 5 0 μ (Dujardin).

Test spherical or almost so, smooth and membranous or covered sparsely by siliceous particles; pseudopodia l o n g, ofen longer than shown, anastomosing; cytoplasm yellowish. Fresh water. There are also closely related genera and species in s a l t water; often classed as Foraminiferida.

2b Pseudopodia filose, sometimes simply branched, no anastomoses.
Family ARCELLIDAE

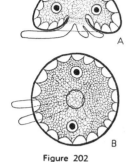

Fig. 202. *Arcella vulgaris*, 30-100μ (Leidy).

Test transparent, yellow to brown (when old), circular in top view, dome-like on top, concave on bottom with central opening. Ameba does not fill test; two nuclei. Fresh water. A. Side view. B. Top view. *Arcella discoides* is very similar, 70-260μ, and flatter (fig. 1).

Figure 202

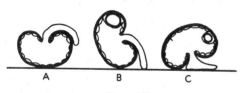

Fig. 203. *Arcella vulgaris* using a unique manner of turning itself over.

A. The animal has been placed on its back, and the pseudopodia are not long enough to reach the

Figure 203

substrate. B. The animal secretes a gas bubble which raises one edge, thereby permitting attachment of the pseudopodium to the substrate. C. The pseudopodium has contracted, and the gas bubble, no longer useful, is being dissolved. If a thick culture of *Arcella* is available this can easily be observed; find a specimen that is upside down and beginning to form a gas bubble and watch it turn over (provided, of course, that the cover slip is high enough to permit it to turn).

Fig. 204. A. *Arcella mitrata*, 100-145μ (Leidy).

Differs from *A. vulgaris* in shape of test which is constricted at bottom.

Figure 204

Fig. 205. *Arcella dentata*, 95μ (Leidy).

Test circular with 15-17 large spines. A. Top view. B. Side view.

The test is easily distinguished from those of other species by the spines which are sometimes directed more laterally than shown and sometimes almost directly upward.

Figure 205

3a Test arenaceous, usually with sand grains, sometimes other particles.   Family DIFFLUGIIDAE

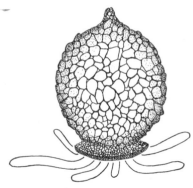

Figure 206

Fig. 206. *Difflugia urceolata*, 200-230μ (Leidy).

Shell rotund with very short neck and a rim around the aperture. Sand grains usually completely cover the test. Easily overlooked on a slide because on superficial examination it looks like a pile of sand grains; close inspection, however, often discloses the ameba. Fresh water.

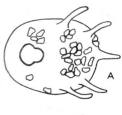

Figure 207

Fig. 207. *Centropyxis aculeata*, 100-150μ (Leidy).

Test oval, 4-6 spines toward one end, aperture toward the other, semi-transparent brown or opaque, with few or many sand grains or diatom shells attached. A. Top view, with few sand grains. B. Side view. Fresh water.

3b Test composed of uniform siliceous scales or plates, cemented together. Family EUGLYPHIDAE

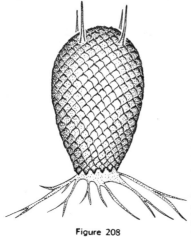

Figure 208

Fig. 208. *Euglypha alveolata*, 125-160μ (Leidy).

Test hyaline, regularly ovoid, with aperture at narrow end; aperture bordered by 4-12 serrated siliceous plates; remainder of test composed of ovate siliceous plates, broader above with a minute median point; 4 to 6 long spines on top of test in largest specimens. In small specimens the pattern of plates is not so well defined. Plates are secreted in the cytoplasm, passed to the surface and then cemented in position. Filopodia. Fresh water.

ORDER FORAMINIFERIDA

The foraminiferans are testate rhizopods, mostly marine, with rhizopodia. The test is of one to many chambers and may be gelatinous, chitinoid, calcareous, siliceous or arenaceous. The calcareous material is calcite and may be granular, hyaline, alveolar, fibrous, or porcellaneous in appearance. All types of test except the arenaceous ones are secreted; and arenaceous materials may be attached to any of the other types.

The chambers are known as *locula*, and the first chamber formed is the *proloculum*. The chambers connect with each other by means of large pores known as *foramina*, and with the outside by means of

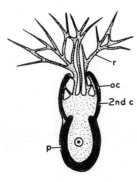

Figure 209

minute pores or *perforations*. The opening of the last chamber to the outside is known as the *aperture*. As the test is built chamber by chamber each temporary aperture of each chamber except the last becomes a foramin as a new chamber is added; the last or definitive aperture is often different in form from the earlier ones. The test is not external, but internal and is covered by a thin layer of cytoplasm. Fig. 209 shows a young *Nodosaria* adding a second chamber (2nd c) to the proloculum (p). The outer layer of cytoplasm (oc) covers the entire test; the rhizopodia (r) are branched and pointed and form anastomoses.

Tests vary greatly in shape. Fig. 210 shows three of the more common fundamental types: A, B, linear as seen in *Nodosaria*, *Orthocerina*, and *Dentalium*. C, a leaf-like shape with new chambers added to the two outside edges only, as seen in *Frondicularia* and *Flabellina*. D, a spiral type as seen in *Elphidium*, *Discorbis*, *Hantkenina*.

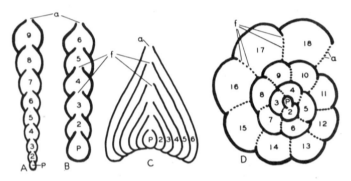

Figure 210

In Fig. 210, A, the proloculum is relatively small; the individual is multinucleate and is referred to as *microspheric*. In B the proloculum is large; the individual is mononucleate and is referred to as *megalospheric*. Both may be the same species. The nucleus and cytoplasm of the microspheric individual divide repeatedly to form many small amebas, each of which secretes a proloculum and grows into a megalospheric individual. The nucleus and cytoplasm of the megalospheric individual then divide repeatedly to form thousands of biflagellate gametes which fuse with gametes from other individuals to form a zygote. The zygote loses its flagella, secretes a proloculum and develops into a microspheric individual. This seems to be a true *alternation of generations;* the microspheric individual reproduces asexually, the megalospheric individual sexually, and the gametes are minute in comparison with the size of the "adult."

The foraminifera live mostly on the ocean bottom and their skeletons (tests) form very thick deposits known as "foraminiferan ooze" which cover about a third of the ocean floor and which may later become sedimentary rock. Eventually, through a general rise in the ocean floor and through a series of other geological changes, this sedimentary rock, formed on the ocean floor, may be found far inland either on the surface or submerged under later rock formations.

When oil wells are drilled in Texas, Oklahoma and elsewhere the borings are carefully examined for Foraminiferida. By identifying these skeletons (and also those of Radiolarida and of non-protozoan

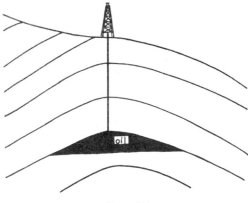

Figure 211

organisms) the geologist is able to identify the particular stratum through which the drill is boring. By comparing the depth of this layer below the surface with the depth of the same stratum in other areas it is possible to plot the contour of the various layers and thereby to predict where oil is most likely to be found. After a few exploratory holes a knowledge of the forams helps put the drill in the right places for finding oil (Fig. 211).

This information is of immense value to oil companies, and the commercial value of such information has greatly stimulated the study of the Foraminiferida. Before this value was generally known the persons who studied the Foraminiferida were thought of as doing "pure research" of no practical importance. Now the same persons (plus many others) carry on the same type of research, and it is considered (and is) highly "practical!"

There are 49 families, only a few of which are represented here. The name of the geological strata in which the species is found is given after each description.

WHAT TO LOOK FOR IN THE FORAMINIFERIDA

Is the test calcareous? If so, is it granular in appearance? Fibrous? Hyaline, i.e., clear, transparent? Porcellaneous, i.e., smooth, shiny, usually white, like porcelain?

How are the chambers arranged? Linearly, i.e., in a line, straight or curved? Biserially, i.e., with two series of linear chambers side by side? Spirally? If so, is the spiral flat or conical?

Are the chambers spherical or almost so? Or are they flattened? Are the *sutures* (lines between the chambers) distinct? If so, how are they arranged?

Figure 212

Fig. 212. *Amnodiscus incertus*, up to 6 mm (d'Orbigny).

Test single chambered, spiral, in one plane, proloculum extended into a simple tube; wall finely arenaceous with much cement. Cold, deep water, usually 3000 to 6000 feet. Jurassic to Recent.

Figure 213

Fig. 213. *Glomospira gordialis*, up to 1 mm.

Similar to *Amnodiscus* but twisted and spiralling in three dimensions instead of in one plane. Cold, deep water, 1000 to 10,000 feet. Jurassic to Recent.

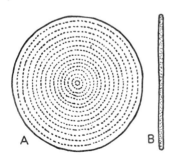

Figure 214

Fig. 214. *Cyclolina cretacea*, (d'Orbigny).

Test discoidal; consisting of annular chambers, proloculum in center; wall porcellaneous; apertures numerous. A. Flat view. B. Edge view. C. Edge view, higher magnification, showing apertures. Shallow water sediments. Upper Cretaceous. Very rare genus. Common related genera are asymmetrical.

131

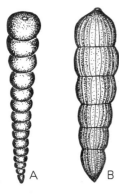

Figure 215

Fig. 215. A. *Orthocerina clavulus,*
1 mm (Lamarck).

Test elongate; multichambered,
linear; wall finely arenaceous.
Shallow water deposits. Eocene
to Recent. B. *Nodosaria raphanus,*
up to 16 mm (Plancus). Test
straight or curved, linear; wall
calcareous, hyaline, longitudinally
ridged; sutures at right angles to
axis. Mostly warm shallow water; but down to 12,000 feet. Triassic to Recent, abundant. C. *Den-
talina communis,* up to 8 mm
(Brady). Test elongate, curved,
linear; wall hyaline; sutures
oblique. Widely distributed geographically and bathymetrically,
more common in warm shallow
water. Triassic to Recent.

Figure 216

Fig. 216. *Tritaxia tricorinata,* 1 mm or more
(Reuss).

Test triangular in cross section; chambers
numerous, coiled three to a whorl, the last
one added linearly; wall finely arenaceous.
1000 to 7000 feet. Upper Jurassic, Lower
Cretaceous to Recent, common in Upper
Cretaceous of Mexico. A, B, two views of
same test.

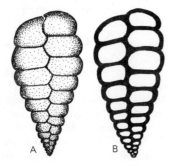

Figure 217

Fig. 217. *Textularia sagittula,* up to
4 mm (Defrance).

Test elongate, tapering, flattened,
composed of two series of alternating
chambers; wall finely arenaceous.
Mostly in shallow tropical seas. Jurassic to Recent. A. Whole test. B.
Section showing arrangement of
chambers.

Figure 218

Fig. 218. *Cribrostomum textulariforme,* up to 2 mm or more.

Test with biserial arrangement as in *Textularia* but not so flattened; wall finely arenaceous and thick; numerous apertures, terminal or nearly so. Limestones and shales. Carboniferous to Permian. It is possible that this organism is merely a stage in the development of the genus *Climacammina,* which is very similar in appearance except that the arenaceous material is coarser.

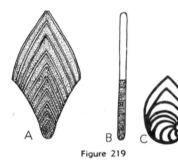

Figure 219

Fig. 219. *Flabellina rugosa,* up to 4 mm or more (d'Orbigny).

Test flattened; chambers added to two edges only as in *Frondicularia* (fig. 210) except for the first few chambers. Mostly shallow water. Jurassic to Cretaceous, common; Tertiary and Recent, rare. A. Flat view. B. Edge view. C. Enlarged section of first few chambers. *Frondicularia* is somewhat similar and is shown in section in fig. 210.

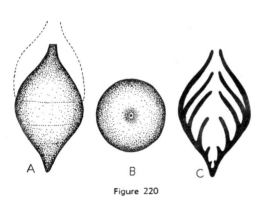

Figure 220

Fig. 220. *Glandulina laevigata,* up to 2 mm or more (d'Orbigny).

Spindle - shaped, circular in cross section, calcareous. Chambers arranged somewhat as in *Frondicularia* except that each new chamber is built completely around the apertural end of the preceding instead of on only two sides as in *Frondicularia* and the older chambers of *Flabellina*. A. Whole test, the place of the next chamber indicated by dotted lines. B. Apertural view. C. Longitudinal section. Littoral to 12,000 feet; mostly 1800 to 3000. Triassic to Recent.

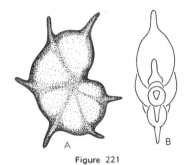

Figure 221

Fig. 221. *Hantkenina alabamensis*, up to 1 mm (Cushman).

Test spiral in one plane, about 3 whorls, rapidly increasing in size, each chamber with a hollow spine; wall hyaline. Shallow water sediments. Upper Cretaceous to Upper Eocene. A. Side view. B. Edge view.

Fig. 222. *Elphidium crispa*, to 4 mm (Brady).

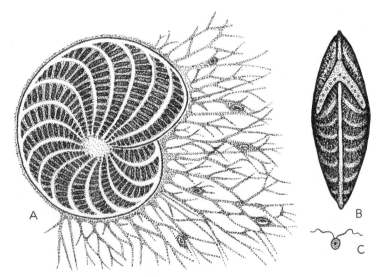

Figure 222

A. Whole animal showing rhizopodial network with several food vacuoles containing copepods and other small animals and plants. This type of rhizopodial network is characteristic of all Foraminiferida. B. Test in edge view. C. Gamete. Life history involves alternation of generations as described on pages 25 and 129. Test spiral; wall calcareous with numerous indentations on surface, as shown; numerous apertures. Cold to warm shallow water. Jurassic to Recent. This genus was first seen by Leeuwenhoek who found the shells inside the stomach of shrimp.

Fig. 223. *Globigerina bulloides*, up to 2 mm; average 0.5 mm (d'Orbigny).

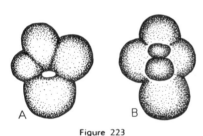

Figure 223

Chambers spherical, spirally arranged, not closely appressed, sutures evident; wall calcereous, hyaline. Pelagic in all oceans, and benthozoic; abundant in warm water. Middle Jurassic to Recent. The skeletons are so numerous on some parts of the ocean bottom that the mud is called "globigerina ooze."

Fig. 224. *Camerina laevigata* (Lamarck), formerly called *Nummulites*, up to 107 mm.

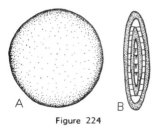

Figure 224

Test discoidal, bilaterally symmetrical, calcareous. Chambers numerous, spirally arranged. A. Side view. B. Edge view. One of the largest of Foraminiferida. Warm shallow water deposits. Jurassic to Miocene, abundant in Eocene. This genus is the principal component of the "nummulitic" limestone of Europe. Found in the limestone of the Egyptian pyramids.

Fig. 225. *Discorbis vesicularis*, to 1 mm (Cushman).

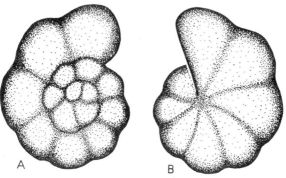

Figure 225

Test plano-convex, ventral side flattened, dorsal side convex; test calcareous, perforate; size of the newest chambers increases rapidly with size of animal; chambers often arranged so as to cover partially the umbilical area; aperture at base of umbilical margin on ventral side. A. Dorsal side. B. Ventral side. Lower Jurassic to Recent.

ORDER MYCETOZOIDA

The Mycetozoida are commonly known as Mycetozoa or Myxomycetes, are usually studied by botanists, and are often classified with the fungi. At one stage in their life history they are small amebas, at another they are small flagellates, at another they are immense amebas, inches or more in diameter and often holozoic, and at still another they are complex masses of spores which remind the observer of fungi. The spore masses persist for a longer period of time than the ameboid or flagellated stages, and the organisms are identified on the basis of the structure of the spore and the spore masses.

A typical life history is shown in fig. 226. If a spore (1) is placed in a moist medium the spore covering becomes cracked (2) and permits the escape of a small ameba, called a myxameba (3). The myxameba develops a flagellum, thereby becoming a myxoflagellate (4) which ingests bacteria and which may divide by binary fission to form more myxoflagellates. The myxoflagellates may then fuse in pairs to form ameboid zygotes (6). The zygote nucleus divides repeatedly and the cytoplasm increases to form a small plasmodium (7) which may fuse with other plasmodia to form a larger one which continues to grow until it may be several inches or more in diameter (8). This large plasmodium usually is a large rhizopodial network with thousands of nuclei, and lives in decaying wet logs, leaves, twigs, manure piles, or soil. It travels through the cavities and crevices in search of food; it is both holzoic and saprobic.

For all of the stages described above (1-8) a very high humidity and a wet medium are required. If the medium in which the plasmodium is living happens to become dry the organism may form sclerotia (9-10). A sclerotium consists of a number of nuclei and a small bit of cytoplasm surrounded by a resistant wall (10). When moisture again becomes available a sclerotium may develop into a plasmodium (10, 11, 8). It is possible to obtain dried sclerotia commercially, and these can be grown into plasmodia on agar.

Eventually, and usually in darkness, the plasmodium forms spores. The protoplasm may flow into certain areas (12) and form upward finger-like projections (13, 14) which may then become spheres on the end of a stalk (15). The remainder of the plasmodium becomes the base, or hypothallus. The mass on the stalk (s) becomes the sporangium (16) which is a mass of spores, embedded in a fibrous network, the capillitium (c), and often covered by an outer membrane, the peridium (p). In 16 the spores fill all of the blank spaces and have been omitted from the drawing. The spores may be dried for years and still remain viable, hatching into myxamebas when placed in water.

The spore masses may be in the form of : 1) *sporangia*, as described above and shown in fig. 226; 2) *aethalia*, in which the whole

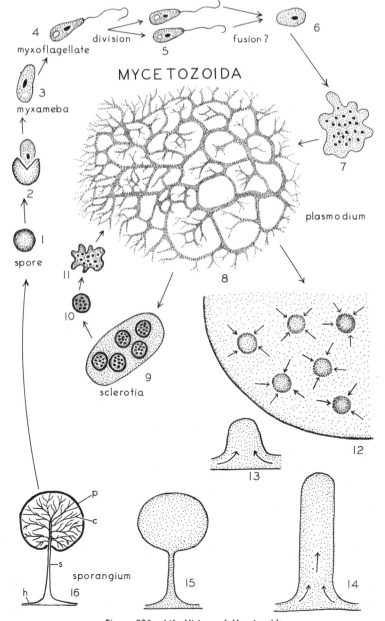

Figure 226. Life History of Mycetozoida.

plasmodium becomes a compact mass which develops into a number of sporangia tightly packed into one structure with the intervening walls incomplete (fig. 228); 3) *plasmodiocarps*, which are formed by the protoplasm accumulating in a few of the larger veins of the rhizopodial net, and these veins may develop as an aethalium; 4) *sporophores*, in which the spores are borne on very small stalks attached to the outside of finger-like processes which grow out from the plasmodium (fig. 227).

1a Spores on sporophores.   **Genus CERATIOMYXA**

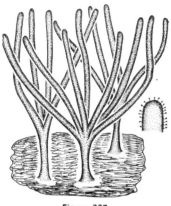

Figure 227

Fig. 227. *Ceratiomyxa fruticulosa*, 2-3 mm. high; white; sometimes the masses are several feet long, covering decaying logs, especially in wooded ravines.

One of the most common and easily detected genera. Insert shows sporophores on end of filament.

The plasmodium lives inside of sodden wood and emerges only to form the spores. The arrangement of the spores is entirely different from that of all other mycetozoa. Several varieties described; world wide in distribution.

1b Spores not on sporophores; in aethalia, plasmodiocarps, or sporangia. 2

2a Spores violet-brown or purplish-gray........................3

2b Spores variously colored but not as above..................4

3a Sporangia (peridium or capillitium, or both) provided with lime (calcium carbonate).   **Suborder PHYSARINA**

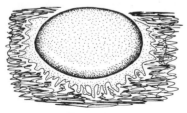

Figure 228

Fig. 228. *Fuligo septica*, aethalium 2 mm. to 30 cm. in diameter, outer covering impregnated with lime and usually various shades of whitish yellow, but also greenish, reddish, or brown.

Lime granules in the capillitium. Has a superficial resemblance to a macaroon. Spores violet.

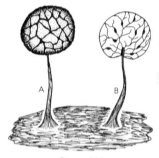

Figure 229

Fig. 229. A. *Physarum viride* (After Macbride and Martin).

Sporangia 0.3 to 0.5 mm; stalked; peridium yellow to orange, later becoming cracked, thereby exposing the mass of brownish or violet-black spores. B. Section of sporangium to show capillitium which bears numerous lime granules (shown black in drawing) in yellow to orange nodes.

Figure 230

Fig. 230. *Physarum didermoides.*

Sporangia ovoid to cylindric, 0.4-0.6 mm broad; stalk short; hypothallus white, reticulate or sheet-like; peridium white, with much lime; capillitium with white lime knots. Drawing shows two complete sporangia, two with peridium partly removed, and one in section with the lime knots visible. Spores purplish brown. (Macbride and Martin).

3b Sporangia without lime.

Suborder STEMONITINA

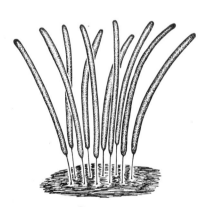

Figure 231

Fig. 231. *Stemonitis fusca.*

Sporangia slender, cylindrical, numerous, 5-20 mm tall, dark brown; capillitium of slender dark anastomosing threads; stalk 1/4 to 1/5 total height. Very common.

Many species. The sporangia are composed of a surface network of fibers which are formed by the repeated lateral and apical branching of a central internal stalk. Sporangia usually numerous and in closely packed groups.

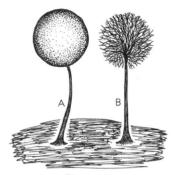

Figure 232

Fig. 232. *Comatricha elegans.*

Sporangium spherical, purplish brown, 0.3-0.5 mm in diameter, 1-2 mm total height; stalk black, dividing repeatedly to form a capillitium; spores pale brownish violaceous. A. Complete sporangium. B. With peridium and spores removed, showing capillitium (Hagelstein).

4a Capillitium scanty or lacking.   **Suborder LICEINA**

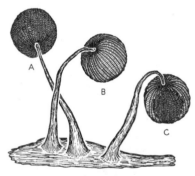

Figure 233

Fig. 233. *Dictydium cancellatum.*

Sporangia distinct, subspherical, numerous, brown, 5-6 mm in diameter; stalk long, slender; peridium thin, membranous, evane s c e n t, strengthened by meridional ribs connected to each other by fine transverse threads; no internal capillitium. A. Sporangium full of spores. B. Sporangium with peridium missing and all spores discharged. C. Sporangium with peridium missing, spores partly discharged. (Crowder).

Figure 234

Fig. 234. *Tubifera ferruginosa.*

Sporangia cylindrical, v e r y crowded, convex or conical above, sometimes perforated, 3 mm by 0.4 mm, forming brown cushions, 1-15 cm long; rufous brown spores; capillitium lacking; hypothallus thick, white, spongy.

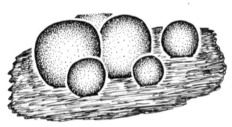

Figure 235

Fig. 235. *Lycogala epidendrum.*

Aethalia solitary or clustered, 3-15 mm in diameter, olive colored to blackish, minutely warted; peridium thin but t o u g h and persistent; spore mass rosy to purplish gray; capillitium scanty. The most common slime mold in the world.

4b Capillitium thread-like, either free or forming a network; spores pallid or yellow.

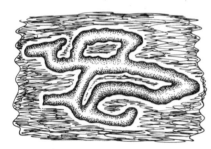

Figure 236

Fig. 236. *Hemitrichia serpula.*

Sporangia forming elongate, winding, branched plasmodiocarps 0.4 to 0.6 mm wide, golden yellow to yellowish brown, often on reddish brown hypothallus; capillitium an elastic tangle of twisted, sparingly branched yellow or orange threads. Spores yellow. (Macbride and Martin).

Figure 237

Fig. 237. *Arcyria denudata.*

Sporangia 2-3 mm high, cylindrical, numerous, brick red to reddish brown; capillitium an elastic network; other species are yellow to red-brown. Very common.

Capillitium is an elastic network which is "spongy" in appearance and to the touch. The peridium completely disappears in the mature sporangium except near the stalk where it forms a cup-like base for the capillitium. This base is much larger in certain other species.

141

SUBPHYLUM SPOROZOA

The Sporozoa are, without exception, parasitic and have a complicated life cycle. This life cycle, which in many species involves an alternation of sexual with asexual reproduction, is one of the principal bases of classification. Many species are transmitted from one host to another by means of spores (e.g., *Eimeria*, the cause of coccidiosis in chickens). A spore is an infective cell or group of cells (sporozoites) capable of producing a new infection, surrounded by a resistant membrane and formed at a definite stage in the life history of the species. This membrane permits the sporozoite to withstand considerable adverse chemical and physical conditions. Some species which are transmitted directly from one host to another (e.g., *Plasmodium*, the cause of malaria) do not have a spore membrane, and the sporozoites are naked.

Since the observer who is trying to identify a sporozoan seldom has the complete life cycle before him, it is usually necessary to identify the animal on the basis of the most easily and most commonly observed stages. Consequently the structure of the spore for those species which have a spore, and the structure of the growth stages and the position of the parasite in the host for those which do not produce spores are the criteria which are most useful.

Spores may contain one or more polar filaments or they may not. A polar filament is a coiled structure usually inside of a special capsule which is inside of the spore.

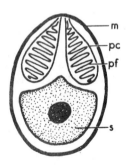

Fig. 238 shows a spore with a polar filament. m, spore membrane; pc, polar capsule; pf, polar filament; s, sporozoite or sporoplasm.

This is the spore of *Myxobolus*, a myxosporidan, of the Class Cnidosporidea, all members of which have at least one polar filament, with or without a polar capsule.

Figure 238

Figure 239

Fig. 239 shows the spore of *Eimeria maxima*, 21-42μ (Becker, Tyzzer) a common cause of coccidiosis in chickens.

This is a typical spore of the Coccidia, and there is no polar filament present. The outer spore membrane (oocyst) contains four inner membranes (sporocysts) and each sporocyst contains two sporozoites, or infective cells.

The Sporozoa which live in the blood stream of vertebrates (Haemosporidia, e.g., *Plasmodium*) do not have spores. The sporozoites are naked and are usually injected by some invertebrate (mosquito, tick, leech) directly into the blood stream of a new host.

The Sporozoa may be separated into three classes.

1a (a, b, c) **Spore with one or more polar filaments.**
Class CNIDOSPORIDEA, p. 161

1b **Spore without polar filament; life history as given below.**
Class TELOSPORIDEA, p. 143

1c **Spore without polar filament; life history incompletely known, but not similar to that of the Telosporidea.**
Class ACNIDOSPORIDEA, p. 168

CLASS TELOSPORIDEA

All of the members of the class Telosporidea have the same general type of life history, but the details vary considerably in the different groups.

The stages in the life history of the Telosporidea are outlined in fig. 240, and the student should identify as far as possible the names of the stages shown in this figure with the drawings of the various stages shown in fig. 241 (*Eimeria*), fig. 246 (*Gregarina*), and fig. 252 (*Plasmodium*). Such a comparison will emphasize both the similarities and the differences of these life histories.

Fig. 240.   The life history of Telosporidea.

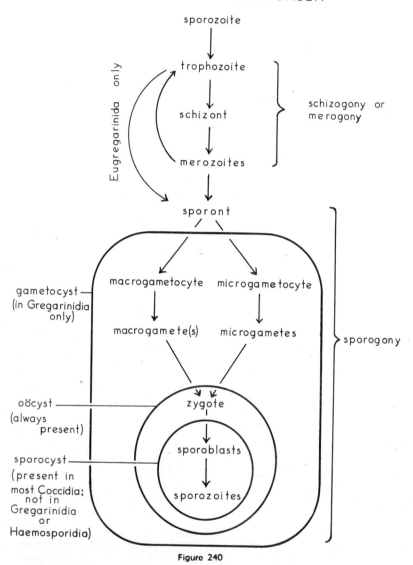

LIFE HISTORY OF TELOSPORIDEA

Figure 240

A *sporozoite*, or infective cell, passes through a growth or *tropho-zoite* stage. The nucleus of the trophozoite may divide repeatedly to form a *schizont* or multinucleate stage; then the cytoplasm divides (multiple fission) to form many small uninucleate cells known as merozoites. This process of division (asexual reproduction) is called *schizogony* or *merogony*. The merozoites may grow into trophozoites, and the schizogony cycle may be repeated time after time (every 2 or 3 days in *Plasmodium*). Eventually some of these merozoites become *sporonts* which develop into *gametocytes*. A gametocyte is a cell which will give rise to the sexual cells or *gametes*. *Microgametocytes* form *microgametes* or sperm; *macrogametocytes* form *macrogametes* or eggs. In one group, the Eugregarinida, the schizogony cycle is omitted and all trophozoites develop directly into gametocytes. In the Eugregarinida two gametocytes (one macro-, one micro-) become attached to each other (process known as *syzygy*) and secrete a membrane, the *gametocyst*. In Coccidia and Haemosporidia the macro- and microgametocytes do not become attached to each other, and there is no gametocyst. Eventually the gametes (one macro-, one micro-) fuse to form a *zygote*, or fertilized egg. The zygote secretes a membrane known as the *oocyst*, and then divides to form *sporoblasts*. Each sporoblast may secrete an inner cyst membrane or *sporocyst* and then divide to form two or more *sporozoites*.

The process of forming gametes is called *gametogenesis*, the process of fusion of gametes is known as *fertilization*, and the divisions of the zygote to form sporozoites are called the *metagamic divisions* or *metagamogony*. Gametogenesis, fertilization, and metagamogony are referred to collectively as *sporogony*.

In Gregarinidia and Haemosporidia and in a few Coccidia there is no sporocyst; in most Coccidia, however, the sporocyst is present. In Gregarinidia the sporozoites are contained in an oocyst when they infect a new host. In Haemosporidia the oocyst becomes broken and the sporozoites are naked at the time they enter a new host. In most Coccidia the sporozoites are surrounded by both a sporocyst and an oocyst at the time of infection.

In all Telosporidea except the Eugregarinida there is a typical alternation of generations. A generation of cells which multiply asexually by multiple fission (schizogony or merogony) is followed by a generation which forms gametes and zygotes, and thereby may be considered to reproduce sexually (sporogony). (See also pp. 21 to 28). In the Eugregarinida there is no schizogony; all multiplication of cells occurs in the sporogony cycle.

The Telosporidea are divided into three subclasses as follows:

1a Mature trophozoite extracellular and large; gametes develop within a gametocyst; zygote not motile; sporozoites enclosed in oocyst.
Subclass GREGARINIDIA, p. 149

1b Mature trophozoite intracellular and small...................2

2a Zygote not motile; sporozoites in oocyst and usually also in sporocyst.   Subclass COCCIDIA, p. 146

2b Zygote motile; sporozoites naked; schizogony in red blood cells or
   endothelial lining of capillaries of vertebrates.
                                              Subclass HAEMOSPORIDIA, p. 153

SUBCLASS COCCIDIA

The coccidians are telosporidian parasites of both vertebrates and
invertebrates. Among the vertebrates they cause many serious and
often fatal diseases, mostly diarrhea and dysentery.

The life cycle follows the general plan shown in fig. 240. In fig.
241 is the life history of *Eimeria schubergi*, found in the intestine of
centipedes of the genus *Lithobius* (after Schaudinn). The centipede

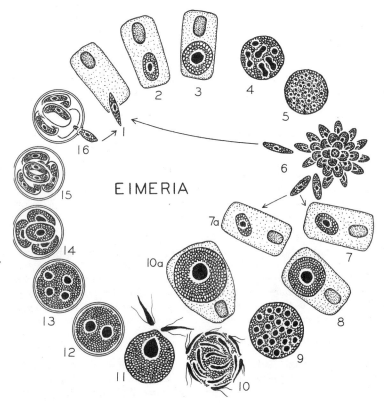

Figure 241. Life History of Eimeria.

ingests an oocyst (15) from which the sporozoites escape (16) and enter epithelial cells (1) where they develop into trophozoites (2, 3), schizonts (4, 5), and merozoites. The schizogony cycle may be repeated several times. Eventually some of the merozoites develop into microgameto-cytes (7) and macrogametocytes (7a) which become flagellated micro-gametes (10) or non-flagellated macrogametes (10a) respectively. Fer-tilization occurs (11), the zygote secretes the oocyst (12), divides into 4 sporoblasts (14) each of which secretes a sporocyst and divides to form two sporooites (15). Oocysts usually pass out in the feces in stage 12 and develop to stage 15 outside the body before they are eaten by another centipede.

In a few coccidians, e.g., Adelea, there is a syzygy similar in cer-tain respects to that of the gregarines (fig. 246). These organisms, however, have been omitted from the present book.

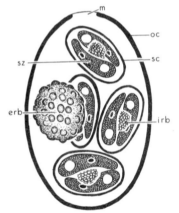

Figure 242

Fig. 242, the detailed structure of a typical coccidian cyst (Becker).

m, micropyle through which the sporozoites escape when the cyst is ingested by a host; sc, sporcyst; sz sporozoite; erb, extra-residual body, cytoplasm left over from the division of the zygote; irb, intra-residual body, cytoplasm left over from the division of the sporoblast.

Figure 243

Fig. 243. Oocyst of Eimeria magna, 21-42μ (Kes-sel and Jankiewicz), a common parasite of the small intestine of rabbits.

Note the broad micropyle. Eimeria stiedae, 28-40μ, with less prominent micropyle, is also common in rabbits, and is found in both the in-testine and the liver where it produces white nodules, some microscopic in size, some as big as a hazelnut. This parasite is very common and usually causes a chronic disease in wild rabbits; heavy infections may cause death in 3 weeks. Every rabbit hunter of note has prob-ably seen the white nodules on the livers of his game. Eimeria perforans, 14-20μ, without micropyle, is also very common but is limited to the intestine.

147

The cyst of Eimeria maxima has already been seen in fig. 239. This is one of seven species of Eimeria that commonly cause coccidiosis of chickens, but not the most fatal. Two other species, E. tenella and E. necatrix usually cause the death of chickens 5-7 days after ingestion of oocyts. Once an epidemic is started in a chicken yard the mortality is usually high unless the chickens are kept on wire mesh. The food and water supplies should also be protected so that they are not commonly contaminated by feces. Other species occur in cats, dogs, ducks, geese, pigeons, pheasants, turkeys, sheep, goats, and a large number of wild animals.

Fig. 244. *Isospora hominis*, 20-33μ (Kudo), the only coccidian which has been reported a number of times from the intestine of man.

Isospora differs from *Eimeria* in that the zygote forms only two sporoblasts and each of these forms four sporozoites. Found in Philippines, southern Asia, to eastern end of Mediterranean. May cause acute diarrhea for several weeks; usually not serious; cure spontaneous.

Figure 244

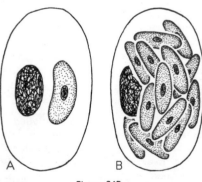

Fig. 245. *Haemogregarina stephanowi* in red blood cells of turtle *Emys*.

A. Young trophozoite in a red blood cell. This organism grows into a schizont which divides. B. Numerous merozoites about to leave the corpuscle. Sporogony occurs in the leech, *Placobdella*, and turtles b e c o m e infected through the bite of the leech, just as man becomes infected with *Plasmodium* by the bite of the mosquito. *Haemo-*

Figure 245

gregarina is similar in many respects to the Haemosporidia, but is not placed in that subclass because syzygy occurs during its development (as in a few coccidia) and because the zygote is not motile. However, no sporocysts are formed as in other Coccidia and neither are they formed in the Haemosporidia. There are several genera and many species related to *Haemogregarina*, and they form a graded series; some have motile zygotes, some do not have syzygy. These species are clearly intermediate between the Coccidia and the Haemosporidia.

SUBCLASS GREGARINIDIA

The gregarines are chiefly coelozoic parasites of invertebrates, especially arthropods and annelids. The mature trophozoites are often large, commonly up to 1 mm, and at certain times of the year are easily obtained for study.

Fig. 246 shows the life history of *Gregarina rigida*, a parasite of grasshoppers which is very common in wild specimens captured late in summer in the northern half of the United States and throughout the entire summer in the southern half, or at any time that grasshoppers are very numerous. The diagrams are based on a study made by Allegre. The grasshopper is infected by ingesting some *spores* (14, 15) along with its food. In the midgut the *sporozoites* (1) escape and enter epithelial cells (2) where they develop into young *trophozoites* (3). These trophozoites increase greatly in size and project into the lumen of the gut (4, 5). The body becomes divided by *septa* (5s) into three sections; an *epimerite* (5e) which serves as an organelle of attachment, a *protomerite* (5p) or middle section, and a *deutomerite* (5d) or posterior section.

Eventually the epimerite is lost, and the adult gregarine is free in the lumen (6) and is then called a sporont. Sporonts become associated in pairs, a process known as *syzygy* (7). Two animals attached in syzygy are called an *association*. The anterior member is called the *primite* (7pr) the posterior member the *satellite* (7sa) . The two associates eventually become folded upon each other and secrete a membrane, the *gametocyst* (8) which contains the two animals, now called *gametocytes*. The gametocytes divide by multiple fission (9) to form many *macro-* and *microgametes* (10) which fuse in pairs to form many *zygotes*. The process of fusion is shown diagrammatically for one pair of gametes in 11, a-c. After fusion of the gamete nuclei (11e), each zygote becomes barrel-shaped and secretes a membrane, the oocyst (12a). Then the nucleus divides three times (12b-d), and the cytoplasm divides to form 8 *sporozoites* (12e).

The gametocyst, which up to this time has been spherical, develops several radial tubes. The oocysts (spores) are arranged in long chains (14) (several inches in length) and are pushed out of the gametocysts through these tubes (13). Each spore is about 8μ in length (the size of a human red blood cell), and many thousand may be formed in one gametocyst.

Stage 8 occurs in the intestine, but stages 9-13 occur in the feces. If infected grasshoppers are kept in the laboratory the feces can easily be collected. Look for white bodies, $300\text{-}500\mu$ in diameter. These are

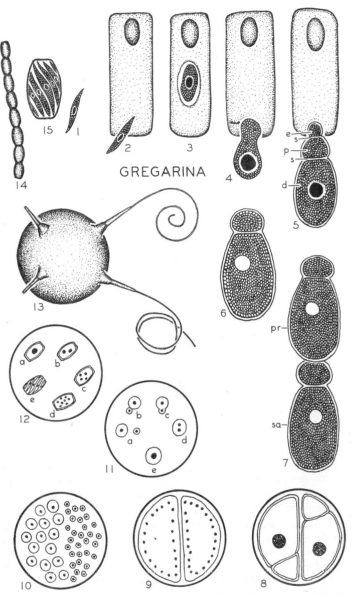

GREGARINA

Figure 246. Life History of Gregarina.

the gametocysts, probably in stage 8 or 9. If these are kept in the open air with the relative humidity at 50% or more they will probably develop into stage 13 in 72-96 hours.

1a With schizogony; asexual as well as sexual reproduction.
Order SCHIZOGREGARINIDA

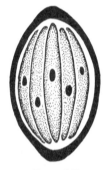

Figure 247

Fig. 247. Oocyst of *Ophryocystis mesnili*, 11μ (Leger) in Malpighian tubules of the meal worm, *Tenebrio molitor*, and other beetles.

An unusually small gregarine. Sporozoites become schizonts which divide to form merozoites which repeat the divisional cycle; syzygy; each gametocyte becomes a single gamete, i.e., one oocyst from each association; 8 sporozoites.

1b Without schizogony; sexual reproduction only.
Order EUGREGARINIDA....2

2a Body of sporont separated by a septum into two compartments, a protomerite and a deutomerite (see fig. 246, 5-6).
Suborder CEPHALINA

Structure and life history are typified by *Gregarina rigida*, fig. 246. Other species of *Gregarina* are common in cockroaches and crickets. Related genera are found in a wide variety of insects.

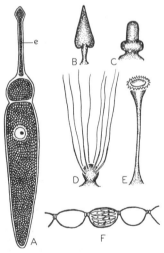

Figure 248

Fig. 248. Various cephaline gregarines (Leger).

A. *Stylocephalus longicollis*, in gut of beetles. Epimerite (e) elongated, nipple-like at end. B. Epimerite of *Pileocephalus*. C. Epimerite of *Sycia*. D. Multiple epimerite of *Cometoides*. E. Epimerite of *Menospora*. F. Chain of oocysts of *Stylocephalus*. Compare with those of *Gregarina*, fig. 246, 14.

One of the principal taxonomic characters of the cephaline gregarines is the size and shape of the epimerite which may be long, short, variously shaped, or divided to form several to many digitate or elongate processes. Two genera develop intracellularly; other genera are identified on the basis of the shape of the spore.

2b Body of sporont not divided by septum.

Suborder ACEPHALINA

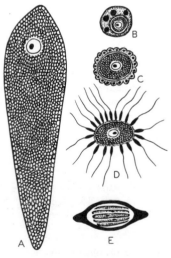
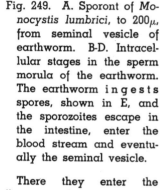

Figure 249

Fig. 249. A. Sporont of *Monocystis lumbrici*, to 200μ, from seminal vesicle of earthworm. B-D. Intracellular stages in the sperm morula of the earthworm. The earthworm i n g e s t s spores, shown in E, and the sporozoites escape in the intestine, enter the blood stream and eventually the seminal vesicle.

There they enter the "sperm mother" cells of the worm at the time the nucleus is undergoing repeated division (4 nuclei in B, many in C). The young trophozoite and the worm sperm develop together. At D the sperm are almost mature and about to leave the trophozoite which then develops into the sporont (A). Syzygy; numerous gametes; numerous zygotes, each with 8 sporozoites, shown at E, $17\text{-}25\mu$. Spores pass into seminal receptacle of another worm and then into the cocoon, where they may infect young worms or they may pass into the soil when the cocoon is broken and infect adult worms. Very common, especially in the spring.

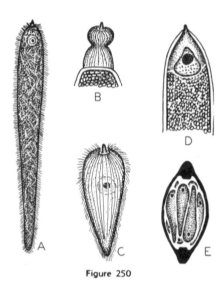

Fig. 250. A. Sporont of *Rhyncocystis pilosa*, 180μ (Troisi) from seminal vesicle of earthworm. Note numerous hair-like processes. B. Anterior end of sporont, showing epimerite-like structure. C. Nipple-like organelle at anterior end, used for boring into sperm morula. D. *R. porrecta*, anterior end of adult. E. Spore of *R. porrecta*.

Figure 250

The genera of the acephaline gregarines are separated partly on the shape of the sporonts and partly on the shape of the spore which may be biconical, round, or oval, and either solitary or in chains.

A very interesting exercise is to examine fresh earthworm seminal vesicles for *Monocystis*, *Rhyncocystis*, and other gregarines. Crush the vesicle on a slide; add drop of physiological salt solution (Ringer's or Belar's solution) and cover slip. Look for the sporonts, gametocysts in stages comparable to fig. 246, 8-12, and loose spores.

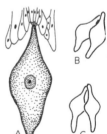

Fig. 251. A. *Enterocystis bulbis*, 275-500μ (Noble) in gut of marine annelid *Urechis*. B, C, animals in syzygy, just before formation of gametocyst.

Other species in mayfly larvae.

Figure 251

SUBCLASS HAEMOSPORIDIA

The haemosporidians have a motile zygote, naked sporozoites, schizogony cycle in the red blood cells or in the endothelial lining of the capillaries of vertebrates, and sporogony in a blood sucking invertebrate. Some of them convert the haemoglobin of the red blood cell into hematin which appears in the form of brownish granules clearly visible in the schizonts.

PLASMODIUM

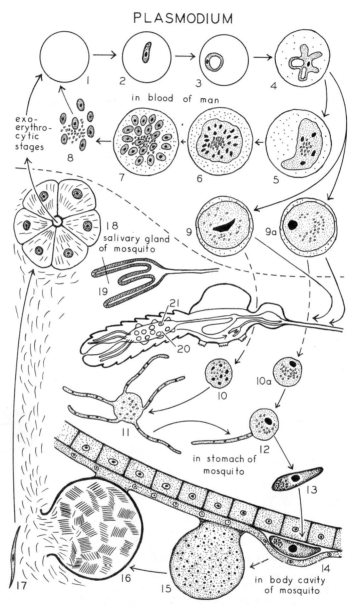

Figure 252. Life History of Plasmodium.

A typical life cycle is that of *Plasmodium vivax*, the cause of benign tertian malaria in man, which is shown in fig. 252. Infection of man begins with the bite of an *Anopheles* mosquito with sporozoites (17) in its salivary glands (18, 19). These sporozoites pass out with the mosquito's saliva into the blood stream from whence they enter the endothelial cells which line the capillaries of the liver, and possibly enter other organs, where they undergo little known stages of development (probably schizogony) called *exoerythrocytic* or *cryptozoic* stages. After several days in the endothelial cells they enter the red blood cells (1) and become trophozoites (2, 3, 4). One trophozoite stage is called a "signet ring" stage because the nucleus and the large vacuole have the general appearance of a ring with a setting. Older trophozoites may develop pseudopodia (4). Later the nucleus divides several times and the parasites become schizonts with as many as 24 nuclei and numerous hematin granules (5, 6). Cytoplasmic division follows (7), the corpuscle is dissolved, and the merozoites are released into the blood stream together with the hematin and the corpuscle fragments. Division is synchronous, i.e., all of the parasites in the blood stream divide at approximately the same time (within a few hours). Some material released at this time causes the fever and chill which is so characteristic of the disease. The merozoites then infect new red blood cells and repeat the cycle.

Some trophozoites develop into macrogametocytes (9a) and some into microgametocytes (9). These are formed in the blood stream but do not develop farther unless ingested by a mosquito. However, if they reach the mosquito's stomach (20) the microgametocyle develops (10) into numerous long thin microgametes (11). The macrogametocyte (9a) becomes a macrogamete (10a) which is fertilized (12) by the microgamete. The zygote (also called an ookinete) is motile and passes through the wall of the mosquito's stomach (14, 21) undergoes repeated nuclear division (15) followed by cytoplasmic division to form thousands of very small motile sporozoites (16), a single one of which is greatly enlarged in 17. These break out of the oocyst, become free in the body cavity, pass forward (note arrow in body of mosquito) to the salivary gland, shown enlarged in 19, and in cross section (denoted by line in 19) in 20. They penetrate into the gland cells and pass into the lumen and thence into the saliva.

The life cycle of *Plasmodium* consists of schizogony primarily in the red blood cells of man and sporogony in the mosquito. This is a true alternation of generations; one asexual, one sexual.

1a **With hematin pigment granules in schizont** 2

1b **Without hematin pigment granules.**

Family BABESIIDAE, p. 158

2a **Schizogony primarily in the red blood cells of vertebrates (2b on p. 157).**

Family PLASMODIIDAE

The genus *Plasmodium* is of very widespread occurrence, both taxonomically and geographically. There are four species in man, fifteen in birds, thirteen in reptiles, four in monkeys, and one or more each in bats, squirrels, buffalo, antelope, and frogs. Malaria is probably the most important of all the diseases of man. The species of *Plasmodium* which cause malaria in man are as follows:

1) *Plasmodium vivax*, the most common cause of benign tertian malaria in which there is a paroxysm (chills and fever) every 48 hours. The life history of this organism is given in fig. 252. A typical fever chart of a patient is shown in fig. 253. The ordinate is the body

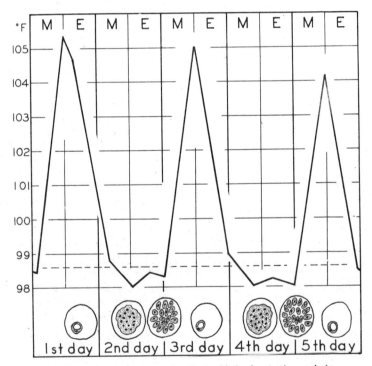

Figure 253.   Fever chart of patient with benign tertian malaria.

temperature, and the abscissa is time in days. M denotes morning hours, E, afternoon and evening hours. At the bottom of the chart is a series of diagrams which show what stage of the schizogony cycle the parasites are in at various times. Note that the rise in body temperature occurs at the time the schizonts are dividing and the corpuscles are dissolving. At this time the patient has chills and thinks he is freezing, and gooseflesh stands out over the body. At the same time his temperature is going up. Then the temperature begins to drop, and he sweats profusely. Compare the diagrams of fig. 253 with those of fig. 252, stages 1-8. During the course of a *P. vivax* infection in man the fevers usually occur every other day for several weeks, slowly decreasing in severity. Several weeks later the fevers may start anew and continue for about two weeks; these recurrences may be repeated. Common throughout most of the tropical and temperate regions of the world except in high mountains.

2) *Plasmodium ovale*, the other cause of benign tertian malaria. Very similar to *P. vivax* in morphology (except for a smaller number of merozoites) and pathology.

3) *Plasmodium falciparum*, cause of malignant tertian malaria, the most deadly of the malarial diseases. The life history of the parasite is similar to that of *P. vivax*. However, the infected erythrocytes tend to stick to each other and to the walls of capillaries, thereby blocking the blood supply to vital organs. The congested condition of the capillaries results in a somewhat asynchronous division of the parasites and a longer duration for the chills and fever (12 to 36 hours instead of 6 to 8 as in benign infections). Mortality about 10%; this is the parasite which accounts for most of the deaths caused by malaria. In 14 southern states over 2500 deaths a year are caused directly by malaria, in India the annual toll is over a million, and in Nyasaland between 40 and 90 percent of the population die of malaria before the age of six years.

4) *Plasmodium malariae*, cause of quartan malaria, a benign disease in which chills and fever occur every 72 hours. This is primarily a tropical disease and as yet occurs in this country only in the vicinity of New Orleans where it was introduced from the West Indies.

Malaria can be treated successfully by several drugs, especially atabrine, quinine, chloroquine, pentaquine, and paludrine, singly or in combination. Prevention consists chiefly in avoiding the mosquito by the use of screens, insect repellants, and especially the newer insecticides (DDT, etc.).

2b Schizogony only in the endothelial cells lining the capillaries of vertebrates.   **Family HAEMOPROTEIDAE**

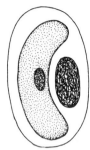

Figure 254

Fig. 254. *Haemoproteus columbae,* in red blood cell of pigeon.

Schizonts in lining of capillaries; gametocytes in red blood cells; sporogony in bloodsucking flies, *Lynchia* and related genera. *H. lophortyx* is found in California quail.

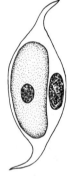

Figure 255

Fig. 255. *Leucocytozoon anatis* in endothelial cell of duck.

Cycle similar to Haemoproteus; transmitted by black fly, *Simulium.* Other species in turkeys and ruffed grouse. High mortality. In Algonquin Park in 1934 *Leucocytozoon* killed 60% of the ruffed grouse; in 1932, 90% of a flock of turkeys in Nebraska.

(from 1b, p. 155)   Family BABESIIDAE

The genus *Babesia* causes a very severe destruction of the red blood cells of susceptible vertebrates. *B. bigemina,* the cause of Texas Fever, killed many thousands of cattle in the United States during the latter part of the 19th century and early part of the 20th century. Southern cattle usually became infected as calves, developed an immunity and became carriers, but northern cattle which later came in contact with these carriers often died in less than a month. Symptoms are a very high fever in 8-10 days, severe loss of red blood cells (anemia) with most of the hemoglobin passing out in the urine, thereby giving rise to the name "Redwater fever."

The discovery of the method of transmission, from one cow to another by means of the tick, *Margaropus annulatus*, was one of the most important discoveries in the history of protozoology. The reason for its great importance is that prior to that time it had never been proven that an arthropod could transmit a protozoan disease. However, Theobald Smith and F. L. Kilbourne in 1893 demonstrated that the tick is the transmitting agent. This work was possible because C. Curtice had just worked out the life history of the tick. This great discovery by Smith and Kilbourne stimulated other workers. In 1895 David Bruce discovered the transmission of African Sleeping Sickness by the tsetse fly (p. 89). In 1898 Ronald Ross discovered the transmission of bird malaria by the *Culex* mosquito, and in 1899 Grassi demonstrated the transmission of the malaria of man by the *Anopheles* mosquito. These discoveries formed the basis for the prevention and control of our more important protozoan diseases transmitted by insects.

Fig. 256. The life cycle of *Babesia bigemina*. 1-4, growth and division into two in a red blood cell. The cell is destroyed (5) and the organism attacks new cells, eventually causing a severe anemia. When a tick sucks blood from an infected cow the parasites enter the tick gut. Here fertilization occurs (7), and the zygote (9) passes through the wall of the gut (10) into an egg inside of the ovary. As the embryo develops the parasite reproduces (11-14), and infects many cells of the young tick. Some of these cells (15) eventually become those of the salivary gland (16) from whence the sporozoites are injected into a new vertebrate host.

At present Texas or Redwater fever of cattle has been virtually wiped out of our southern states, primarily by the almost complete eradication of the tick. This tick, and the disease it carries, has been eliminated by the regular dipping of all cattle in arsenical solutions. This campaign was started in 1906, and by 1940 the tick was almost completely eliminated. However, constant vigilance is necessary to keep it from spreading again.

This is an excellent example of how knowledge of the life cycle of an organism can be put to practical use. When Curtice worked out the life cycle of the tick it was not even known to be dangerous. Now this same type of knowledge is applied to the campaign against malaria, trypanosomiasis, kala-azar, and other diseases, whether they are caused by Protozoa, viruses or bacteria.

Babesia still affects cattle in other parts of the world. Also, there are other species which infect sheep, goats, horses, and dogs.

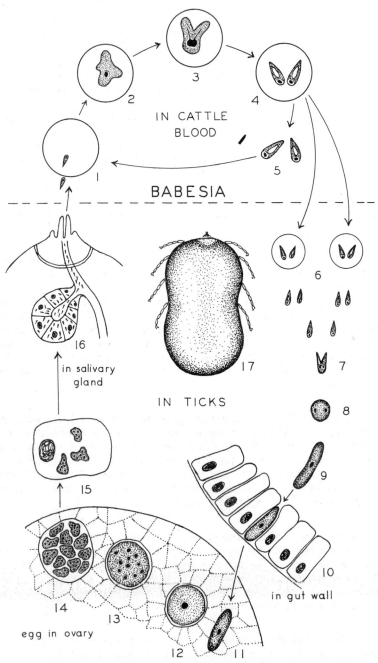

IN CATTLE
BLOOD

BABESIA

in salivary
gland

IN TICKS

in gut wall

egg in ovary

Figure 256.   Life History of Babesia.

CLASS CNIDOSPORIDEA

The cnidosporideans are distinguished by the presence of one to four polar filaments. A typical spore has already been described (fig. 238) and is shown again in fig. 257, 8. It is composed of an outer covering or envelope (e) made up of two parts or valves, a polar capsule (pc) with a coiled polar filament, and a sporoplasm (s).

A typical life history is that of *Myxobolus* as shown in fig. 257 (adapted from Keysselitz, Kudo, and others). A fish becomes infected with *Myxobolus* by ingesting spores (8) either in the body of another fish or free in the water or on the bottom of a pond or lake. These spores consist of a bivalve envelope, two polar capsules with polar filaments, and a sporoplasm, or infective cell, comparable to the sporozoite of Telosporidea. Under the action of gastric and intestinal juices the polar capsules open (9) and the filaments attach the spore to the wall of the fish gut. The sporoplasm escapes (10), enters the blood stream and is carried to some part of the body where it crawls out of the blood vessel and goes in between the host cells.

In *Myxobolus pfeifferi* this sporoplasm (1) becomes lodged in the dermis or skeletal muscle. Here it develops into a histozoic multinucleate ameba (2) and may reach a diameter of 7cm (almost 3 inches!). Then the cytoplasm surrounding most of the nuclei may become separated from the remainder of the mass to form a sporont (3). A single sporont is shown at 4. This undergoes nuclear division until there are 12 nuclei (5). The cytoplasm then divides so that 2 nuclei are in an outer membrane, 4 nuclei are in 2 inner membranes, 2 nuclei form small cells within the inner membrane, and 4 nuclei form 2 binucleate cells, one within each inner membrane (6). The uninucleate cells develop vacuoles (7) and later become the polar capsules (8). The outer membrane dissolves and the inner membrane becomes the envelope of the spore (7, 8). The nuclei of the binucleate cells fuse to form a sporoplasm (7, 8). The spore is now complete and it may remain wherever it is and be eaten by a carnivorous fish or it may be eliminated from the body by various channels, depending upon where it is formed.

This life history bears no close resemblance to any of those of the Telosporidea (figs. 240, 241, 246, 252). For instance, the nuclei and cells which form the outer membrane are destroyed, and those which form the inner membrane which later becomes the envelope are converted directly into the envelope. In the Telosporidea the various coverings are always secreted by cells which continue as ancestors of future generations. Similarly, the cells which form the polar capsules develop directly into the capsules and are thereby removed from the

MYXOBOLUS

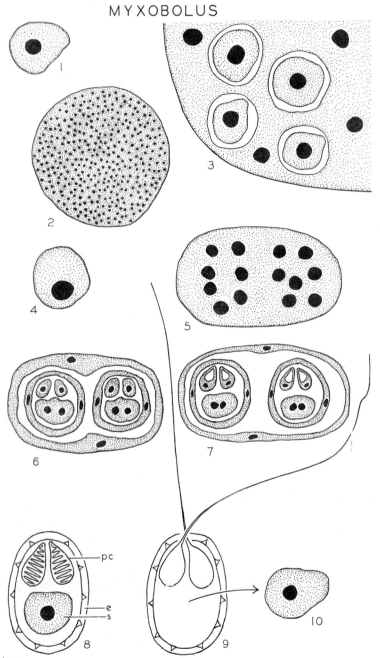

Figure 257. Life History of Myxobolus.

"germ line" or from the role of ancestors. This removal of cells from the "germ line" constitutes the formation of a "soma." However, this "soma" is short lived and serves only one purpose: the protection and transmission of the "germ line" or sporoplasm to a new host. It is possible to discuss the philosophical implications of this type of life history for many pages, but that seems to be somewhat beside the present purpose.

The Cnidosporidea are divided into at least three orders.

1a Spores comparatively large, usually more than 5μ............2

1b Spores comparatively small, usually less than 5μ.
Order MICROSPORIDA, p. 166

2a Shell bivalve; 1, 2, or 4 polar capsules visible in the living spore.
Order MYXOSPORIDA, p. 163

2b Shell trivalve; 3 polar capsules.
Order ACTINOMYXIDA, p. 166

ORDER MYXOSPORIDA

The myxosporidans are primarily parasites of fishes, both fresh water and marine, but a few are found in amphibia. In fishes they may infect almost any part of the body; the skin, muscles, gills, intestine, liver, gall bladder, and urinary bladder are the most common sites. The large tumor-like growths appear as bumps often several centimeters in diameter. Fig. 258 shows a channel cat (about one-half natural size), infected with *Henneguya exilis* (after Kudo).

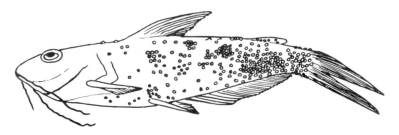

Figure 258

There are at least several very serious diseases of fishes caused by Myxosporida. Examples are: 1) The "boil disease" of the European barbel, caused by *Myxobolus pfeifferi*, usually fatal. 2) The "wormy" halibut of our Pacific coast. The "worms" are elongate amebas of *Unicapsula muscularis* which live in the muscle fibers. 3) The "twist" disease of salmonoid fishes, caused by *Myxosoma cerebralis* which lives in the cartilage and perichondrium and exerts pressure on the central nervous system.

The families, genera, and species are separated on the basis of the structure of the spore.

 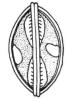

Figure 259

Fig. 259. *Myxobolus okobojiensis,* 12μ (Otto and Jahn), side and polar views of spores. Ameboid forms 250-500μ.

In intestine of the Black Crappie, *Pomoxis sporoides.*

This genus is very common in fresh water fish and is characterized by the shape of the spore and by the presence of a large glycogen vacuole in the cytoplasm which stains brown with iodine.

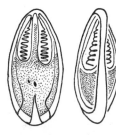
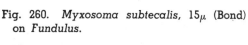

Figure 260

Fig. 260. *Myxosoma subtecalis,* 15μ (Bond) on *Fundulus.*

This genus is similar to *Myxobolus* but does not have vacuoles which stain with iodine as does *Myxobolus.*

Figure 261

Fig. 261. *Myxidium folium,* 11-12μ (Bond).
In *Fundulus,* gall bladder and bile ducts. Two capsules at opposite ends of the spore.

This bipolar arrangement of the polar capsules is characteristic of the family which includes two other genera.

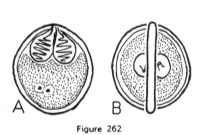

Figure 262

Fig. 262. *Sphaerospora renalis,*
9-10μ (Bond).

In kidney of *Fundulus.* Spore
similar to *Myxosoma* but
spherical. A. Side view. B.
polar view.

Another species, *S. polymor-*
pha, is found in the urinary
bladder of toadfish, *Opsanus*
tau and *O. beta,* and is fre-
quently infected by a micro-
sporidan, *Nosema notabilis.*

Fig. 263. *Ceratomyxa,* spore greatly elongate at right angles to the
suture between the two valves.

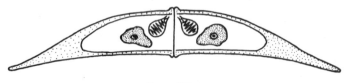

Figure 263

Protoplasm usually does not fill the intrasporal cavity. Numerous
species in gall bladder of marine fish, 30 to 65μ wide.

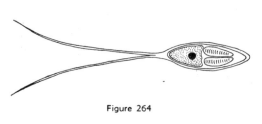

Figure 264

Fig. 264. *Henne-*
guya magna, 87μ
(Rice and Jahn).

On gill filaments
of White (Silver)
Bass, *Lepibema*
chrysops. V a l v e s
greatly elongated to
form two posterior
filaments.

These posterior filaments make recognition of the genus very easy.
Numerous species, mostly in fresh water fish. Iodinophilous vacuole
present. The genus *Agarella* also has long posterior filaments, but it
has four instead of two polar capsules and is recorded only in the
testis of the South American lungfish.

165

Figure 265

Fig. 265. *Chloromyxum trijugum,* 7-8μ (Otto and Jahn).

From gall bladder of Black Crappie, *Pomoxis sporoides.* Similar to *Sphaerospora* but with 4 polar capsules.

Numerous species in fresh water and marine fish and also in amphibia. The genus *Agarella* has four polar capsules, but its general shape is somewhat similar to Henneguya.

ORDER ACTINOMYXIDA

The Actinomyxida differ from the Myxosporida primarily in symmetry. The capsule is trivalve, i.e., composed of three parts, and there are three polar capsules. They have been found only in the body cavity or intestine of fresh water and marine annelids.

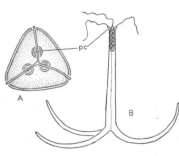

Figure 266

Fig. 266. A. *Sphaeractinomyxon gigas,* 40μ (Granata) in the coelum of *Limnodrilus,* an oligochaete. Spore almost spherical with three polar capsules, shown here in end view. B. *Triactinomyxon ignotum,* 30μ (Leger) in the gut of *Tubifex,* an oligochaete.

The valves are greatly elongated and form three large hooks; 8 sporoplasms; 3 polar capsules, shown here discharged.

ORDER MICROSPORIDA

The microsporidans are minute parasites with a spore usually 3-6μ in length with a coiled filament, a single sporoplasm, and an envelope of a single piece, i.e., not bivalve or trivalve. The filament usually can be seen only in stained specimens.

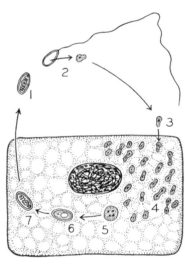

Figure 267

Fig. 267, the life cycle, diagrammatic, of *Nosema bombycis*, the cause of pebrine, a fatal disease of silkworms.

The spore (1) is typical of the order, with a single filament and sporoplasm. Upon ingestion, the filament is extruded (2) and the sporoplasm enters an epithelial cell of the gut (3) where it divides many times to form uninucleate amebas which fill the cell. The cell may become dissolved. Then the amebas attack other cells, perhaps almost all of the cells in the body of the worm. Eventually the parasites form 4-nucleate cells (5), and these develop into the spore (6, 7). Silkworms become infected by eating mulberry leaves or other food contaminated by feces or body fragments of infected worms.

In 1865 pebrine was causing great havoc among the silk factories of France, and Louis Pasteur was appointed by the French government to determine the cause. Pasteur discovered the tiny "corpuscles" in the sick worms and correctly interpreted them as the agent by which the disease was spread. He recommended destruction of all colonies which contained sick worms and certain modifications in the sanitary conditions in the factories. These precautions greatly reduced the loss of silkworms.

Nosema apis is the cause of a serious dysentery of bees. Another species of *Nosema* causes a serious disease of the potato tuber worm. In nature this parasite of the potato tuber worm might be considered helpful to man. However, in the laboratories of the U. S. Department of Agriculture it is a pest because in the laboratory the potato tuber worm is reared in large numbers because it has another parasite, *Macrocentrus ancylivorus*, which attacks the oriental fruit moth. Since potato tuber worms are easier to grow than oriental fruit moths, *Macrocentrus* is grown on the tuber worm and then planted in orchards where it can attack the fruit moths. *Nosema* attacks both the tuber worm and *Macrocentrus*, and greatly inhibits efforts to fight the fruit moth.

167

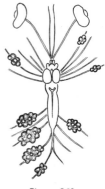

Figure 268

Another species of *Nosema*, *N. notabilis*, is found in the large ameboid trophozoite of the myxosporidan *Sphaerospora polymorpha* which is found in the urinary bladder of the toadfish *Opsanus*, but does not attack the tissues of the fish. (*Sphaerospora*, fig. 262).

Fig. 268. The central nervous system of the fish *Lophius piscatorius*.

The spinal nerves are infected with *Nosema lophii*, and the parasite has caused a great hypertrophy of the host tissue. The infected areas are the dark wart-like enlargements on the nerves (Doflein).

CLASS ACNIDOSPORIDEA

A number of unrelated organisms are provisionally placed in this class. As more is learned about their life history they are usually moved to other groups. Only one example is given.

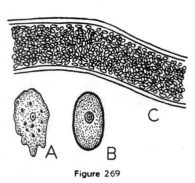

Figure 269

Fig. 269. *Malpighamoeba locustae* in the grasshopper *Melanoplus differentialis* (after King and Taylor). A. Ameboid stage, 5-10μ. B. Spore, 9μ. C. Section of malpighian tubule showing thousands of spores.

The amebas reproduce by binary fission, and many thousand are produced in a single grasshopper. The cysts often cause enlargements of the tubules which can easily be seen with the unaided eye. Occurence in wild grasshoppers, less than 1%; in laboratory colony, 100%.

SUBPHYLUM CILIOPHORA

The ciliophorans possess cilia which serve as organelles of locomotion. In all groups except the Suctorea cilia are present throughout trophic life of the individual; in the Suctorea cilia are present only during early development. Nutrition is holozoic or saprobic.

In all Ciliophora except the Protociliatia there are two types of nuclei (e.g., *Paramecium*, fig. 298). Each animal has: 1) one or more macronuclei which are large and stain solidly with methyl green and other stains and 2) one or more micronuclei, usually very small, not easily seen with methyl green, but they are easily seen in specimens well stained with hematoxylin. The macronuclei control the metabolic activities of the organism, but eventually degenerate and are replaced by micronuclei which increase in size and assume the characteristics of macronuclei. Nuclei of both types normally divide during division of the cell.

1a Cilia present throughout trophic life.

Class CILIATEA....2

1b Adult with tentacles; cilia present only in early developmental stages.   **Class SUCTOREA, p. 222**

2a Two types of nuclei; macro-, and micro-; sexual phenomena, conjugation.   **Subclass EUCILIATIA, p. 170**

2b Nuclei all alike; sexual phenomena involve permanent fusion of cells.   **Subclass PROTOCILIATIA**

The protociliates are almost exclusively found in the Salientia (tailless Amphibians); a few species in tailed amphibians, reptiles, and fish.· No cytostome; nutrition saprobic. Permanent fusion of gametes occurs.

ORDER OPALINIDA

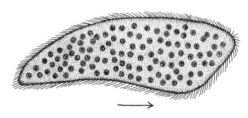

Figure 270

Fig. 270. *Opalina*, 100-840μ, in various species of frogs and toads.

Body very flat in cross section, wider and truncate anteriorly; swims with spiralling motion; many nuclei. Very common in frogs, but often disappear from the intestine

if the animals are kept in the laboratory for weeks before examination. One of the most easily available endozoic Protozoa. Related genera:

Cepedea, circular in cross section, multinucleate; *Protoopalina*, circular in cross section, two nuclei; *Zelleriella*, greatly flattened in cross section, two nuclei.

SUBCLASS EUCILIATIA

The euciliates are characterized by the presence of cilia and of two types of nuclei: macronuclei and micronuclei. The subclass is divided into four orders on the basis of the distribution and types of ciliary organelles. These are exemplified in the four figures below.

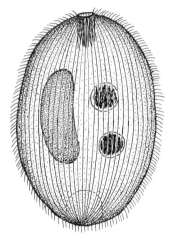

Figure 271

In some organisms all of the cilia are of the same size and there is no special group of cilia around the mouth or the oral groove. Fig. 271 shows *Prorodon discolor*, 100-130μ (Butschli), ovoid, with 45-50 rows of uniform cilia. The mouth is anterior, there is no oral groove and there are no special adoral (i.e., near the mouth) cilia. *Paramecium* (Fig. 298) is also uniformly ciliated with an oral groove but no special adoral cilia. Both *Prorodon* and *Paramecium* belong to the Order Holotrichida, characterized by the absence of special adoral ciliary organelles.

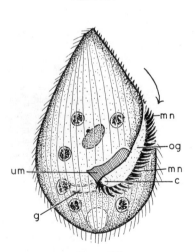

Figure 272

Fig. 272 shows *Blepharisma lateritium*, 160μ (Kahl), a beautiful pink ciliate with three types of ciliary organelles: 1) free cilia for swimming, uniformly distributed over the body; 2) special adoral "cilia" which are really several short transverse rows of cilia, fused together to form larger organelles and which are called *membranelles* (mm). These line one edge of the oral groove (og) and in the direction indicated by the arrow push bacteria and other food particles toward the mouth (c) from whence they pass into the gullet (g). In *Paramecium* the oral groove is lined with the same size free cilia used for swimming. 3) An *undulating membrane* (um) which is formed by two more or less longitudinal rows of cilia fusing together.

These cilia do not beat synchronously, but a wave of activity seems to pass down the row (as in a longitudinal row of free cilia (fig. 19). This asynchronous beat of the cilia causes the membrane to undergo an undulatory motion, hence the name. The undulating membrane helps push food particles toward the mouth.

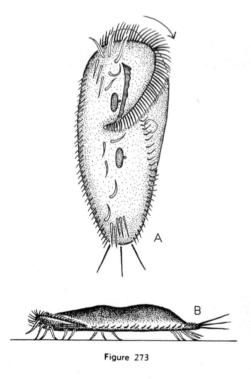

Figure 273

Fig. 273 shows *Stylonychia mytilus;* 100-300μ (Stein, Butschli). A. Ventral view. B. Edge view of animal walking on substrate.

There are no free cilia on the body. There is an adoral zone of membranelles which leads to the mouth and also an undulating membrane. The structures which look like cilia on the ventral surface are really tufts of cilia fused together to form a single structure called a *cirrus.* As can be seen from the edge view all of the cirri are on the ventral surface except for the three at the posterior edge. There are two longitudinal rows near the lateral margins (*marginals*), an anterior group (*frontals*), two posterior groups (five *anals* and three *caudals),* and five scattered over the ventral surface *(ventrals).* Most of the cirri, especially the larger ones, are used very much like legs for walking. The presence of an adoral zone of membranelles and of cirri on the ventral surface of a flattened body is characteristic of the Suborder Hypotrichina.

171

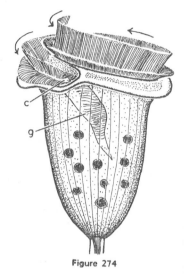

Figure 274

Fig. 274 shows an individual of *Carchesium polypinum*, 80μ (Doflein).

The animal is bell-shaped with at least two distinct rows of cilia which form a spiral just inside of the lip of the bell and lead to the gullet. These cilia are long and thin and loosely fastened together, somewhat less so than an undulating membrane, being found mostly near the base and often free at the distal end, thus forming what are called semi-membranes. The direction of beat is as shown by the arrows; as seen from the anterior end it is counter clockwise to the cytostome. In both *Blepharisma* (Fig. 272) and *Stylonychia* (Fig. 273) the adoral ciliary organelles (membranelles) spiralled clockwise to the cytostome. This difference in direction of spiral is considered an important taxonomic character and is used for separating the Spirotrichida and Chonotrichida (clockwise) from the Peritrichida (counter clockwise).

WHAT TO LOOK FOR IN A CILIATE

In the classification of ciliates the arrangement of cilia and the grouping of cilia to form more complex organelles is of primary importance.

Does the animal under consideration have an adoral zone of membranelles? If so, it is not a holotrich but may belong to any of the other orders. If so, does the zone wind clockwise or counterclockwise to the cytostome? A less formal way of stating the same question is "Does the body resemble that of *Vorticella* (fig. 358)? If so, (membranelles counterclockwise), Peritrichida. If not, Spirotrichida.

If the animal is a holotrich does it have a mouth? If not, Astomina. If so, one of the other suborders. Where is the mouth? Is it on the body surface (fig. 271), or at the base of a peristome (fig 296)? Is it surrounded by undulating membranes? If so, Hymenostomina. By free cilia? If so, Trichostomina. By neither? If neither, Gymnostomina. Does it have a zone of large thigmotactic (i.e., used for holding on to surfaces) cilia? If so, and it was found in the gill cavity of mussels, Thigmotrichina.

If the ciliate is a spirotrich, is it ciliated over all or part of the body surface? Or does it have cirri? If ciliated, Heterotrichina. If with cirri, Oligotrichina, or Hypotrichina. If marine, with lorica, Tintinnina. If in digestive tract of herbivores, probably Entodiniomorphina.

If the animal is a heterotrich what is its shape? And how large is the adoral zone? If it is a hypotrich, how many cirri of each type (fig. 330) does it have?

Where is the contractile vacuole? And what type is it? These are characters which do not appear in the key but which are often useful in checking an identification. For instance, in many ciliates the contractile vacuole is always posterior and there are other genera or species which bear a superficial resemblance to those with a posterior vacuole but which have the vacuole or vacuoles elsewhere. An example of this resemblance is found in *Prorodon* and *Ichthyophthirius*. *Prorodon* (fig. 271) has a single posterior vacuole; *Ichthyophthirius* (fig. 288) is superficially very similar but has numerous contractile vacuoles in the adult and a single lateral vacuole in the young stages. By observing the contractile vacuole the student can easily tell whether he has *Prorodon* or *Ichthyophthirius*.

The type of vacuole is also of importance. Some vacuoles are fed by long canals which empty into vesicles which fuse to form the large vacuole. This is shown for *Paramecium* in fig. 300.

Most contractile vacuoles, however, are directly vesicle fed and do not possess radiating canals. The mechanism of the discharge of the vacuole of *Paramecium trichium* is shown diagrammatically in fig. 275 (after King). A. The vacuole at full diastole, the stage at which

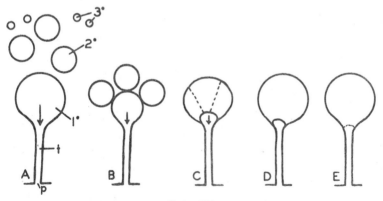

Figure 275

it is completely filled. The vacuole in this species is connected to the outside by a permanent tube (t) at the end of which is a permanent pore (p). The vacuole connected to the tube is known as the primary vacuole (1°). Secondary vacuoles (2°) are smaller and are nearby in the cytoplasm. These are formed by the fusion of several still smaller tertiary vacuoles (3°) scattered in the cytoplasm. B. Later stage in which the primary vacuole is partly contracted and the secondary vacuoles have moved closer to the primary. C. Later stage in which the secondary vacuoles are fusing with each other and with the remnant of the primary vacuole. D. Later stage with fusion complete but the new primary vacuole formed by fusion of the secondary vacuoles is not yet open to the outside. E. Wall of old primary vacuole is disintegrating so that the new primary vacuole can empty to the outside as at A.

Figure 276

Many vacuoles of ciliates and also those of flagellates and Sarcodina are similar in structure to that of *Paramecium trichium* except that the canal is absent. This is shown diagrammatically for *Blepharisma* in fig. 276 (See fig. 272 for details of animal). The tertiary vacuoles fuse to form secondaries, the secondaries fuse to form a primary, and the primary opens to the outside. In *Paramecium caudatum* (fig. 300) the vacuole is similar except that the secondary vacuoles are filled by canals.

In some ciliates (e.g., *Spirostomum*, fig. 319, and *Stentor*, fig. 327) there is a long longitudinal canal leading to a large posterior vacuole. Small vacuoles fuse with the canal, the liquid flows to the large vacuole, and the large vacuole empties to the outside.

In addition to ciliary organelles many ciliates have trichocysts and trichites. Trichocysts are organelles of protection which are found just under the pellicle in *Paramecium* and in the normal condition appear to be short rods. Fig. 277 A. shows a longitudinal section through

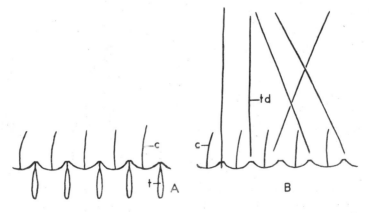

Figure 277

174

the pellicle of *Paramecium*. There are numerous small hexagonal depressions on the surface and these are shown here in section. A cilium (c) arises from the center of each depression. A trichocyst (t) is found just under each transverse ridge. Upon suitable stimulation (e.g., attack by a *Didinium*, the trichocysts are discharged and some of them are thrown completely free of the animal (td) as shown in fig. 277 B and in fig. 283.

Trichites are rods superficially similar to trichocysts but usually longer. Trichites are not discharged, but usually form a skeletal structure for supporting the rim of the mouth. Fig. 271 shows a number of rods which are located around the mouth perpendicular to the surface and which are not connected to each other. When the mouth opens the trichites support the lip and permit the mouth to open widely enough to engulf large objects. The trichites of *Spathidium* are shown in fig. 280 and those of *Trachelius* in fig. 294. *Didinium* has a group of trichites similar to those of *Prorodon*.

Some ciliates have oral trichites which are fused together to form a pharyngeal basket which also serves as a skeletal structure. The pharyngeal basket of *Chilodonella* is shown in fig. 297, and those of *Nassula* and *Paranassula* in fig. 296.

KEY TO THE ORDERS OF EUCILIATIA

1a Without adoral zone of membranelles or semi-membranes.
Order HOLOTRICHIDA, p. 175

1b With adoral zone of ciliary organelles....................2

2a Adoral zone winds counterclockwise to cytostome.
Order PERITRICHIDA, p. 216

2b Adoral zone winds clockwise to cystostome................3

3a Peristome extending out like a funnel.
Order CHONOTRICHIDA, p. 216

3b Peristome not extending beyond general body surface..
Order SPIROTRICHIDA, p. 198

ORDER HOLOTRICHIDA
KEY TO THE SUBORDERS

1a Without cytostome.   Suborder ASTOMINA, p. 176

1b With cytostome 2

2a Cytostome small rosette-like structure.
Suborder APOSTOMINA
(marine organisms, omitted from this book)

2b Cytostome not rosette like................................3

3a With well developed thigmotactic ciliated field; commensal in mussels. Suborder THIGMOTRICHINA, p. 197

3b Without special thigmotactic ciliated field 4

4a Cytostome on body surface or in peristome, without strong ciliary organelles. Suborder GYMNOSTOMINA, p. 176

4b Cytostome in peristome bearing special cilia or undulating membranes 5

5a Peristome lined with rows of free cilia. Suborder TRICHOSTOMINA, p. 186

5b Peristome with undulating membrane(s); with or without free cilia. Suborder HYMENOSTOMINA, p. 194

SUBORDER ASTOMINA

Members of this group have no cytostome, are saprobic commensals or parasites in various invertebrates, especially annelids and molluscs, and in amphibia. They can easily be distinguished from Opalinida by staining with methyl green. Astomina have a large macronucleus and one or more small micronuclei, difficult to find; Opalinida have two or many nuclei, all similar in appearance.

Figure 278

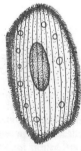

Fig. 278. *Anoplophrya orchestii*, 6-68μ (Summers and Kidder) in gut of the sand-flea, *Orchestia agilis*.

With 7-45 longitudinal rows of cilia, large macronucleus, several contractile vacuoles. *A. marylandensis* is 36-72μ and occurs in the intestine of several species of earthworms.

SUBORDER GYMNOSTOMINA

1a Cytostome at or near anterior end. Tribe PROTOSTOMATA, p. 177

1b Cytostome not at or near anterior end 2

2a Cytostome lateral, narrow or round. Tribe PLEUROSTOMATA, p. 184

2b Cytostome ventral, in anterior half. Tribe HYPOSTOMATA, p. 186

TRIBE PROTOSTOMATA

1a Free living 2

1b Endozoic in mammalian intestine; ciliation over entire body or in few zones.   Family BUTSCHLIIDAE

Fig. 279.   *Blepharoprosthium pireum,* 54-86μ (Hsiung).

Body pear-shaped; circular cytostome at smaller anterior end; anterior half ciliated, posterior end without cilia except for caudal tuft. In cecum and colon of horse.

Figure 279

2a Cytostomal region not compressed........................3

2b Cytostomal region compressed; bearing trichites.
                              Family SPATHIDIIDAE

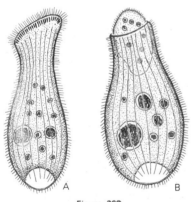

Fig. 280.   A. *Spathidium spathula,* up to 250μ (Woodruff and Spencer).

Body flask-shaped, expanded anteriorly; with trichites around the mouth; contractile vacuole posterior. B. *Spathidium* ingesting a *Colpidium.* The trichites form a supporting structure for the lips of the cytostome.

Very common; numerous species which differ mostly in shape of body. The genus *Paraspathidium* is more elongate and has a more slit-like mouth.

Figure 280

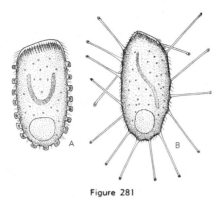

Figure 281

Fig. 281. A. *Legendrea bellerophon*, 100-180μ (Penard).

Somewhat similar to *Spathidium* except that the body has numerous projections which contain trichocysts. These projections are extensible, can be greatly elongated (as shown in B), and can be used as tentacles for the capture of prey. These tentacles inject trichocysts into the prey and then pull the victim toward the mouth, which opens as in *Spathidium*.

3a Cytostome not at tip of apical cone.............................4

3b Cytostome at tip of apical cone.   Family DIDINIIDAE

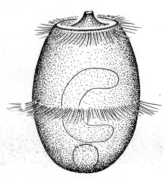

Figure 282

Fig. 282. *Didinium nasutum*, 80-200μ.

Body ovoid, circular in cross section, flattened anterior, with projecting cone with mouth at tip. Two bands of cilia around body, one anterior and one around middle. Carnivorous, and lives almost exclusively on *Paramecium*. This animal, if present in a culture of *Paramecium*, will usually multiply rapidly and eat almost all of the paramecia within a few days, no matter how numerous they were at first. It is a very voracious feeder, and a single *Didinium* will ingest one *Paramecium* immediately after another.

Fig. 283 is a series of diagrams showing how a *Didinium* ingests a *Paramecium*. A. The initial attack. The mouth of *Didinium* is at-

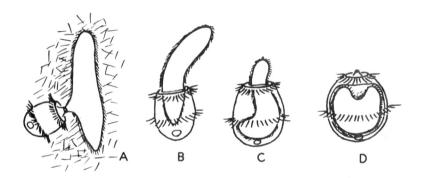

Figure 283

tached to the side of the paramecium. The mouth widens and at the same time sucks the victim inward. The paramecium discharges its trichocysts, and some of these enter the didinium. However, the trichocysts apparently do no harm, and the attack continues. B. Mouth expanded and paramecium partly in. C. Later stage. D. *Paramecium* completely ingested. *Didinium* returning to normal shape and getting ready for the next victim. The entire process of ingestion as shown here sometimes requires only a minute. Note the increase in size of *Didinium* between A and D.

It is very interesting to watch didinia attack and ingest paramecia. If you have a culture of *Paramecium* which has just been cleaned out by didinia and in which the didinia are still active it is usually exciting to place a number of didinia on a slide and then to add a few drops of a thick culture of *Paramecium*. If the didinia have been without food for a few hours they will vigorously attack the paramecia and ingest one immediately after another. If deprived of food for several days *Didinium* usually falls to the bottom of the culture and encysts. A fresh *Paramecium* culture added to an old *Didinium* culture will usually cause excystment of the *Didinium*, followed by an attack on the paramecia and a rapid decrease in their numbers.

179

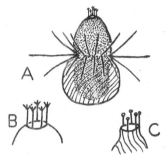

Figure 284

Fig. 284. A *Mesodinium pulex*, 20-38μ, (Noland).

Body ovoid, with equatorial furrow; conical anteriorly, spherical posteriorly. Double ring of cilia around middle. Tentacle-like retractile processes around the cytostome. Freshwater or marine. B. Anterior end, higher magnification. C. Anterior end of *M. acarus*, 10-16μ (Noland). Marine.

4a Cytostome does not open into anterior receptaculum..........5

4b Cytostome opens into anterior receptaculum; with lorica.
Family METACYSTIDAE

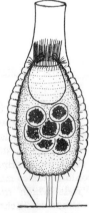

Figure 285

Fig. 285. *Vasicola ciliata*, 100μ (Kahl).

Ovoid; with flask-shaped lorica with numerous rings. Cytostome anterior with four rows of long cilia on lip; shorter cilia on body; long caudal cilia. Large cavity (receptaculum) just within mouth.

Macronucleus round, central. A rapid feeder, usually with numerous food vacuoles. Fresh or salt water.

5a Body not covered with plates. 6

5b Body covered with regularly arranged, perforated, ectoplasmic plates.
Family COLEPIDAE

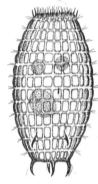

Figure 286

Fig. 286. *Coleps octospinus*, 80-110μ (Noland).

Body barrel-shaped, with 8 posterior spines, 12 circular and about 24 longitudinal rows of platelets, dark in color. Mouth at anterior end. Newly divided organisms may appear half dark and half light in color. This is caused by the fact that at division the anterior filial cell receives the anterior 6 rows of dark platelets and has to grow some new ones on the posterior end. The posterior cell receives the posterior 6 rows and must regenerate the anterior ones. Several common species in fresh and salt water.

6a With radially arranged tentacles.   **Family ACTINOBOLINIDAE**

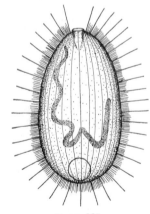

Figure 287

Fig. 287. *Actinobolina vorax*, 100-200μ (Wenrich).

Body ovoid, pale yellowish brown in color; mouth anterior, about 30 rows of cilia and of tentacles. The tentacles are not knobbed (as are those of the Suctorea) and are not used for sucking or grasping. They contain toxic material in the form of rods which are called toxicysts (in contrast to trichocysts, which are probably purely mechanical). Fresh water.

6b Without tentacles.   **Family HOLOPHRYIDAE**

Fig. 288. *Icthyophthirius multifiliis.* 1. Free swimming individual, 100-1000μ,.body ovoid, mouth anterior, no trichites, uniform ciliation, numerous contractile vacuoles.

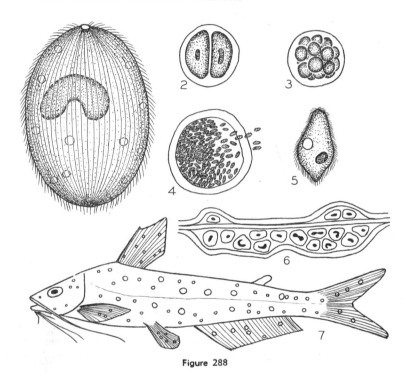

Figure 288

A common parasite of fresh water fish in open ponds and in home aquaria. This is the cause of white pustules up to several millimeters in diameter which often occur in tropical fish aquaria. The large free swimming form encysts on the bottom of the aquarium and divides in the cyst as shown in 2-4 to form as many as 1000 small ciliates, 18-22μ, shown at 5. These small ciliates bore into the skin of the fish and grow into large ciliates as shown in 1. A section of a fin with numerous developing ciliates is shown at 6, and an infected catfish at 7. 1-5, Butschli; 6, Kudo; 7, Stiles).

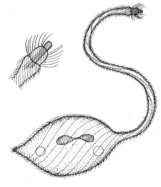

Figure 289

Fig. 289. *Lacrymaria olor*, up to 500-1200μ when extended.

Long, flexible, extensible and very active anterior end. Often known as the "swan animalcule." Mouth at end of the long "neck"; details shown in insert. The oblique lines in the drawing are myonemes or contractile elements, which permit rapid movement of the neck which can be vigorously lashed about or can be held partly contracted, straight and almost rigid for swimming. Under high power the "head" is seen to be very definitely marked off from the "neck." Fresh or salt water.

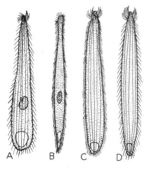

Figure 290

Fig. 290. A. *Trachelocerca conifer*, 140μ (Kahl). B. *T. subviridis*, 320-380μ (Noland). C. *Chaenia simulans*, 250-350μ (Kahl). D. *C. teres*, 150μ (Kahl).

Both genera are elongate, vermiform or slightly flask-shaped, with more or less extensible anterior end without the definite ring-like furrow which marks the "head" of *Lacrymaria*. In *Chaenia* the "head" is spirally furrowed; in *Trachelocerca* it is not furrowed or has slight longitudinal furrows.

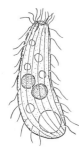

Figure 291

Fig. 291. *Rhopalophrya salina*, 29-55μ (Kirby).

Cylindrical, slightly asymmetrical, mouth anterior. In California brine pool.

TRIBE PLEUROSTOMATA

1a Cytostome on convex ventral surface......................2

1b Cytostome on concave ventral side.　　　Family LOXODIDAE

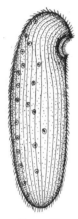

Figure 292

Fig. 292. *Loxodes magnus*, to 700μ.

Body dark brown; anterior end hook-like. Mouth crescent-shaped; 5-25 vesicles in cytoplasm. Fresh water. *L. vorax*, 125-140μ is yellowish brown.

The genus is easily identified by means of the indented subterminal oral region. The vesicles, known as Muller's vesicles, contain a clear fluid and one to several refractile spherules. According to some investigators these serve as balancing organelles.

2a Cytostome a long slit.　　　Family AMPHILEPTIDAE

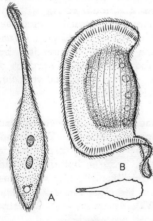

Figure 293

Fig. 293. A. *Lionotus fasciola*, 100μ.

Body with long flattened neck, bent toward dorsal side. Cytostome a long slit. No cilia on dorsal side of neck. Contractile vacuole posterior. Fresh water. c, mouth; g, gullet; c.v, contractile vacuole; v, cytoplasmic vacuole.
B. *Bryophyllum lieberkuhni*, 400-600μ.

Body thick in center with flange-like protection on three sides, continuing posteriorly. Mouth a long slit on the edge without a flange. Flange bears numerous trichocysts. Several contractile vacuoles. Lower figure shows cross section of body. Fresh water.

2b Cytostome round, at base of trichocyst bearing neck.

Family TRACHELIDAE

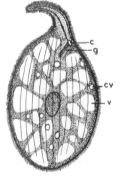

Figure 294

Fig. 294.　*Trachelius ovum*, 200-400μ.

Body ellipsoidal, curved neck with a longitudinal groove. Mouth circular, surrounded by trichites. Cytoplasm highly vacuolated so that granular material seems to be in bands. Numerous contractile vacuoles. Fresh water.

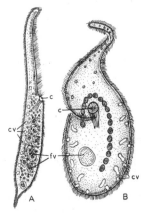

Figure 295

Fig. 295.　A. *Dileptus anser*, 250-500μ (Hayes).

Body elongate, pointed posteriorly, with long neck. Mouth round with trichites. Numerous contractile vacuoles. B. *Paradileptus robustus*, 180-450μ. (Wenrich). Mouth central, surrounded by raised rim that continues forward as a curved neck. c, mouth; fv, food vacuole; cv, contractile vacuole.

These genera are readily recognized once the mouth is located. The round mouth of *Dileptus* easily separates it from *Lionotus*, and the spirally curved "neck" of *Paradileptus* easily separates it from both of the other genera. *P. conicus*, 100 to 200μ, is similar to *P. robustus* but is conical posteriorly.

185

TRIBE HYPOSTOMATA

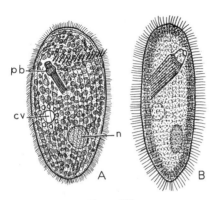

Figure 296

Fig. 296. A. *Nassula aurea*, 200-250μ (Schewiakoff).

Oval to elongate; ventral surface flat, dorsal convex. Usually brightly colored by partially digested algal food material; green, yellow to red food vacuoles. Mouth surrounded by trichites which are fused together to form a pharyngeal basket (pb). Fresh water.

B. *Paranassula microstoma* 80-95μ (Noland). Similar to *Nassula*. Pharyngeal basket with small opening. Pellicle roughened by numerous circular and longitudinal furrows. Marine.

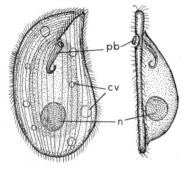

Figure 297

Fig. 297. *Chilodonella cucullulus*, 130-150μ.

Body ovoid with point to one side of anterior end; thick in middle, thin toward edges. Pharyngeal basket (pb) curved, and protrusible on ventral surface. Numerous contractile vacuoles (cv). Nucleus (n) posterior. Very common in stagnant water, especially on the surface of the water just under thin bacterial scum.

SUBORDER TRICHOSTOMINA

The Trichostomina comprise 14 families with many genera, of which only a few are herewith represented.

Paramecium is probably the most intensively studied protozoan genus. It is discussed in all elementary zoology and biology books, and many hundreds of papers have been written on its morphology, physiology, sexual phenomena and genetics. There are at least nine species of which four are relatively common.

Fig. 298 shows the four most common species of *Paramecium.*

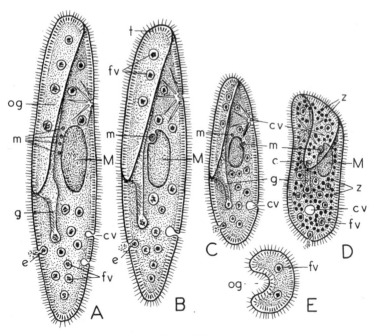

Figure 298

A. *P. multimicronucleatum,* 200-350μ; four or more very small vesicular micronuclei, visible only in well stained specimens; 3 or more contractile vacuoles. B. *P. caudatum,* 180-300μ, slightly more pointed posteriorly than *P. multimicronucleatum* or *P. aurelia;* one compact micronucleus which is in a pocket in the macronucleus and which can easily be stained with methyl green; two contractile vacuoles. C. *P. aurelia,* 120-180μ, quite rounded posteriorly; two very small vesicular micronuclei visible only in well stained specimens; two contractile vacuoles. D. *P. bursaria,* 100-150μ, cell flattened, truncated anteriorly; single compact micronucleus; numerous zoochlorellae which make the organism appear green. E. Cross section of any of the three organisms shown in A, B, and C taken through the middle of the oral groove. c. cytostome; cv, contractile vacuole; e, food vacuole emptying through the anal spot; fv, food vacuole; g. gullet; m, micronucleus; M, macronucleus; t, trichocysts; z, zoochlorellae. (A-D, after Wenrich).

The genus *Paramecium* is easily recognized by its shape, which is very similar to figure 298, A-C, or D. The oral groove is very prominent, the body is uniformly ciliated and has trichocysts just under the entire surface. The two contractile vacuoles with radiating canals are found in all species except *P. putrinum* and *P. trichium.*

The identification of the species of *Paramecium* is relatively easy and should be attempted routinely by every student. If an animal under observation belongs to the genus *Paramecium,* is green with zoochlorellae and is shaped like the drawing of *P. bursaria,* then it is *P. busaria.* If it has this shape but no zoochlorellae it is probably *P. calkinsi, woodruffi, trichium, putrinum,* or *polycaryum,* all relatively rare species. *P. putrinum* has one very slowly acting contractile vacuole in the center with no radiating canals; *P. trichium* has two such vacuoles; *P. woodruffi, polycaryum,* and *calkinsi* have two vacuoles with canals.

If the *Paramecium* has the elongate cylindrical shape it must be *P. caudatum, P. multimicronucleatum,* or *P. aurelia.* If it is less than 180μ and rounded posteriorly it is *P. aurelia.* If over 180μ it may be either *P. caudatum* or *multimicronucleatum; P. caudatum* is more pointed posteriorly than *P. multimicronucleatum.* If acidulated methyl green is added to the slide the nuclei will stain. If you can find a micronucleus as shown in fig. 298B, m, the animal is *caudatum;* if you examine a dozen well stained specimens and can not find the micronucleus then it is probably *P. multimicronucleatum.*

Paramecium has trichocysts just under the entire outer surface of the cell (fig. 277, 298). These can be caused to discharge in a variety of ways. The following method is useful because it permits staining of the cilia and also of the discharged trichocysts.

Add a small drop of red record ink to several drops of a thick *Paramecium* culture on a slide. Wait five minutes. Then add a cover slip. (The animals should still be alive; if they are dead, clean the slide and start over again with less ink). Then add a drop of permanent blue-black record ink at the edge of the cover slip. As the blue ink diffuses under and reaches the animals they will discharge their trichocysts and die. The trichocysts will be stained blue and may still be attached to the animal or may be free in the water. The cilia should be stained red.

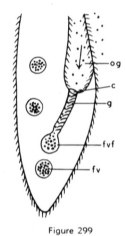

Figure 299

Another interesting exercise is to watch *Paramecium* ingest colored material as shown in fig. 299. Add a mixture of powdered carmine or Chinese ink and water to a drop of culture on a slide. Watch the carmine or ink particles get swept into the oral groove (og) by the cilia and enter the cytostome (c) and pass along the gullet (g) by means of the membranelles in the gullet. The particles are packed into the base of the gullet; when a number of particles has accumulated the base of the gullet constricts off to form a food vacuole (fv). A food vacuole in the process of formation is shown (fvf). *Paramecium* ordinarily ingests bacteria and small algae exactly the same way it ingests carmine or ink particles.

Another interesting exercise is to watch the contractile vacuole contract. Upon examination under the high power lens the vacuoles may be seen as clear round structures which seem to have a very faintly pinkish tinge of coloring. As the vacuole contracts there are six or seven feeding canals which become very prominent. These can be seen in fig. 298, A-D, in the anterior vacuoles; in this figure the radiating canals of the posterior vacuoles are not shown.

The details of how the vacuole contracts can be seen in fig. 300 (after King). Here there are four stages in the cycle of contraction, shown in both side and surface views. For the sake of simplicity all but two of the six or seven canals have been omitted. A. Upper figure shows side view and lower figure the surface view of the vacuole at the stage of greatest size, i.e., at full diastole. Note that the pore is permanent and appears in all four stages and that the radiating canals are also permanent and go to the inner margins of the pore. The canals are much longer than shown and may be about a third as long as the animal. B. Vacuole during contraction. Arrows show direction of flow. The large vacuole, shown with a dash line is emptying to the outside and more liquid is moving up the canals toward the pore and is causing a great distention of the canals. C. Later stage. Large vacuole is completely empty and canals are distended near the pore. The liquid from the canals now flows back into the cytoplasm, as indicated by arrows, to form smaller vesicles. D. Two small vesicles have been formed and they contain the liquid that was in the canals. These vacuoles fuse with each other to form one large vacuole as shown at A, and the cycle is repeated.

With a high power (4 mm.) lens it is possible to find the permanent pore very easily in *Paramecium caudatum* or *P. multimicronucleatum*. Find an animal that is only slightly flattened by the cover slip so that it is free to rotate slowly. When the vacuole is uppermost focus on the upper surface of the animal. It is best to focus on the large vacuole as shown at fig. 300, A, and then to raise the focus and look for a

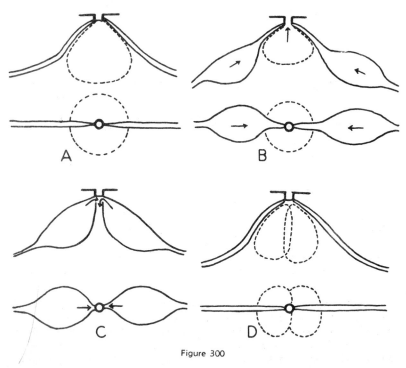

Figure 300

clear ring which seems to have a different refractive index. When you find this you will be looking down into the permanent pore. The canals are very small when not distended, and only rarely and perhaps only with an oil lens is it possible to see them in the living animal.

Count the number of contractions in ten minutes. Does the anterior vacuole contract more rapidly than the posterior one? If the osmotic pressure of the medium is raised the rate of contraction will decrease and eventually may stop. If the temperature is increased the rate of contraction will increase (up to 35°C); a decrease below room temperature will likewise cause a decrease in the rate.

The function of the contractile vacuole seems to be primarily that of a bailing pump in a leaky boat. The osmotic pressure of the cytoplasm is higher than that of the medium, and consequently water enters the cell through the pellicle. Considerable water also enters through the wall of the food vacuoles. This water is taken up by the radial canals and pumped out through the contractile vacuole in somewhat the same way that the mammalian kidney secretes urine into the bladder. Soluble materials such as carbon dioxide and urea are dissolved in the liquid when it leaves the cytoplasm, and this is eventually passed to the outside. Therefore the contractile vacuole can be considered as a respiratory and excretory organelle as well as a bailing device; it has at least these three functions.

Division and conjugation of *Paramecium* are often observed in cultures (fig. 15).

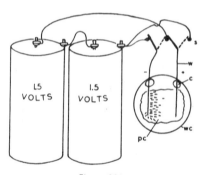

Figure 301

The movement of *Paramecium* is easily controlled by an electric current as shown in fig. 301. If an electric current from one or two dry cells is passed through a *Paramecium* culture the organisms will accumulate at the negative wire, i.e., *Paramecium* is negatively galvanotropic. This can easily be demonstrated by fastening two wires (w), preferably but not necessarily of platinum, to a watch glass or caster dish (wc) by means of some cement (c) insoluble in water. Attach the wires directly to two dry cells or preferably through a reversing switch (s). The paramecium culture (pc) covers both free ends of the wires and carries the current between them. The paramecia collect at the wire connected to the negative side of the battery. By reversing the current by means of the switch (so that the connections are as shown by the dash lines) the other wire becomes negative and the paramecia turn around and go to the new negative wire.

The mechanism of this galvanotropism is shown in fig. 302. The negative wire is on the right; the positive on the left. The cilia on the side of the animal nearer the negative wire are reversed. In A the cilia on the right are reversed, those on the left beat normally. This causes the animal to turn to the right as shown by the arrow. In B the same animal now faces the negative pole and is going to-

191

ward it. A few cilia at the anterior end are beating in reverse, but those along both sides are beating normally and the animal moves directly to the negative wire. If the current is very strong (more batteries!) most of the cilia may be reversed as shown at C. This causes the animal to swim *backwards* toward the *positive wire*. Sometimes the animals hit the negative wire and then become much more sensitive to the current so that they swim backwards to the positive pole even though the current has not been increased.

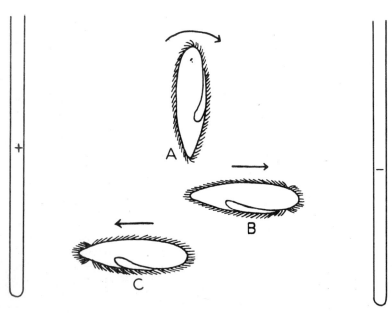

Figure 302

A dissecting microscope is useful but not necessary for watching galvanotropism of *Paramecium*. If a piece of black paper is placed under the dish the migration can easily be seen with the unaided eye. Many other Protozoa besides *Paramecium*, especially other ciliates, are galvanotropic. Once this apparatus is set up it can be used for studying galvanotropism of a variety of Protozoa. Some species are positively galvanotropic, i.e., they go to the positive wire even with small currents. Other species apparently do not respond to electric currents. *Spirostomum*, however, undergoes a definite and continuous series of bending and straightening movements in response to electric current.

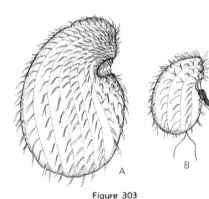

Figure 303

Fig. 303 A. *Colpoda cucullus*, 40-110µ (Burt).

A very common ciliate, the genus of which is easily determined by its kidney-like **s h a p e** with the indented mouth slightly anterior to the middle. Free cilia around mouth; about 12 longitudinal rows of paired cilia, as shown. Stagnant water. B. *C. steini*, 15-40µ (Burt). Similar to *C. cucullus*, but smaller, with fewer rows of cilia. two long posterior cilia, and the postoral cilia more or less fused to form a "beard." Fresh water and in organs of the land slug, *Agriolimax*.

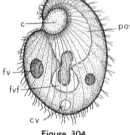

Figure 304

Fig. 304. *Bresslaua insidiatrix*, 500µ.

Similar in general appearance to *Colpoda* but with very large cavity or postoral vacuole (pov) behind the mouth (c). This postoral vacuole is useful in capturing smaller ciliates. In the figure a small *Colpoda* is entering a future food vacuole (fvf). cv, contractile vacuole; fv, food vacuole.

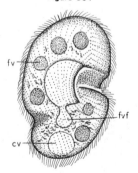

Figure 305

Fig. 305. *Tillina canalifera*, 130-200µ (Turner).

Similar to *Colpoda* except that the peristome is curved and there is a pharynx which ends in a cavity, from which the food vacuoles are formed (fvf). cv, contractile vacuole; fv, food vacuole.

T. magna, up to 400µ, is similar. In both species the pharynx may be seen as an internal curved tube which is first directed anteriorly, and curves a full 180° to the cavity where the food vacuole is formed. Stagnant water and coprozoic.

SUBORDER HYMENOSTOMINA

This suborder consists of 5 families and many genera of which only a few are represented herewith. The one character which all genera possess is the presence of at least one and usually two or more undulating membranes in or on the margin of the peristome or mouth. In many genera these membranes are large and obvious; in others they are small and distinguishable only with an oil lens.

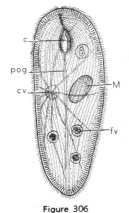

Figure 306

Fig. 306. *Frontonia leucas*, 150-600μ (Kahl).

Body ovoid, and dark in color. Cytostome (c) close to anterior end with a posterior oral groove (pog) and three small undulating membranes on the left margin. Trichocysts under entire surface of pellicle. Contractile vacuole with permanent pore and numerous canals. *F. atra*, 150μ, is very similar but very black and with pointed posterior end.

Fig. 307. Four common species of small ciliates which are often confused and very difficult to distinguish. A. *Leucophrys patula*, 80-160μ. B. *Tetrahymena geleii*, 40-60μ C. *Glaucoma scintillans*, 45-73μ. D. *Colpidium campylum*, 50-70μ. All four genera have an undulating membrane on the right margin of the mouth and three membranelles

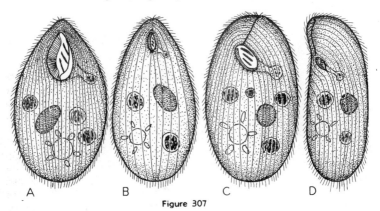

Figure 307

on the left. The size of the mouth is different in different genera, but at least in *Tetrahymena* this varies with the state of nutrition. The best way to distinguish the genera seems to be by counting the rows of cilia (indicated by lines in the drawing) which begin at the mouth and go posteriorly. There are 5 in *Leucophrys*, 2 in *Tetrahymena*, 7 in *Glaucoma*, and 1 in *Colpidium*. Any small ciliate of this group on which the postoral ciliary rows can not be counted usually can not be identified with certainty.

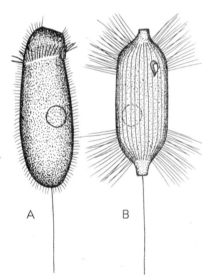

Figure 308

Fig. 308. A. *Loxocephalus plagius*, 50-65μ (Stokes).

Body ovoid-cylindrical; dark in color. No cilia at anterior end; a single transverse row of larger cilia near anterior end; one long posterior cilium. Mouth small, near anterior end, with 2 small membranes. Very common among decaying vegetation. B. *Balanonema biceps*, 42-50μ (Penard). Body cylindrical with plug - like, sharply tapered ends. No cilia in middle of body; one long caudal cilium. Mouth small with membrane about ¼ of body length from anterior end.

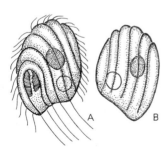

Figure 309

Fig. 309. *Cinetochilum margaritaceum*, 15-45μ (Kahl).

Body oval, truncated posteriorly. Cytostome in posterior half of body, with undulating membranes on both edges; 3-4 long caudal cilia. A. Ventral view. B. Dorsal view, cilia not shown.

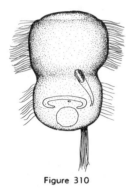

Figure 310

Fig. 310. *Urocentrum turbo*, 50-80μ.

Body shaped like two spheres, closely appressed, with a band of cilia about each. Mouth with double undulating membrane on left edge just behind constriction of body. Caudal tuft of cilia. Body quite clear, contractile vacuole posterior; macronucleus C-shaped. Animal swims very rapidly in an irregular spiral fashion, hence the specific name. Very common, especially in pond vegetation a few days after it is brought into the laboratory.

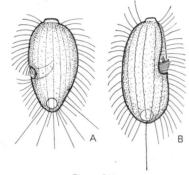

Figure 311

Fig. 311. A. *Uronema pluricaudatum*, 25μ (Noland).

Body ovoid, flat anteriorly, with spiral peristome; membrane small; about 8 caudal cilia; contractile vacuole posterior. Marine. B. *U. marina*, 30-50μ (Kahl). Similar to *U. pluricaudatum* but only one caudal cilium.

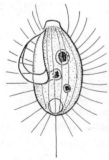

Figure 312

Fig. 312. *Cyclidium glaucoma*, 25-30μ (Kahl).

Body ovoid, flattened anteriorly; long peristome with very large undulating membrane which is extended when animal is feeding; long cilia; one long caudal cilium; posterior contractile vacuole. Animal moves primarily by "jumping" with rapid movements of the long cilia; seldom seen swimming. Easily recognizable by its shape, the long cilia which can been seen individually under high power, and the "jumping" movement. Very common in putrid cultures.

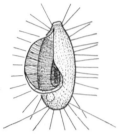

Figure 313

Fig. 313. *Pleuronema setigerum,* 40-50μ (Noland).

Body ellipsoidal, long peristome with large membrane, long cilia, and several very long caudal cilia. Marine.

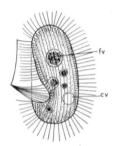

Figure 314

Fig. 314. *Pleuronema crassum,* 100μ (Kahl).

Body ovoid; long peristome; large membrane, uniformly long cilia; trichocysts over entire body surface. Marine. cv, contractile vacuole; fv, food vacuole.

SUBORDER THIGMOTRICHINA

Most of the ciliates placed in this suborder inhabit the mantle cavity of fresh water and marine mussels. The character which is common to the group is the possession of special long cilia which are used for attachment to the gill or to the mantle wall. There are 6 families of which only one is represented herewith.

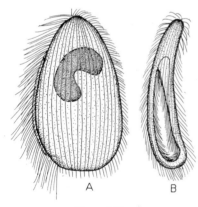

Figure 315

Fig. 315. *Ancistruma mytili,* 52-74μ (Kidder) in the marine mussel, *Mytilus edulis,* on our northeastern coast.

Body ovoid, flattened, concave ventrically, convex dorsally; thigmotactic cilia on left margin, peristome on right. Peristome long, with cytostome near posterior end of body. A. dorsal view. B. view of right edge showing peristome with cilia on both margins.

197

ORDER SPIROTRICHIDA

The spirotrichs have an adoral zone of membranelles which are used for directing food particles toward the mouth. Separation into suborders is made on the basis of ciliary organelles present elsewhere on the body.

KEY TO THE SUBORDERS

1a With only free cilia on body; or with small groups of cirrus-like projections in addition to cilia.........................2

1b Cirri only, on ventral side; dorsal side usually with rows of short bristles.   Suborder HYPOTRICHINA, p. 205

2a Body more or less uniformly ciliated.
                          Suborder HETEROTRICHINA, p. 198

2b Body ciliation much reduced or absent....................3

3a Rounded in cross section; adoral zone encloses a non-ciliated peristomal field, usually spiral............................4

3b Body compressed, carapaced, peristomal field reduced to 8 membranelles which lie in oval peristome.
                          Suborder CTENOSTOMINA, p. 216

4a Free living 5

4b Endozoic in rumen of ruminants or in colon of other herbivores.
                          Suborder ENTODINIOMORPHINA, p. 211

5a Without lorica.   Suborder OLIGOTRICHINA, p. 211

5b With lorica.   Suborder TINTINNINA, p. 215

SUBORDER HETEROTRICHINA

The body is uniformly ciliated, except in two families which have been omitted. Separation into families is made mostly on the basis of the shape and location of the peristome.

1a Peristome not sunk into a funnel-like cavity at anterior end, but leads to a short and narrow oral funnel (absent in one family)...2

1b Peristome sunk in a funnel-like cavity at anterior end, thus mostly covered.   Family BURSARIIDAE

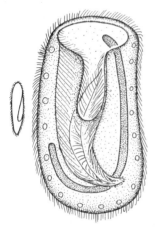

Figure 316

Fig. 316. *Bursaria truncatella*, 500-1000μ (Kahl).

Ovoid; truncate anteriorly; with large anterior oral cavity, often large enough so that paramecia may swim about freely within the cavity. Cavity divided by longitudinal ridge. Cytostome at base of cavity, near middle of body, leads to pharynx which continues almost to posterior end. Ciliation complete and uniform. Macronucleus very long, C-shaped. Many contractile vacuoles on lateral and posterior borders. A voracious feeder, ingests ciliates as large as *Paramecium* one immediately after another.

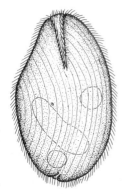

Figure 317

Fig. 317. *Balantidium coli*, 40-80μ (Wenyon) from human intestine.

Ovoid, numerous oblique rows of cilia, peristome anterior with inconspicuous cytostome and cytopharynx at inner end of peristome and not shown in figure. Macronucleus large. Two contractile vacuoles, one posterior, one in middle. Cytopyge near posterior tip. Food consists of erythrocytes, host cell fragments, starch grains, fecal debris, and similar substances.

This organism lives in the cecum and colon of man and causes balantidial dysentery. The ciliate forms deep ulcers similar to those of amebic dysentery, and the dysentery is usually chronic. Often a serious disease; rather unusual in the United States, more common in the Philippines; no effective treatment known. The ciliate is often found in hogs where it usually is not pathogenic. Cysts pass out in hog feces, and man usually becomes infected by contamination of food or drinking water.

Other animals harbor various species of *Balantidium*, and guinea pigs serve as a good source of laboratory material.

2a Peristome at anterior region 3

2b Peristome at posterior end.　　　Family **CLEVELANDELLIDAE**

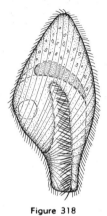

Fig. 318. *Clevelandella panesthiae*, 87-156μ (Kidder).

Body fusiform, bluntly pointed anteriorly, truncate posteriorly; peristome and cytostome posterior, peristome nearly enclosed. Macronucleus large, supported by sheet like karyophore (nuclear support) which separates the endoplasm into two parts; food vacuoles posterior. In the gut of wood-eating roaches of the genus *Panesthia*.

Figure 318

3a A narrow non-ciliated zone on right of adoral zone; usually an undulating membrane or ciliary row to right of this non-ciliated zone and anterior to cytostome; a small peristomal field between the membrane and adoral zone 4

3b Without the non-ciliated zone on right of adoral zone; a large peristomal field with a half or completely spiral adoral zone...5

4a Adoral zone parallel to body axis on flat ventral surface, turns somewhat to right of cytostome; oral funnel distinct; typically an undulating membrane or a double ciliated furrow in front of cytostome.

FAMILY SPIROSTOMIDAE

Fig. 319. *Spirostomum ambiguum*, 1-3 mm. (Kahl).

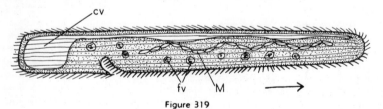

Figure 319

One of the largest Protozoa common in fresh water. (See size range, p. 12). Body elongate, cylindrical, somewhat flattened; ectoplasm with highly developed myonemes which permit contraction to ¼ or less of normal body length; contractile vacuole (cv) large, posterior, connected to longitudinal canal; macronucleus (M) bead-like; caudal cilia thigmotactic; peristome ¾ of body length; length to width ratio, about 10 to 1. *S. intermedium*, 400 to 600μ, is similar in appearance with peristome slightly more than ½ body length. *S. teres*, 150-400μ, has one oval macronucleus, peristome only ½ body length. A thick culture of *Spirostomum* is suggestive of a dish of spaghetti.

Fig. 320. *Blepharisma steini*, 180μ (Kahl).

Body elongate ovoid, peristome about ½ body length; membranelles on left edge of gullet, large membrane on right; contractile vacuole posterior. Ordinarily the pellicle is pink to bright rose in color, but may be colorless if grown in bright sunlight (Giese). *B. lateritium*, 130-200μ (fig. 272) is similar in color and structure but is pear-shaped.

Under the influence of certain chemicals *Blepharisma* can be made to cast off the pink pellicle and is then a colorless ciliate. As found in ponds, however, the animal is usually pink. Whenever a student finds a pink ciliate the first guess at the genus should be *Blepharisma*; other pink ciliates are rare.

Figure 320

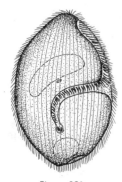

Fig. 321. *Nyctotherus cordiformis*, 60-200μ (Wenyon).

Body oval, flattened; peristome begins at anterior end, runs along one edge to middle; cytostome central, elongate curved tube with undulating membrane; large macronucleus anterior. In colon of frogs and toads, common. *N. ovalis*, 90-185μ or larger, in cockroaches and millipedes.

Figure 321

4b Adoral zone extends diagonally to posterior-right on ventral surface; some highly developed forms with long zone twisting spirally around body.   **Family METOPIDAE**

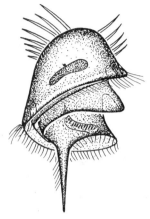

Fig. 322. *Caenomorpha sapropelica,* 200μ (Kahl).

Bell-shaped with long posterior spike; strong marginal or adoral zone of about 8 rows of cilia is very obvious and surrounds the body; cytostome posterior; cytopharynx directed anteriorly; 2 rows of large dorsal cilia. In oxygen deficient ponds. Superficially similar to *Metopus intercedens* (fig. 324).

Figure 322

Fig. 323. *Metopus es,* 120-200μ (Kahl).

Body elongate, tapered posteriorly; peristome conspicuous, diagonally spiral; contractile vacuole posterior. In putrid plant infusions and in bogs which contain hydrogen sulfide and little oxygen. *M. fuscus,* 180-333μ, is similar in shape but broader posteriorly.

Figure 323

Fig. 324. *Metopus intercedens,* 90-140μ (Kahl).

Body very broad, almost umbrella-like anteriorly, tapered posteriorly, with very prominent peristome. Posterior cilia are thigmotactic. In oxygen deficient ponds. *M. campanula,* 40-90μ, is similar in shape.

Figure 324

5a Peristomal field ciliated; without undulating membrane 6

5b Peristomal field not ciliated; with large undulating membrane on right edge. Family **CONDYLOSTOMIDAE.**

Fig. 325. *Condylostoma arenarium,* 400-700μ.

Body elongate, uniformly ciliated; peristome prominent, undulating membrane prominent. Other species range from 100 to 900μ, and the smaller ones have a proportionately larger peristome. Stagnant water.

Figure 325

6a Peristomal field drawn out into 2 wings; with thin flask-shaped transparent lorica. Family **FOLLICULINIDAE**

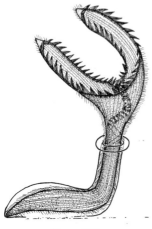

Fig. 326. *Folliculina aculeata,* 500μ (Dewey).

Lorica attached on broad surface, neck oblique, with collar. Peristome with two long wings; gullet spirals inside of body. Marine.

Figure 326

The large size, the most unusual winged peristome, the spiral gullet, and the lorica make this genus particularly interesting from the viewpoint of morphology. There are several related genera: *Microfolliculina,* with small sac-like protruberances on the lorica. *Pseudofolliculina,* vertical, attached to substratum by posterior end of lorica.

Parafolliculina, neck of lorica with basal swelling, attached on side or on end.

6b Peristomal field not drawn out into 2 wings; free swimming or with gelatinous lorica. Family STENTORIDAE

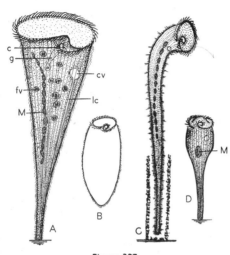

Figure 327

Fig. 327. A. *Stentor coeruleus,* 1-2 mm., extended.

Body trumpet - shaped, attached at narrow end, uniformly ciliated, including peristomal field, peristome around rim, cytostome (c) at end of small spiral on one edge of rim, leading to short gullet (g); macronucleus (M) bead-like; contractile vacuole (cv) anterior, with longitudinal canal (lc); food vacuoles (fv) numerous; pellicle a dark blue in color, hence the specific name. Under certain unknown conditions the ciliate may shed the pellicle and thereby become colorless (cf. *Blepharisma,* fig. 320). B. *S. coeruleus,* free swimming, contracted form. The pellicle contains many myonemes which permit considerable change of shape. However, the animal can usually be identified by the doubly spiral peristome. C. *S. mulleri,* 200μ, (Kahl). Similar to above, but thinner, not colored, with a few longer cilia on body, and sometimes attached in a gelatinous tube. D. *S. igneus,* 300μ, (Kahl). With oval instead of bead-like macronucleus.

Figure 328

Fig. 328. *Climacostomum virens,* 100-300μ (Kahl).

Similar to *Condylostoma* but without undulating membrane, and with peristomal field ciliated; macronucleus band form. With or without zoochlorellae. Fresh and brackish water.

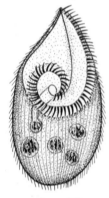

Figure 329

Fig. 329. *Fabrea salina*, 120-220μ (Kirby).

Body pear-shaped, narrowed anteriorly; peristome 2/5 of body length, with posterior portion in spiral. In salt marshes, salinity of 7.5 to 20 per cent, California.

SUBORDER HYPOTRICHINA

The hypotrichs possess an adoral zone of membranelles and usually cirri on the ventral surface. The suborder is divided into families and genera on the basis of the distribution of these ciliary organelles.

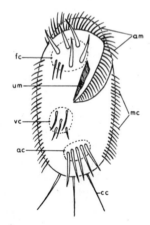

Figure 330

Fig. 330 shows the nomenclature of the various types of ciliary organelles in *Stylonychia* (after Kudo). ac, anal cirri; am, adoral zone of membranelles; cc, caudal cirri; fc, frontal cirri; mc, marginal cirri; um, undulating membrane; vc, ventral cirri. This genus is characterized by the possession of 8 frontals, 5 ventrals, 5 anals, numerous marginals and 3 caudals.

1a Adoral zone fully formed..............................2

1b Adoral zone reduced.   Family ASPIDISCIDAE

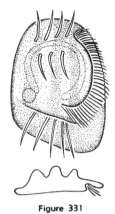

Figure 331

Fig. 331. *Aspidisca lynceus*, 30-50μ (Stein).

Body ovoid, inflexible, convex dorsally with as many as 5 conspicuous ridges, adoral zone on lateral edge but not anterior; 7 fronto-ventrals, 5 (or more) anals. Lower figure shows cross section. Numerous species; some marine. Very common among vegetation on which it crawls with great rapidity.

2a Cirri on ventral surface...............................3

2b No ventral cirri, but ventral cilia and caudal cirri.
Family PARAEUPLOTIDAE

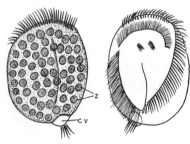

Figure 332

Fig. 332. *Paraeuplotes tortugensis*, 85μ (Wichterman).

Ovoid; adoral zone well developed; two ciliary rows, one anterior transverse, one longitudinal; two ciliary tufts; 5-6 caudal cirri; contractile vacuole (cv) posterior; zooxanthellae (z) present; in a coral, *Eunicea*.

3a Ventrals and marginals not in longitudinal rows.
Family EUPLOTIDAE

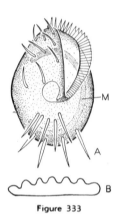

Figure 333

Fig. 333. *Euplotes patella*, about 90μ (Pierson).

Body ovoid, inflexible, flattened ventrally, convex and longitudinally ridged dorsally; 9 fronto-ventrals, 5 anals, 4 scattered caudals; macronucleus band-like. The body is very clear, and the cirri are large and easily seen. Therefore, this genus is excellent for beginners to study the distribution of cirri. B. Cross section to show 6 conspicuous longitudinal ridges. *E. woodruffi* has eight low inconspicuous ridges; *E. eurystomus* and *E. aediculatus* have a variable number of inconspicuous ridges or none.

3b Ventrals in rows, although reduced in some; 2 rows of marginals.

Family OXYTRICHIDAE

Figure 334

Fig. 334. *Oxytricha fallax*, 150μ (Stein).

Body ellipsoid, flexible, flattened ventrally, convex dorsally; 8 frontals, 5 ventrals, 5 anals, short caudals, marginals continuous around posterior border (not so in some other species), 2 macronuclei.

Many species. More common ones are: *O. bifaria*, 250μ, with posterior end slightly pointed, fresh water. *O. ludibunda*, 100μ, fresh water. *O. setigera*, 50μ, 5 frontals, extra rows of very long marginals in addition to those shown for *O. fallax*.

Figure 335

Fig. 335. A. *Urosoma cienkowskii*, 150-300μ, (Kowalewski, Kahl).

Similar to *Oxytricha* but posterior end narrowed and greatly elongated. In oxygen deficient ponds. B. *Gonostomum affine*, 90-115μ (Kahl). Similar to *Oxytricha*, 8 or more frontals, long adoral zone. In fresh water and soil.

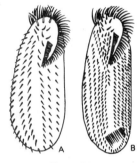

Figure 336

Fig. 336. A. *Kahlia acrobates*, 100-200μ (Kahl).

Frontal margin with 3-4 strong cirri; 5 ventral rows (up to 8 in other species); marginals; no anals or caudals. In soil infusion. B. *Urostyla grandis*, 300-400μ (Kahl). Body ellipsoid, flexible, with several rows of ventrals, 2 or marginals, 5-12 anals.

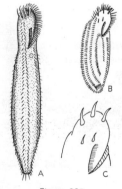

Figure 337

Fig. 337. A. *Uroleptus limnetis*, 200μ (Stokes).

Body elongate; 3 frontals, 2 rows of ventrals, 2 of marginals; no anals; sometimes rose or violet colored. B. *U. coei*, 200μ (Turner). Similar to *U. limnetis*, but with 4 rows of ventrals, 6 anals. C. Anterior region of *U. coei*.

Numerous species, most of which have the posterior end attenuated. *U. halseyi*, 160μ by 20μ, has micronucleus divided into as many as 26 parts; posterior end tapered, pointed, and permanently curved more than 45° toward the ventral side.

Figure 338

Fig. 338. *Kerona polyporum*, 120-200μ (Stein).

Body slightly kidney-shaped; 6 oblique rows of fronto-ventrals; no caudals. Ectozoic on *Hydra* (as is *Trichodina*, fig. 355). Very common. Often seen on *Hydra* obtained from commercial sources for use in elementary zoology laboratory studies. These ciliates may be seen crawling along the body surface of *Hydra* and may readily be distinguished from *Trichodina* by the shape of the ciliate body.

Figure 339

Fig. 339. *Stylonychia pustulata*, 150μ (Roux).

Body ovoid, not flexible, ventral surface flat, dorsal convex; 8 frontals, 5 ventrals, 5 anals, marginals, 3 caudals. Common in fresh water. This genus can usually be identified by the 3 caudal cirri. *S. pustulata* is also shown in fig. 331; *S. mytilis*, 100-300μ, in fig. 273.

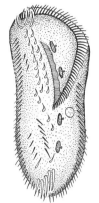

Figure 340

Fig. 340. *Onychodromos grandis*, 100-300μ (Stein).

Body somewhat rectangular, not flexible, truncate anteriorly, flat ventrally, convex dorsally; 3 frontals, 3 rows of ventrals parallel to right edge of peristome, 5-6 anals, marginals uninterrupted; 4 macronuclei.

This large ciliate is often confused with *Stylonychia* but is easily distinguished by the absence of the three long caudal cilia present in *Stylonychia*.

Figure 341

Fig. 341. A. *Stichosticha secunda*, 130-200μ (Kahl).

Body slender fusiform, peristomal part narrowed, not flexible; usually 4 spiral rows of cirri; often tube dwelling; tube often found among plant debris in fresh water. Animal usually darts rapidly part way out and then back into the tube. B. *Strongylidium californicum*, 250μ, (Kahl). Body elongate; 2-5 spiral rows of ventrals, 4-5 frontals; not tube dwelling. Shape of body and length of peristome permits distinguishing it from *Stichosticha*.

Figure 342

Fig. 342. *Hypotrichidium conicum*, 90-150μ.

Two rows of ventrals and marginals spirally arranged, body bulges between rows; peristome large with large undulating membrane; 2 macronuclei. Fresh water.

SUBORDER OLIGOTRICHINA

Free living ciliates, without lorica, with adoral zone, with body cilia greatly reduced or absent.

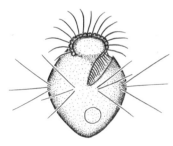

Figure 343

Fig. 343. *Halteria grandinella*, 25-50μ (Kahl).

Body spherical or almost so, with conspicuous adoral zone, and an equatorial band of 7 groups of 3 cirri each. Very common in pond water plant infusions the first few days they are kept in the laboratory. The ciliates are easily identified by a "bouncing" movement produced by the equatorial cirri which are used for "springing." The movement is characteristically that of a bouncing ball.

SUBORDER ENTODINIOMORPHINA

Body cilia absent, with obvious adoral zone, with or without tufts or rows of cirri elsewhere on body. In rumen and reticulum of ruminants, colon of other herbivores, universally present. Very numerous, 100,000 to 400,000 per cc. or a total of 10 billion or more for a cow.

The ciliates of ruminants eventually pass into the omasum, abomasum and intestine and are digested. The ciliates feed on bacteria and plant fragments, and when the ciliates are digested this material becomes available for nutrition of the host. However, the Protozoa do not seem to be essential to the cattle. Evidence consists of the fact that cattle may be freed of ciliates by feeding copper sulfate and may be kept in good health without ciliates for more than a year, and under these conditions have a growth rate at least as high as normal. Whatever benefit cattle derive from the presence of ciliates seems to be incidental. The ciliates of cattle, however, are well adapted to life in the rumen, do not live elsewhere and have never been successfully maintained in culture.

Fig. 344. *Epidinium ecaudatum*, 130μ (Sharp), shows the typical structure of this interesting group of ciliates.

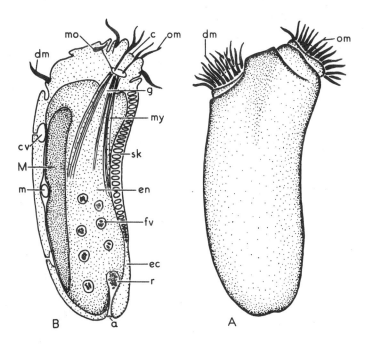

Figure 344

A. View of entire animal, showing oral (om) and dorsal (dm) membranelles. **B.** Longitudinal section, showing: a, anus; c, mouth; cv, contractile vacuole which opens to outside by means of a short tube; ec, ectoplasm; en, endoplasm; fv, food vacuole; dm, dorsal membranelle; M, macronucleus; m, micronucleus; mo, motorium or "nerve center" which sends a fiber to a ring around the pharynx; my, myonemes; om, oral membranelles; r, rectum, food vacuole about to empty through anus; sk, skeletal plates near ventral surface. In cattle, and reindeer.

This is a good example of the complexity of a protozoan. This animal has organelles for locomotion (dm), for feeding (om), for swallowing (g), for contraction (my), for maintenance of form (sk), for digestion (fv), for storage of food residue (r), for egestion (a), for excretion (cv), for maintenance of metabolic functions (M), for direction of locomotion and ingestion (mo), and for conservation of its germplasm (chromatin material) for future generations (m). All of this is contained in the simplicity (? !) of a single cell!

Figure 345

Fig. 345. *Epidinium parvicaudatum,* 70-120μ (Kofoid and Christenson).

Similar to *E. ecaudatum* but with 5 posterior spines, one very long. From wild ox, other species in cattle and sheep.

Figure 346

Fig. 346. *Ophryoscolex bicoronatus,* 120-170μ (Dogiel).

With adoral and dorsal zones of membranelles, dorsal zone encircling ¾ of the body circumference. Posterior end with numerous spine-like projections. Various species of this genus in sheep, goats, cattle.

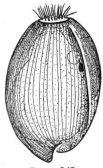

Figure 347

Fig. 347. *Entodinium costatum,* 20-40μ (MacLennan).

Without dorsal zone, otherwise similar to *Ophryoscolex.* Some species have posterior spines. *E. costatum* in mule deer; other species in cattle and sheep.

Common species are: *E. caudatum,* 50 to 80μ, with one long posterior spine, in cattle and sheep. *E. bursa,* 55-114μ, no posterior spines, in cattle.

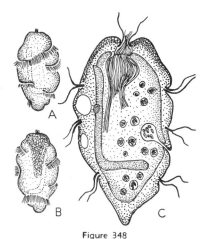

Figure 348

Fig. 348. *Troglodytella abrassarti*, 120-160μ.

A. Ventral view. B. Dorsal view (Brumpt and Joyeux). C. Longitudinal section (Swezy). Adoral zone, and three additional zones of membranelles. Section shows contractile vacuoles, food vacuoles, macro- and micronuclei, mouth, gullet, anus, ectoplasm, a n d endoplasm. Compare with *Epidinium*, fig. 344. In colon of chimpanzees; other species in other apes.

Figure 349

Fig. 349. *Tetratoxum unifasciculatum*, 230μ (Davis). Two anterior and two posterior zones of membranelles. In colon of horse.

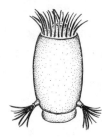

Figure 350

Fig. 350. *Cycloposthium bipalmatum*, 80-127μ (Bundle). Body elongate barrel-shaped; cytostome in center of retractile conical anterior elevation, two groups of membranelles near posterior end. Very common in **cecum** and colon of horses; numerous other species.

SUBORDER TINTINNINA

Body conical or trumpet-shaped; attached inside a lorica of gelatinous material, with or without foreign particles; longitudinal rows of cilia on body; with very large adoral zone of bushy membranelles; usually 2 macronuclei. More than 300 species, comprising 51 genera and 12 families. Pelagic; mostly marine, a few in fresh or brackish water.

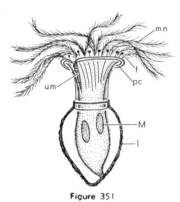

Figure 351

Fig. 351. *Tintinnopsis,* 100μ (Campbell), diagrammatic.

l, lorica; M, macronucleus; pc, peristomal collar; mn, adoral membranelles; t, tentacles; um, undulating membrane.

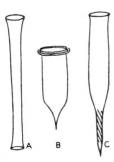

Figure 352

Fig. 352. Loricas of various Tintinnina (after Kofoid).

A. *Tintinnus.* B. *Cymatocyclis.* C. *Xystonellopsis.* The loricas vary greatly in shape in different species. Some are transparent, others highly arenaceous.

SUBORDER CTENOSTOMINA

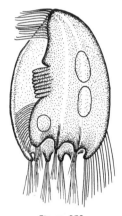

Body flattened, with rigid pellicle, very sparse ciliation, exclusively free living, in water deficient in oxygen.

Fig. 353. *Epalxis mirabilis*, 38-45μ (Roux).

Body rounded triangular, pointed anteriorly, dorsal surface convex; several median teeth, posterior teeth without spine, comb-like structure posterior to mouth. Fresh water. Many species. *Saprodinium* is similar except that some of the posterior teeth have spines.

Figure 353

ORDER CHONOTRICHIDA

Attached to aquatic animals, especially crustaceans. Body is vase-shaped with an apical peristome with an outer ectoplasmic collar and an inner deeply located cytostome. Not common.

Fig. 354. *Spirochona gemmipara*, 80-120μ (Stein).

Peristome funnel spirally wound with ciliary zone on floor of the funnel; body typically vase-shaped; attached to the gill plates of *Gammarus*.

Other genera have wider funnel-shaped peristome, up to 3 times width of body, some with spines on the periphery. Some genera with short or long stalk.

Figure 354

ORDER PERITRICHIDA

The peritrichs possess an enlarged disc-like anterior region which is conspicuously ciliated, usually with three semi-membranes. The adoral zone winds counterclockwise to the cytostome as viewed from the anterior end. Body ciliation is very limited, usually absent. Most species are stalked. The stalked forms may develop a posterior ring of cilia and lose the stalk and thereby become a free swimming stage known as a telotroch.

1a Free swimming, but with highly developed attaching organelles on aboral end.

SUBORDER MOBILINA

Fig. 355. *Trichodina pediculus*, 50-70μ. A. Top view (Mueller). B. Side view (James-Clark).

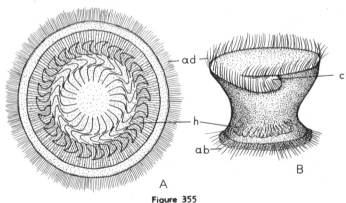

Figure 355

On *Hydra* and amphibia; common in skin folds and on gills of Necturus and on frog tadpoles. Body shaped like a thick disc, constricted on edges; two rings of cilia, one on upper or adoral surface (ad), one on attached or aboral surface (ab); the adoral zone leads to the mouth (c) on one edge of the upper surface. The aboral surface bears a ring of about 24 hooked teeth by which the ciliate may become attached to its host.

1b Attached to submerged objects; usually no body cilia except in telotroch stage which possesses a posterior ciliary ring.

Suborder SESSILINA....2

2a With definite lorica.   **Tribe LORICATA**

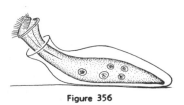

Figure 356

Fig. 356. *Platycola longicollis*, 126μ (De Fromental).

Lorica clear, yellow to brown in color, attached to substrate for greater part of its length. *Vaginicola* is similar except that the lorica is vase-like and attached only at the end.

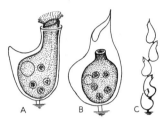

Figure 357

Fig. 357. *Cothurnia variabilis*, 70-100μ.

Lorica yellow to brown, irregularly shaped, with much variation, with short stalk. On gills of crayfish, sometimes in numbers sufficient to make the gills appear yellow. Sometimes colonial, with one lorica attached upon another as shown at C. A and B show the typical lorica shapes, with animal expanded in A, contracted in B.

2b Without lorica, with or without stalk.

Tribe ALORICATA

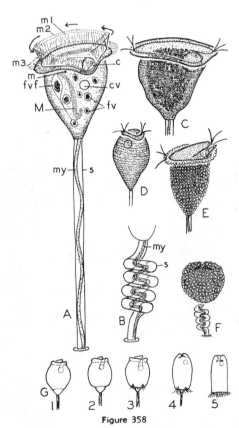

Figure 358

Fig. 358. *Vorticella* (After Noland and Finley).

A. Diagram of typical normal animal to show structure. Adoral zone consists of three semi-membranes, m1, m2, and m3. Arrows show direction of beat. Body bell-shaped, attached to stalk (c), no body cilia. Stalk possesses internal myoneme (my) which is capable of contracting. c, mouth; cv, contractile vacuole; fv, food vacuole; fvf, food vacuole in process of formation; M, macronucleus which is band- or C-shaped; m, micronucleus. B. Stalk in contracted condition. The myoneme (my) shortens but the sheath of the stalk (s) merely coils like a spring, without actual shortening. C. *Vorticella campanula*, 50-150μ. D. *V. microstoma*, 35-80μ, note small peristome. E. *V. monilata*, 50-75μ, with small bumps on pellicle. F. *V. monilata*, contracted. G. Formation of telotroch in *V.*

218

microstoma. A posterior ring of cilia develop (1-3), the animal becomes elongate and cylindrical (4), and eventually free swimming (5). See also fig. 15, D.

The genus is easily recognized by the fact that the stalked form is not branched. *Vorticella* is often found in clusters, but these clusters are not colonies, i.e., the stalk of each organism is attached directly to the substrate. In other genera described below the stalk is branched, and may be non-contractile *(Epistylis, Opercularia)* or contractile only as a single unit, i.e., the whole colony contracts at the same time *(Zoothamnium)*, or each branch contractile as an independent unit *(Carchesium)*.

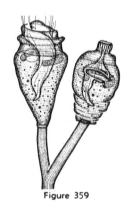

Figure 359

Fig. 359. *Epistylis chrysemydis,* 230-250μ (Bishop and Jahn).

Expanded form on left, contracted on right. Note an extra collar around the rim of the bell when expanded. The gullet is very large and in the expanded form the opening to the gullet is partly covered by a large flap; in the contracted form this flap is seen in the center of the animal. The stalk is dichotomously branched and is non-contractile, i.e., without a myoneme. On carapace of Western Painted Turtle, *Chrysemys picta bellii.*

Figure 360

Fig. 360. *Epistylis cambari,* bell 50μ (Kellicott).

On gills of crayfish. Very common. The dichotomous branching of the non-contractile stalk is characteristic of the genus.

Fig. 361. A. *Epistylis niagarae,* to 180μ (Bishop and Jahn).

L e f t individual expanded, right one contracted. On Western Painted Turtle. B. *E. urceolata,* 160μ (Bishop and Jahn). On the larva of *Chironomus,* very common.

Figure 361

Fig. 362. *Opercularia ramosa,* 140μ (Bishop and Jahn).

Genus differs from *Epistylis* in that there is no separation of the peristome from the body, i.e., no thickening around the rim of the bell. Left individual fully expanded with peristomial cap protruded; middle individual partly expanded with cap inside body; right individual more contraced. On carapace of Western Painted and Snapping Turtles.

Figure 362

Fig. 363. *Carchesium polypinum,* body 100-125μ (Stein).

Colonial, with myonemes in the stalk. The myonemes are not continuous so that the part of the stalk immediately attached to any individual can contract without causing contraction of the whole colony.

Figure 363

Figure 364

Fig. 364. *Zoothamnium adamsi*, body 60μ, colony up to 250μ, on *Cladophora*.

Similar to *Carchesium* except that the entire colony of many individuals has a single branched myoneme system. All of the myonemes contract simultaneously, thereby causing contraction of the entire colony. *Z. arbuscula* may have hundreds of individuals in a colony which may be 6 mm. in diameter

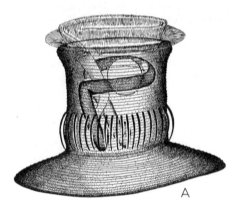

A

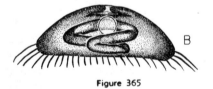

B

Figure 365

Fig. 365. A. *Scyphidia ameiuri*, 34-45μ (Thompson, Kirkegaard, a n d Jahn).

Body cylindrical, without stalk; peristome similar to *Vorticella*; single row of cilia around middle; basal end greatly expanded to form a sucking disc which is attached to the gill filaments of the Bullhead, *Ameiurus melas melas*. In young catfish caught on drying mudflats the ciliate has been found to cover as much as 1/3 of the gill surface. B. Telotroch which is formed simply by the detachment of the attached form and the contraction of both the peristome and the sucking disc.

The formation of the telotroch may be observed by placing a piece of infected catfish gill on a slide (with a coverslip). After a short while, possibly because of the changing gaseous content of the liquid, the attached form may become detached, may fold in its broad base, and may then become free swimming. Most other species of *Scyphidia* are attached to inanimate submerged objects and do not have a median row of cilia.

CLASS SUCTOREA

The suctoreans possess cilia only during the early growth stages. The adult has sucking tentacles by means of which it can extract the cytoplasm from its prey.

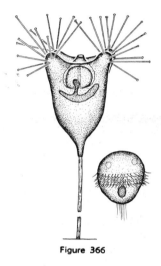

Figure 366

Fig. 366 shows a typical suctorean, *Tokophrya quadripartita*, body 100-175μ, with sucking tentacles and long stalk, several times length of body.

The tentacles are in four groups, or fascicles. At the distal end is an opening which is the *birth pore*. Below the birth pore is a cavity in which can be seen a small ciliate which is being constricted off from the parent, and which will contain one lobe of the macronucleus (and one or more micronuclei, not shown). This young ciliate will soon be free swimming. Insert at lower right shows the free swimming form with several median bands of cilia and a caudal ciliary tuft, but no tentacles. This animal becomes attached by means of the caudal cilia and then grows tentacles, loses all cilia, and secretes a stalk.

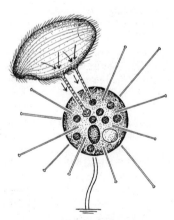

Figure 367

Fig. 367. *Podophyra fixa*, 10-28μ.

Body spherical with short stalk. This specimen has caught a small ciliate, *Tetrahymena*, to which it has attached two tentacles. The suctorean is sucking the *Tetrahymena* cytoplasm which is flowing as indicated by arrows, and which is filling food vacuoles at the basal ends of the tentacles. Very common. Fresh water.

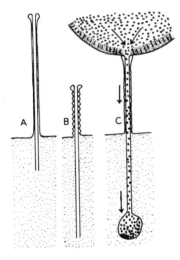

Figure 368

Fig. 368. Diagrams to show the action of sucking tentacles.

A. Extended tentacle, consisting of semi-rigid tube and outer pellicle covering. B. Tentacle retracted. Note that the tube projects farther into the cytoplasm and that the pellicular covering is wrinkled. C. Tentacle attached to *Paramecium*. The *Paramecium* cytoplasm is flowing through the tentacle and forming a food vacuole inside the suctorean.

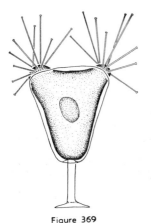

Figure 369

Fig. 369. *Acineta limnetis*, 35-55μ (Goodrich and Jahn).

Body with thin lorica, two fascicles of tentacles, and heavy stalk with broad base. Attached to algae on carapace of turtles.

Embryo formation as in **Tokophrya**. Numerous species, most of which are attached to fresh water algae. There are also several closely related genera with species which grow on marine hydroids, on the shells of fresh water snails, on copepods, and on other microcrustacea. *Acinetopsis tentaculata* is found on the stalks of *Obelia* at Woods Hole.

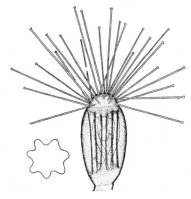

Figure 370

Fig. 370. *Anarma multiruga,* 70-150μ (Goodrich and Jahn).

Body cylindrical with seven or eight longitudinal ridges as shown in insert; tentacles in one group at dome-shaped distal end; no stalk; attachment by small base to peritrich stalk or algal filaments on carapace of turtles or directly to the carapace.

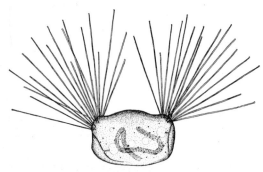

Figure 371

Fig. 371. *Anarma brevis,* 125μ wide, 75μ high, (Goodrich and Jahn).

Body low and flat; attached directly to carapace of turtles; one or two groups of tentacles.

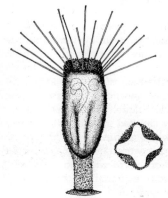

Figure 372

Fig. 372. *Squalorophrya macrostyla,* body 90μ, with heavy stalk ¼ to ¾ body length, which is continuous with a transparent lorica to which considerable debris is usually attached.

Tentacles at distal end only; with four longitudinal folds in basal part of body as shown in cross section in insert. On algal filaments on turtles.

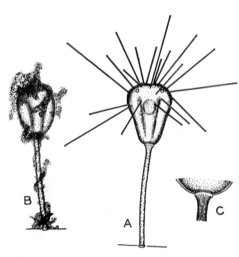

Figure 373

Fig. 373. *Squaloro-phrya stenostyla,* body 40μ (Hamilton and Jahn).

Similar to *S. macrostyla* but stalk is longer (1½ times body length) and is not continuous with lorica. End of stalk bears cup-shaped structure in which the end of the body is attached. On algal filaments on turtles.

Young individuals which have just secreted the stalk and lorica have little or no debris. However, apparently because of the sticky surface of these structures the debris is rapidly accumulated so that at first glance only an experienced observer would readily recognize the organism as a suctorean.

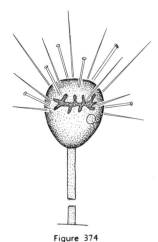

Figure 374

Fig. 374. *Ephelota gemmipara,* 250μ, stalk up to 1.5 mm.

Body bears two types of tentacles: sucking as described above (fig. 368) and piercing. Prey is impaled by the piercing tentacles and the sucking tentacles extract the victim's cytoplasm. Macronucleus greatly branched; reproduction by external budding, as many as two dozen small buds being formed in a circle around the distal end of the parent (fig. 13). Marine; often found on colonies of *Obelia* and other hydroids. The prepared slides of *Obelia* used in elementary zoology courses usually have *Ephelota* and peritrichs attached to the *Obelia* stalks.

Probably the most dependable source of fresh water suctoreans for study is the "moss" on the backs of turtles. This "moss" consists mostly of a filamentous alga, *Basicladia*, and a variety of peritrichous ciliates (p. 220), especially *Epistylis* and *Opercularia*. The suctoreans are attached to the algal filaments, to the peritrich stalks, and directly to the carapace or skin folds around the neck and limbs.

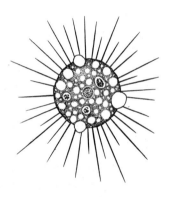

INDEX AND PICTURED GLOSSARY

A

Acantharina (see Actipylina) 105
Acanthocystis turfacea, 104
Acanthodesima, 107
Acanthometron elasticum, 105
Acellular, 5
Acephalina, 152
Acineta limnetis, 223
Acinetopsis, 223
Acnidosporidea, 168
Actinobolina vorax, 181
Actinobolinidae, 181
Actinocoma ramosa, 108
Actinomyxida, 166
Actinophrys sol, 102, 103
Actinopodea, 101
Actinosphaerium, 102
arachnoideum, 102
eichhorni, 102
Actipylina (or Acantharina), 105
Adelea, 147
ADORAL: near the mouth; adoral cilia, 170
AETHALIA: structures with incomplete intervening walls containing sporangia, found in some of the Mycetozoida, 138
Agarella, 165, 166
Agriolimax, 193
Aloricata, 218
Ameba, what to look for in an, 110, 111
AMEBIASIS: infection with a pathogenic ameba, e.g., Entamoeba histolytica in man, 113, 114
Ameiurus melas melas, 221
Amnodiscus incertus, 131
Amoeba carolinensis, see Chaos carolinensis, 121
Amoeba proteus (Choas diffluens) 120
Amoebida, 110
Amoebidae (or Chaidae), 117
Amphileptidae, 184
Amphimonadidae, 93
Amphimonas globosa, 93
Anarma, 224
brevis, 224
multiruga, 224
ANAYODIN: organic iodine compound used in treatment of amebiasis, 113
Ancistruma mytili, 197
Anisonema, 72
Annulus, 47, 58
Anoplophrya, 176
marylandensis, 176
orchestii, 176
Anthophysis vegetans, 94
Apostomina, 175
Arcella, 3, 126, 127
contracting, 3
dentata, 127
discoides, 126
mitrata, 126
vulgaris, 126
Arcellidae, 126

Archetista, 7
Arcyria denudata, 141
Ascoglena vaginicola, 69
Aspidisca lynceus, 206
Aspidiscidae, 205
ASSOCIATION: two cells attached in syzygy, 149 Fig. 375

Figure 377

Figure 375

Astasia dangeardi, 71
Astasiidae, 70
Astomina, 176
Astramoeba radiosa, 119
ATABRINE: drug used in treatment of malaria, 157; in eradication of Giardia, 97
Aulacantha scalymantha, 107
Autogamy, 28
AXOPODIA: long, thin, unbranched projections of cytoplasm, not locomotor in function, 99 Fig. 376

Figure 376

B

Babesia, 158, 159
bigemina, 158, 159
Babesiidae, 158
Balanonema biceps, 195
Balantidium coli, 199
Basicladia, 226
Bees, dysentery caused by Nosema, 167
Bicosoeca, 86
Bicosoecidae, 86
BINARY FISSION: equal division of an organism to form two individuals, 21 Fig. 377

BLACKHEAD: a disease of turkeys caused by Histomonas, 83
Blepharisma, 170, 201
lateritium, 170, 201
steini, 201
Blepharoprosthium pireum, 177
Bodo edax, 94
Bodonidae, 94
Boil disease, of fish, 163
Bresslaua insidiatrix, 193
Bruce, David, 159
Bryophyllum lieberkuhni, 184
BUDDING: unequal cell division, either internal or external, 24
Bursaria truncatella, 199
Bursariidae, 198
Butschliidae, 177

C

Caenomorpha sapropelica, 202
Camerina laevigata, 135
Cannopylina (see Tripylina), 106
CAPILLITIUM: fibrous network in which spores are embedded in the Mycetozoida, 136
Carbarsone, used in treatment of amebiasis, 113
Carchesium polypinum, 172, **220**
Carotenoids, 44
Carteria cordiformis, 81
Carteriidae, 81
Cell, definition, 4
CELL WALL: a secreted closely fitting external covering, (a), 47 Fig. 378

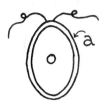

Figure 378

Figure 379

Figure 380

Figure 381

Figure 382

Figure 383

INDEX

Figure 384

E

F

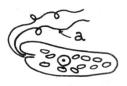

Figure 385

229

INDEX

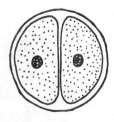

INDEX

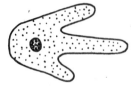

INDEX

multimicronucleatum, 187, 188, 190
  polycarum, 188
  putrinum, 188
  trichium, 173, 174, 188
  woodruffi, 188

PARAMYLUM: a carbohydrate similar to starch, 45
Paranassula microstoma, 186
PARASITIC: living on or in another organism to the detriment of the latter, 19
Paraspathidium, 177
Pasteur, Louis, 167

PEBRINE: disease of silkworms, 12, 167
Pellicle, 36
Pelomyxa carolinensis, see Chaos carolinensis, 121
Pelomyxa palustris, 123

PENTAQUINE: treatment of malaria, 157
Peranema trichophorum, 48, 72
Peranemidae, 72

PERFORATIONS: small pores by which chambers of test of foraminiferans open to outside, 128
Peridinium wisconsiense, 59

PERIDIUM: outer covering of the capillitium in Mycetozoida, 136
Peripylina (or Spumellina), 106
Peritrichida, 172, 216
Permanent fusion, 25
Petalomonas, 48, 74
  alata, 74
  asymmetrica, 74
  bicarinata, 74
  mediocanellata, 74
Phacotidae, 79
Phacotus lenticularis, 47, 79
Phacus, 46, 67, 68
  acuminata, 46
  agilis okobojiensis, 46
  longicauda, 67
  monilata, 67
  pleuronectes, 67
  pyrum, 68
  quinquemarginatus, 68
  torta, 67
  torta v. tortuosa, 67
  trimarginatus, 46, 68
  warszewiczii, 68
Phaeodina (see Tripylina), 106
Phalansteriidae, 84
Phalansterium digitatum, 84

PHARYNGEAL BASKET: skeletal structure of some ciliates formed by fusion of oral trichites, 175

PHOSPHORESCENCE: light produced by an organism, e.g., by Noctiluca, 61
Phototrophic (synonyms, holophytic or photosynthetic), 19
Physarina, 138
Physarum, 139
  didermoides, 139
  viride, 139
Phytomastigophorea, 51-81

Phytomonadida, 75
Phytomonas, 91
Pileocephalus, 151
Placobdella, 148
Plasmagel, 36
Plasmasol, 37
Plasmodiidae, 155

PLASMODIOCARPS: in Mycetozoida, formed by protoplasm accumulating in a few veins of rhizopodial network, 138
Plasmodium, 154-157
  falciparum, 157
  malariae, 157
  ovale, 157
  vivax, 154-157
Platycola longicollis, 217
Platydorina caudata, 76
Pleodorina, 77
  californicus, 77
  illinoisensis, 77
Pleuronema, 197
  crassum, 197
  setigerum, 197
Pleurostomata, 184
Podophyra fixa, **222**

POLAR CAPSULE: in the spore of some of the Sporozoa, a capsule containing coiled filament, 142 Fig. 389

Figure 389

POLAR FILAMENT: coiled structure held within capsule in spores of some Sporozoa, 142, 143
Polychaos dubia, 123
Polykaryomastigina, 97
Polymastigida, 94
Polyoeca dichotoma, 86
Polytomella agilis, 81
Pomoxis sporoides, 164, 166
Potato tuber worm, role in control of fruit moth, 167
Poteriodendron petiolatum, 86
Pouchetia fusus, 61

PRIMITE: anterior member of an association in gregarines, 149

PROLOCULUM: the first chamber of the test in foraminiferans, 128
Prorodon discolor, 170
Proteomyxida, 108
Protista, 7

Protochrysis phaeophycearum, 57
Protociliatia, 169
Protomastigida, 84
Protoopalina, 170

PROTOPLASMIC COLLAR: a collar-like projection of protoplasm which surrounds the flagellum of choanoflagellates, 49, 85

PROTOPLASMIC WAVES: wave-like extensions of the protoplasm, resulting in locomotion without formation of pseudopodia, 99
Protospongia haeckeli, 86
Protostomata, 177
Protozoa, 3-16
  not simple unicellular animals, 3-8
  collection of, 10
  culture methods, 11
  equipment for study, 9, 10
  habitat, 8, 9
  size, 12
  size, estimation of, 13-15
  staining of, 15, 16
Pseudofolliculina, 203

PSEUDOPODIUM: a "false foot," an elongated protoplasmic process resulting from the flow of protoplasm, 36, 37; various types, 99-110
Pteromonas aculeata, 79
Pusule, 58
Pyorrhea, relationship of Entamoeba gingivalis to, 114
Pyramimonas tetrahynchus, 81
Pyrenoids, definition of, 45

Q

Quinine, treatment of malaria, 157

R

Rabbits, coccidia of, 147
Radiolarian ooze, 104
Radiolarida, 100, 104
Rapidophrys pallida, 103

"RED EUGLENAS": species of Euglena which form a red scum on ponds during very hot weather, 65, 66
Red Tide, 58, 59
Red Water, 60
Redwater fever, or Texas fever of cattle, 158, 159

REPRODUCTION: the process of increasing numbers of an organism, either sexually or asexually, 21-29
Reservoir, 46
Rhabdomonas, 48, 71
  incurva, 71
Rhizochrysidina, 55
Rhizochrysis scherfelli, 55
Rhizomastigida, 82
Rhizopodea, 108

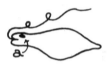

INDEX

TEST: a loosely fitting external covering within which the organism is free to move, (a), 47. Fig. 392

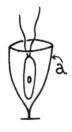

Figure 392

TRICHITES: rods which form a skeletal structure for supporting rim of mouth in ciliates, 175

TRICHOCYSTS: dart-like protective structures found in many cilates, 174, 175, 179, 188. Fig. 393

Figure 393

TROPHOZOITE: an active or growth stage in the life history of an organism, 44, 144

TSETSE FLY: vector in transmission of T. gambiense and T. rhodesiense, 89

Twist disease, of salmonoid fishes, 163

UNDULATING MEMBRANE: in ciliates formed by two more or less longitudinal rows of cilia fused, 171. In flagellates, a thin double layer of pellicle by which flagellum is attached along length of body, 87.

UROID: posterior protoplasmic mass of amebas, often slightly separated from body by a constriction, 111 Fig. 394

Figure 394

VIOFORM: organic iodine compound used in treatment of amebiasis, 113

XYLOPHAGOUS: wood eating, as are termites and certain cockroaches, 20

ZYGOTE: fertilized egg, 145